Colonial Inscriptions

Central Kenya circa 1925

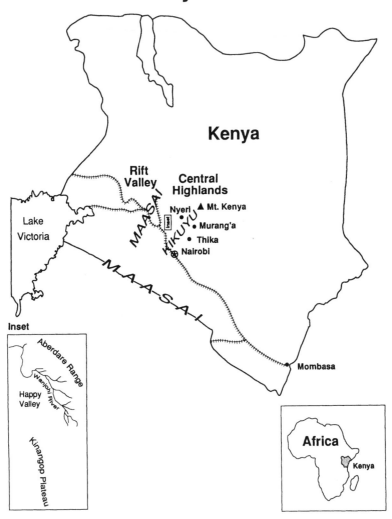

Kenya

Rift
Valley

Central
Highlands

Nyeri ▲ Mt. Kenya

• Murang'a

Lake
Victoria

• Thika

⊕ Nairobi

MAASAI

Inset

• Mombasa

Inset

Aberdare Range

Wanjohi River

Happy
Valley

Kinangop Plateau

Africa

Kenya

Colonial Inscriptions

Race, Sex, and Class in Kenya

Carolyn Martin Shaw

University of Minnesota Press
Minneapolis
London

Grateful acknowledgment is made for permission to reprint the following:
"Land and Food, Women and Power in Nineteenth Century Kikuyu,"
Africa 50, 4 (1980): 357-70, the journal of the International African Institute;
"Louis Leakey as Ethnographer: *On The Southern Kikuyu before 1903*,"
Canadian Journal of African Studies 23, 3 (1989): 380-98, by permission of
the Canadian Association of African Studies.

Published by the University of Minnesota Press
111 Third Avenue South, Suite 290, Minneapolis, MN 55401-2520
Printed in the United States of America on acid-free paper
Second printing 1997
Library of Congress Cataloging-in-Publication Data

Shaw, Carolyn Martin, 1944–
    Colonial inscriptions : race, sex, and class in Kenya / Carolyn
Martin Shaw.
        p.   cm.
    Includes bibliographical references (p.   ) and index.
    ISBN 0-8166-2524-7 (acid-free paper) ISBN 0-8166-2525-5
(pbk. : acid-free paper)
        1. Kenya—Social conditions. 2. Kenya—History—1895–1963.
3. Power (Social sciences)—Kenya. 4. Kenya—Colonial influence.
5. Women—Kenya—Social conditions. I. Title.
HN793.A8S54 1995   94–36180
306'.096762—dc20

Contents

Acknowledgments   vii

Chapter 1. Introduction: Social Theory and Colonialism   1
Colonial Discourse/Colonial Culture   4
Social Theory and the Colonial Encounter   13
Culture and Colonialism in Kenya: The Book   25

Chapter 2. The Production of Women: Kikuyu Gender and Politics
      at the Beginning of the Colonial Era   28
Piecework: Constructing the Past   29
The Kikuyu   33
The Political Economy of the Nineteenth-Century Kikuyu   36
Women's Contribution to the Political Economy   40
Food Presentation for Work Parties and for Hospitality   42
Women as Objects or Subjects in the Political Economy   46
The Lost Sister   47
Piecing It Together   58

Chapter 3. Kikuyu Women and Sexuality   60
Women as Allegory: Leakey   60
Kenyatta on Women   63
Malinowskian Functionalism in Support of Clitoridectomy   67
Kikuyu Sexual Morality   71
The Conduct of Virginity   72
Clitoridectomy and Sexuality   76
Kikuyu Virginity within a Broader Context   82
Virginity and Clitoridectomy   85
The Achievement of Virginity   88
The African Contrast with Europe and Asia   89

Contents

Chapter 4. Louis Leakey and the Kikuyu   95
     The Excursion   95
     Louis Seymour Bazette Leakey   100
     Louis Leakey's Ethnography of the Kikuyu   106

Chapter 5. The Ethnographic Past: Jomo Kenyatta and Friends   118
     The Ethnographic Past   118
     Jomo Kenyatta: Author, Authentic Native   123
     Facing Mount Kenya   131
     Speaking for the African: The Professional Friend   138
     The Future in the Past   143

Chapter 6. Mau Mau Discourses   149
     Mau Mau   150
     Mau Mau: Fiction and Fact   159
     Mau Mau News   170

Chapter 7. Race, Class, Empire, and Sexuality   179
     Colonial Landscapes   180
     The Politics of Representation in Colonial Kenya   185
     Living Off the Land   192
     Racial Aesthetics in Colonial Kenya   196
     African Discourses on Tribe and the Other   203
     The Air up There: The Visible Minority of Socialite Settlers   209
     Noble Savage, Spiteful Servant, Socialite Settler: Sex and
       Power in Kenyan Colonial Discourses, A Summary   216

Notes   219

Bibliography   225

Index   243

Acknowledgments

"I don't know nothin' 'bout birthin' no books," resounded in my mind as I began the final push to finish this project. The line is, of course, a paraphrase of "Ah doan know nuthin' 'bout birthin' babies!"—which Butterfly McQueen, playing Prissy in *Gone with the Wind*, said, much to my embarrassment. When I saw the classic Civil War film as a youngster, I was embarrassed by Prissy's simplemindedness and embarrassed to have found her character funny, despite the stereotype of the stupid, willful, and deceitful servant. How could the person playing that role be the sister of my dignified high school drama coach? My feelings about the Butterfly McQueen character changed over the years to anger at the early and persistent representation of black people as cowardly, lazy, untrustworthy. I must admit, though, that I directed most of my anger to Hattie McDaniel's Academy Award-winning portrayal of Mammy as loyal, abnegating guardian of standards of white gentility. "I don't know nothin' 'bout birthin' no books" jangled in my head. I felt I had been headstrong in embarking on this task, that this black woman from Virginia was not meant to write this book. As the process of publishing *Colonial Inscriptions* neared its end, I knew, as Butterfly McQueen did, that there were far too many things to orchestrate all at once before this work could be crowned.

But I am here celebrating the fruition of long labor and I am fortunate to have had the help of friends, family, colleagues, and students to make this happen. Some of the ideas in this book I have struggled with for almost twenty-five years. Others are newer. I have learned from many people, in many situations; it is impossible to acknowledge them all. I can mention the names of only a few who made direct contributions to this book, but I do thank those who over the years of its production have comforted and nourished, poked and prodded, and showed me the way.

Much of my work on gender and political economy, virginity and sexuality, history and ethnography, and social theory and discourse analysis was tested in graduate and undergraduate classes at the University of California, Santa Cruz, and developed in conversations with generous colleagues, especially May N. Diaz, Barbara Joans, Joan Larcom, Triloki Pandey, Richard Randolph, and Mario Davilla. Important lessons on human sexuality, anatomy, and physiology were given me by physical anthropologists Adrienne Zihlman and Lorraine Heidecker. Anna Tsing introduced me to a new language and coached me through the harmonies and counterpoints of this critical moment in anthropology. Others from outside of anthropology provided broader contexts for my work. I am particularly grateful to students in literature, sociology, and history of consciousness whose graduate committees I was a member of, and to political scientist I. Leonard Markovitz, whose National Endowment for the Humanities summer seminar I attended.

The University of California, Santa Cruz, is an ideal place to do what I call Tina Turner anthropology: nothing is ever "nice and easy," but always "nice and rough." I have been a member of two writing groups at UCSC that have been very important in helping me get my work out. Participating in a writing group is never easy—finding the time to read other people's work and the courage to share yours is rough. I sometimes left the meetings feeling sad and depressed, but just as often—perhaps more often, since I persisted, and I like to think of myself as more of a pleasure seeker than a pain seeker—I went feeling sad and depressed and left energized and hopeful. Members of my first writing group, which called itself Mahvajyna, included Mischa Adams, Nancy Heischman, Katie King, Aliki Maris, Jan Pearson, Ellen Rifkin, and Lynn Woodbury. My second writing group was drawn from the Anthropology Board at UCSC: Shelly Errington, Diane Gifford-Gonzalez, Olga Najera-Ramirez, and Anna Tsing. I gratefully acknowledge their contributions to this project. In other quarters on this campus, discussions at conferences sponsored by the Center for Cultural Studies and the Feminist Studies Focused Research Activity, where I presented papers, engaged scholars from a wide range of perspectives and often challenged my working premises. Some people were moved to send written comments on my conference papers, especially Robert Stevens, Gary Lease, and David M. Schneider. I could not follow up on all the issues they pointed out but would like to acknowledge the good effect their interest had on my work. A colleague in community studies, Carter Wilson, read a complete draft of an earlier version of this book and kindly provided me with excellent writerly and anthropological feedback. Diane K. Lewis inspired me to bring some of my work back home by reflecting on myself and the black community.

Research on this project was supported by small grants from the University of California, Santa Cruz. UCSC graphic designer Helen Cole produced the Kenya map for me, and the Word Processing Center helped with the production of the manuscript. Graduate research assistants Ron Eglash and Lena

Acknowledgments

Sawyer and undergraduate research assistants Ruth Mathis and Susie Bullington were crucial in keeping me on track in the final stages of this work. Susie
Bullington's dedication in checking my facts and my style gave me the extra
push I needed at the end. Critical comments on an earlier version of this book
were provided by Betty J. Harris, Naomi Katz, and Deborah S. Rubin. Janaki
Bakhle at the University of Minnesota Press was ever encouraging, and the
comments of the anonymous readers she corralled led me to make significant
improvements in the manuscript.

My daughter, Koren Fatimah Clark, went through her childhood and ado-
lescence with her mother talking constantly, and critically, about virginity and
sexuality. I appreciate her interest and her forbearance. Friends of mine, especially Nubra Floyd and Julie Dodd Tetzlaff, have endured long letters from me
from Zimbabwe and Germany, not about those countries or my experiences
there, but about virginity, Louis Leakey, and the uses of history and culture. I
am grateful to them for allowing me to work out my ideas with them, and for
responding by telling me what was going on in their lives. My colleague in the
UCSC Academic Senate Office, Julie Dryden, shared her dreams with me and
cheered me.

William H. Shaw, my husband, a much-published philosopher, reminded
me that this project would only get done by my "putting in time in the chair."
His optimism and good humor helped me to sit, and his delight in my work,
his confidence in me, gave me something to lean against. Bill got me to stop
snatching defeat from the jaws of victory. Thank you.

This book is dedicated to the memory of two deceased colleagues, feminist
anthropologist Nancy Tanner and literary critic and revolutionary Roberto
Crespi.

1

Introduction: Social Theory and Colonialism

The colonial period was a brief, violent, constitutive moment in the history of Kenya, ending in 1963; it lasted about sixty years.[1] People, ideas, and practices forced together in colonial Kenya gave rise to discourses that shape inequalities, rivalries, adventures, and fantasies to this day in Kenya. The social imagery that Kenyan colonialists used to represent the native other, to construct narratives of domination and subordination, can best be understood as emanating from social processes taking place in the borderland between European and African knowledge and experience. This borderland is a space of *interculturality*, of overlapping "part" societies and local communities influenced by local traditions, colonial innovations, metropolitan mores, and international politics and economics. In this work, I concentrate on the Central Highlands, also known as the White Highlands, on British socialites and bourgeoisie, on one lone Dane who settled there, and on the Kikuyu, who were there when it all started.

This book is primarily a study of writings on Kenya, by Kenyans—such as Jomo Kenyatta, anthropologist and first president of the country, and Louis Leakey, paleohistorian and ethnographer—by people who settled in Kenya for long periods, like British memoirist Elspeth Huxley and Isak Dinesen (the pen name of Danish novelist Karen Blixen), and by those who, like me, made shorter forays into Kenya, including the sensationalistic American novelist Robert Ruark. I also comment on commercial films on colonial Kenya, European creations of African images consumed worldwide. These texts are part of colonial discourse in Kenya, the not always systematic relations of power, language, and knowledge through which objects, individuals, and groups are invested with meanings that define and mobilize native peoples as subjects in and subject to colonialism, while simultaneously creating colonialists with varying degrees of freedom and constraint from the metropole, the colony, each other, and the native peoples. Enduring metaphors, instructive imagery, and compelling figures in Kenyan colonial discourse—the white hunter, the noble sav-

1

age, the dedicated white farmer, the detribalized native, the African terrorist, the kindly missionary, the harmonious little community, and the beleaguered colony—reveal themselves in my study of histories, ethnographies, novels, and memoirs. These images, this discourse, developed in the Kenya colony in a context in which Europeans strove to bring the progress of enlightenment to the dark continent and in the process to live out their own nostalgic and lustful fantasies. Europeans caught in their own contradictions caused irreparable damage to the progress of African lives, and at the same time created in those lives new tastes and sensibilities, desires and commodities, and joys and suffering. Kenyan colonial discourse established particular styles of domination and subordination through the contradictions of colonization.

Turning first to the Kikuyu of the Central Highlands of Kenya, I probe two major themes differently represented in ethnographies and histories: the Kikuyu as the harmonious little community and as egalitarian society. In the "little community" everyone is taken care of and order and peace reign supreme, while in the egalitarian society there are no structured inequalities; all *men* are equal. My writing is informed by my fieldwork in Kenya, which explored family relations, the choices and justifications made as family members negotiated competing demands within a restrictive framework of economic, political, and cultural resources.[2] The approach I took led me to rethink Kikuyu history and social organization, to ask questions about gender politics and the ways in which women's power, greatly derived from their productive activities, shaped the inequalities of male patron-client relationships. In highlighting relations between patrons and clients and the political importance of women's domestic activities, my ethnography of the Kikuyu differs considerably from older sources.

Older sources, especially Louis Leakey's and Jomo Kenyatta's ethnographies, are the ground for many of my reinterpretations of Kikuyu life, but they also are the basis for much of my critique of colonial discourse. The work and life of Jomo Kenyatta spans almost the entire colonial period: he was a political activist in the first decades of the twentieth century, a Kikuyu ethnographer in the late 1930s, a symbol of the anticolonial Mau Mau movement in the 1950s, and, at the end of the colonial period, a leader of independent Kenya. Kenyatta offers a unique angle of vision of African nostalgia, revolution, and accommodation. I criticize the cultural nationalism of Kenyatta's ethnography, a cultural nationalism curiously shaped and supported by his mentor, pioneer anthropologist Bronislaw Malinowski. I expose American colonial discourse in the racial politics of the coverage of Kenyatta and the Mau Mau movement in popular media in the United States.

In the late 1930s both Kenyatta and Louis S. B. Leakey produced works on the Kikuyu of central Kenya: Leakey, a three-volume ethnography, *The South-*

ern Kikuyu before 1903 (1977), and Kenyatta, the functionalist and cultural nationalist ethnography, *Facing Mt. Kenya* (1938). But the writers themselves—an iconoclastic son of missionaries and a mission-educated firebrand—are also a part of the story, as are the social and political conditions in which their works were constructed. Major controversies in the histories revolve around the nature of precolonial Kikuyu society (Was it egalitarian or dominated by large landowners?) and of Mau Mau (Was it a syncretistic religious movement or the Land and Freedom Army?). Using methods that draw out the poetics and politics of their representations of the Kikuyu, I argue that understanding the subject position of the writers, as well as the local and international influences at the moment of production, effectively situate their knowledge, enabling me to assess their contribution to shaping the image and culture of the Kikuyu and of Kenya.

In Leakey's and Kenyatta's ethnographies, women are more metaphor than social actors, symbols used in a battle against real and imagined enemies. Both ethnographers allegorize Kikuyu women, Leakey in his quarrel with conventional European sexual mores and Kenyatta in his bid for recognition and respect for "traditional" Kikuyu beliefs and customs. My chapter on virginity, a comparative study that focuses on female premarital virginity among the Kikuyu, makes clear that it is not just in colonial discourse's pitting of the metropole against the natives that women are used to symbolize the strength and integrity of the group. Discourses on power, prestige, and status within certain African societies were framed in terms of kinship, honor, and the purity of women. The comparative material suggests that female premarital virginity was even more highly valued as a prize for family honor in some European and Asian societies (Ortner 1978 and 1981; Schneider 1971; Goody and Tambiah 1973). The cultural meaning and conduct of virginity varies. Sub-Saharan African virgins were not forced to chastity through clitoridectomy, nor were they chaperoned and secluded—they achieved their virginity in sexually charged environments.

Colonial and metropolitan discourses and images of sexuality and gender influenced relations between local groups, as did the discourse and images of race and class. Kenya's particular history involves events as disparate and unexpected as dissolute aristocratic settlers admiring the free-living Maasai and building Orientalist pleasure domes, a Kikuyu modernist movement in favor of clitoridectomy, and a vindication of open sexuality and polygamy as a defense of men's privilege and women's rights. I suggest that Europeans brought with them to Africa powerful discourses of inequality that both offered a coherent scheme for distancing the alien and suggested distinctions among subordinate others. Thus, varied forms of representation catalogued the degenerate lower classes: the foul Jew, the indolent southerner, and the contrasting stereotypes of black American and red Indian. These representations, often coded as racial within European contexts, were assimilated and transformed to the needs of colonialist hegemony. In colonialist imagery the Kikuyu and the Maasai form a contrasting pair similar to the black American slave and the wild Indian in American folklore. I argue that the images and stories created about the Maasai and Kikuyu construct them as particular colonial subjects—the noble savage and the deceitful servant—and influenced colonial land and labor policies. The African landscape also played on the colonialist imaginary, setting off against one another freedom and control, proficiency and passion, and civilization and nature. European fantasies of the tropics inspired the flaunting of metropolitan mores as well as a fearful, strict adherence to metropolitan precepts and rigid enforcement of the color bar.

Colonial Discourse/Colonial Culture

Part Societies/Tribes

Colonial Kenyan society was made up of many communities, or partial societies. Some were based on African ethnic groups or tribes, some on Indian immigrant populations who maintained some ethnic boundaries while contravening others. Others were formed around European class and ethnic groups, such as Afrikaner farmers, British aristocrats, and British colonial officers. I call them partial societies to emphasize both the permeability of their borders and the variety of ways that local groups may be linked together at different levels to form tribal, regional, national, colonial, imperial, and world systems. Partial societies are not peculiar to colonies. Social historians (N. Davis 1975; Thompson 1966; Scott 1988; Braudel 1975, 1981) and historically minded anthropologists, especially Wolf (1982), urge an appreciation of the intersection of microlevel processes, interactions among individuals at grassroots levels, and macroprocesses, institutional and opportunistic initiations and responses up to international levels, in an effort to understand how specific histories of peasants and tribal peoples connect to European colonialization, the development and spread of capitalism, and the establishment of imperialism. Eric Wolf, in criticizing the tendency of contemporary anthropologists to "[divide their] subject matter into distinctive cases: each society with its characteristic culture, conceived as an integrated and bounded system, set off against other equally bounded systems" (1982: 4), points to the influence of the Atlantic slave trade on African peoples as a counterexample:

> From Senegambia in West Africa to Angola, population after population was drawn into this trade, which ramified far inland and affected people who had never even seen a European trader on the coast. Any account of Kru, Fanti, Asante, Ijaw, Igbo, Kongo, Luba, Lunda or Ngola that treats each group as a

"tribe" sufficient unto itself thus misreads the African past and the African present. (1982: 4)

The idea of tribe and tribalism holds fast in the Africanist imagination. In *Culture and Imperialism* (1993), Edward Said argues that conceptions of primitivism associated with Africanist discourse—Africa for the West—produced essentialist and reductive philosophies of African identity as tribalistic, vitalistic, and originary. Said concludes that "so productive and adaptable was this notion of African identity that it could be used by Western missionaries, then anthropologists, then Marxist historians, then antagonistically, even liberation movements"(1993: 193). Increasingly, however, Western scholarship on Africa emphasizes the lack of tribal distinctiveness and the interrelationship of local-level groups (Kratz 1980; Hobsbawm and Ranger 1988; O'Brien and Roseberry 1991; Lawren 1968; Spear and Waller 1993). The question posed by Kratz's (1980) article "Are the Okiek Really Masai? Kipsigis? or Kikuyu?" for instance, takes up the issue of the tribal identity of a little-studied hunter-gatherer group and shows that it is the very blend of different languages, rituals, and everyday practices that define this group as Okiek.

Ironically, during the colonial period many more local groups were brought into contact with each other, enhancing the possibility of intercultural exchange; at the same time, colonial governments worked against this exchange by establishing tribal chiefs and headmen as well as tribal reservations—clearly bounded territories for the exclusive preserve of particular named tribes. The colonial inventions of well-demarcated tribal groupings, part and parcel of British indirect rule—commanding through "African" lines of authority— called on European models of subservience, extending a rigid feudal-patriarchal ethic in the face of customary African flexibility (cf. Ranger 1988: 220, 236, 247).

Europeans did not find Africans in neatly bounded self-sufficient tribal groups:

> Almost all recent studies of nineteenth-century pre-colonial Africa have emphasized that far from there being a single "tribal" identity, most Africans moved in and out of multiple identities, defining themselves at one moment as subject to this chief, at another moment as a member of that cult, at another moment as part of this clan, and at yet another moment as an initiate in that professional guild. (Ranger 1988: 248)

By rewarding and heightening internal political and economic differences, by recognizing big men or wealthy landowners over elders' councils and men over women, by establishing feudal relations to whole groups of people through the vassalage of their appointed leader, colonialists tried to create effective tribes to rule.

The Kikuyu of Kenya are prime examples of the social transformations that can take place as natives respond to the alien's request to "take me to your leader." The Kikuyu population was scattered throughout the forested hillside ridges of the Central Highlands in Kenya, living primarily in large family compounds organized around a father and his sons or a set of brothers.[3] Sections of the population defined by residence on a particular ridge or near a river fought against each other and against the nearby Maasai and Kamba peoples. In some areas, especially in the north where the Kikuyu confronted the Maasai on the open plains, the Kikuyu retreated to the forest in fortified villages composed of several family groups. The Kikuyu age grade system united men and women across the widest range of territory. Men's elders' councils drawn from all the men of the age grade and led by men who distinguished themselves in wisdom, in wealth, and in managing a large family made political and religious decisions. Comparable women's elders' councils arbitrated domestic disputes and organized particular religious rituals for the community, from the smallest to the largest groupings.

When European explorers and colonialists entered into this environment, they demanded to be taken to the person in charge. The names of a few very wealthy men appear again and again in the early records of these travelers and colonialists.[4] Many of these big men later became the paramount and district chiefs of the Kikuyu. Given symbols and oaths of office by the colonialists, they were paid for their services, which included conscripting labor for the colonial government or for individual colonialists. Chiefs and their families often were exempt from corvée, or forced labor. The colonial system established a system of chiefs and subchiefs, regularized all male judiciary councils, codified Kikuyu customary law, and through many commissions and much testimony mapped the extent of the Kikuyu tribal reserve.

What was once a fluid system of community relations became—though never totally and never successfully—an official tribe. This officializing discourse (cf. Bourdieu 1990: 107–10), created against a very different reality, represented the natives to the colonialists and ultimately became a part of the self-representation of Africans. The Kikuyu can be characterized as part societies despite official colonial and anthropological delimitation, including my own use of the definite article *the* in discussions of them. The kind of part societies created in colonial Kenya depended on this "definition" of peoples as the Kikuyu, the Maasai, the Kamba, the Luo, and so on. Africans learned to see themselves as members of a discrete group among many such groups.

Part Societies/Fracturing White Solidarity

But it is not just for the Africans that I refer to colonial society as being made up of part societies and local communities. According to Dane Kennedy's engaging study of colonialists in Kenya and Zimbabwe (Southern Rhodesia), *Islands of White: Settler Society and Culture in Kenya and Southern Rhodesia, 1890-1939*, European colonialists in Kenya represented themselves as "virtually classless collectives of immigrants" (1987: 183). European colonialists emphasized their sameness as whites over and against the Africans' blackness, but within their communities well-defined lines of difference demarcated interactive groups. Kennedy contends that "if the social distinctions *within* the settler community were subordinated to the requirements of the colonial system, the social distinctions between settler communities were accentuated by the same requirements" (192). In the process of putting Africans into tribal groups, Europeans did not put themselves into bounded cultural groups. Rather, I will argue, differences of class, ethnicity, nationality, religion, and appetite cracked the white solidarity colonialists imagined as a prime requirement of the colonial system.

In Kenya, colonialists who owned land and managed estates for the first time came into social contact with sons and daughters of the European landed gentry who were colonial officers or large-scale farmers and ranchers themselves. Colonialists of many different stripes came together in the settler organizations or clubs that threatened local rule against the colonial government; they hunted wild animals together, savored each others' stories and stories about each other, and struggled to make something out of Africa, its land and people. But the story of the Kenya colony is not one of embattled white colonialists against the darkness of Africa. Instead the story tells of colonialists who worried over or enjoyed their class position, who were fascinated with the noble savage, and whose invented traditions, both metropolitan and colonial, forged colonial culture.

In the late nineteenth century Kenya was colonized by a British "migratory elite":

> These were persons of middle- and upper-class backgrounds (termed the "migratory elite" by one scholar), motivated to emigrate either because their traditional social standing had deteriorated in a changing Britain or because they possessed certain educational or professional skills in high demand in developing countries. (Kennedy 1987: 6)

Kennedy holds that these Kenya colonialists, a white minority in a black land, were preoccupied with security and with the maintenance of white culture and prestige in the face of the black peril (1987: 6–7). I see it differently. An upwardly mobile middle class, rather than all colonialists and most definitely not the aristocrats, was most concerned with white prestige, and it was this group that felt most threatened by Africans and by poor whites. They wanted a clear distinction between themselves and blacks that was thwarted by poor whites:

"By subsisting at a level barely distinguishable from that of the indigenous population, poor whites undermined the very foundation of the colonial relationship," Kennedy (1987: 168) concludes. Poor whites challenged the hegemony of white prestige and economic dominance, while the socialite settlers and white Afrikaners challenged the notion of European moral superiority.

An imperative for the British middle class was to maintain the prestige and standing of the white race, to protect white privilege through control of morality and control of the means of production. But such a neat moral order could not be maintained in the face of aristocratic dissoluteness, Afrikaner degeneracy, middle-class downward mobility, and the demands of Africans for more land and cultural autonomy. White prestige was built on middle-class morality and discipline, and on the maintenance of distinct boundaries between the colonizer and the colonized. This boundary was transgressed by poor and uneducated whites. The existence of second-generation British youth who could achieve little more than artisan status and the influx of minimally educated Afrikaners from South Africa threatened colonialist hegemony. The place of white South African settlers of Dutch heritage, Afrikaners, the quintessential poor whites in the Kenya colony, though it cannot be taken up in detail here, is instructive of the differences among white colonialists, the boundedness of their societies, and the permeability of part societies.

Afrikaners posed an interesting problem: they were white and therefore had the right of dominance. But in their everyday lives, their bare feet, their overabundant fertility, and their contempt for civilized manners, they represented an undeniable link to the African continent. They were degenerate Europeans, and descriptions of them in Elspeth Huxley's memoirs (1987) intimate a cultural aesthetics in which the lower classes are a different race. Unlike the British and continental Europeans, who required a considerable outlay of money to reach Kenya and purchase land there, Afrikaners came up by wagon train from the south. Huxley describes the towns and churches devoted to "Dutchmen" and "Boers" and in one fond remembrance of an Afrikaner farmer evidences their association with coarseness and backwardness:

> What is so interesting about Kenya's history is that events belonging by rights to a bygone century, to the era of covered wagons and the Oregon Trail, should have taken place, albeit on a relatively tiny scale, within the lifetime of people still alive. Cecil Hoey [an Afrikaner] had come to East Africa at the turn of the century [and had reached his farm by wagon train]. He was a burly man, rather slow of speech, with a quiet humour and strong fixed opinions. Times were to change more quickly than his powers to adjust to such changes. (1987: 25-26)

In *The Flame Trees of Thika* Huxley remembers another Afrikaner neighbor as a mysterious, somewhat frightening man who lacked the refinement of civilization: home, garden, and breeding. Of home she states: "He scarcely had what we would call a house, it was a hut like the natives', only with a sort of veranda on one side and a fireplace made of scraps of corrugated iron on the other" (1959: 167). Of his garden she says: "It was strange to see a European's dwelling without a garden, not even a few salvias or daisies, or an attempt at a lawn" (167). Civilization had been bred out of him or else not bred into him: "[Thinking like a leopard] sounded as easy as making a pot of tea, and perhaps it was to Mr Roos, whose own wildness had not quite been bred away, and who used a rifle as if it were an extra limb" (177). Afrikaners, individuals and communities at the bottom of white society, like the figure of the Africanized European and the skilled backwoodsman, were ingredients in Kenyan colonial culture, colonial discourse. They are used here only as an example of a contested border between white colonialists and black Africans. Socialite settlers, in their contempt for middle-class morality and admiration for the freedom and autonomy of pastoralists like the Maasai, engaged in skirmishes at another front of this border. I will take up the case of socialite settlers as a part society in chapter 7.

Colonial Encounters/God's Disease

Both African and colonialist communities had varying degrees of openness and boundedness, and the intensity and depth of their interactions with each other varied with time, place, and situation. Karen Blixen, who wrote under the name Isak Dinesen, in *Out of Africa* (1937) is fascinated by the perception of the European as god she imagines natives hold (cf. Obeyesekere [1992: 122-25], who suggests that myths of the Europeans as gods are more European inventions than the natives'). In likening the natives' image of the colonialists to "the brass serpent" and to "acts of God," Dinesen insinuates that Africans find pragmatic uses for the power of Europeans or else feel themselves at the mercy of unassailable power. The brass serpent, the sensible, manipulable presence of god in the midst of humanity, could by its very presence heal the sick and change the course of human life.[5] Despite the advantages of civilization that Europeans brought, it is their value as physical symbols of ultimate authority from which Africans got the most use. Dinesen explains that Europeans can do little to resist Africans' using them as brass serpents:

> Because of their gift for myths, the Natives can also do things to you against which you cannot guard yourself and from which you cannot escape. They can turn you into a symbol. I was well aware of the process, and for my own use I had a word for it,—in my mind I called it that they were brass-serpenting me. Europeans who have lived for a long time with Natives, will understand what I mean, even if the word is not quite correctly used according to the Bible. I believe that in spite of all our activities in the land, of the scientific and mechani-

9

cal progress there, and of Pax Britannica itself, this is the only practical use that the Natives have ever had out of us. (1989 [1937]: 101-2)

The climactic scene in the film *Out of Africa* (released in 1985), in which Meryl Streep playing Karen Blixen kneels before the colonial governor, represents a narrative of an actual event when Blixen begged permission for her squatters (Kikuyu tenant farmers) to stay together and not be sent to the reservation after she sold the farm where they had lived. This plea was motivated by her imagination that the natives perceive their fate as unfathomably bound with the luck and misfortune of Europeans, that they think of Europeans as gods: "In some respects, although not in all, the white men fill in the mind of the Natives the place that is, in the mind of the white men, filled by the idea of God" (1937: 358). Her failure to maintain the farm was to them, Dinesen asserts, an act of god—"what is completely unforeseeable, and not consonant with rule or reason, that is an act of God" (358). Blixen's sympathy for Africans who saw themselves so unalterably in her power compelled her to plead for them, as did her appreciation of herself as a god. Colonial culture and colonial discourse included imagery, metaphors, and narratives sometimes unilaterally derived from interaction across the borders of partial societies.

Perhaps more than the African perceptions of Europeans, Dinesen captured the European colonialists' sense of themselves; as Said (1993: 23) puts it, "Europeans performing acts of imperial mastery and will in (or about) Africa." Still, Dinesen does capture something of the African response to the colonial arrogance. On the whole, conquered and colonized Africans were not admitted to the inner sanctum, did not sit in the boardrooms, attended no family meetings, voted on nary a colonial ballot, advised on no administrative appointments, contended at none of the club meetings, and counseled no one about their own welfare. They were denied access to their own land, could not grow certain cash crops, were limited in the ownership of property, were forced into unpaid labor, and had little freedom to conduct their own affairs. Their powerlessness to legitimately control their own lives left them on the other side of a chasm whose expanse was as great as that between god and worshipper. Moreover, the paternalistic demand that Africans follow European rules and standards, simply because the orders came from Europeans, inculcated authoritarian discipline in subordinate Africans. By maintaining social distance, political hegemony, control of the distribution of resources, and disciplinary codes of behavior, colonialists gave themselves the aura of gods and brass serpents.

Getting a sense of what Africans thought of the early colonialists is not easy. Histories and ethnographies are obsessed with what happened rather than with the constitution of African subjectivity and production of colonial discourse through African representation of the other.[6] While I was in Murang'a in the

Introduction

Central Highlands of Kenya in 1971-72 I took life histories of Kikuyu men and women who had been children around the turn of the century. The first thing that almost all of them said to me in talking about the coming of white people was that the colonialists brought chiggers, sometimes called jiggers, a mite that infected their toes, causing severe itching and leading the way to infectious disease. For women this story accompanied their telling of working as porters for caravans or working and raising their families on European farms. While I was in the field I never understood why the chigger had a place of such importance in the history of colonial contact, but on further reflection I see it both symbolically and literally as significant in the constitution of the body of the colonial subject. This bloodsucking insect interfered with mobility at a time when Kikuyu were being pressed into the service of whites; it was irritating and debilitating, but it did not prevent African subservience. Distance from whites was rewarded with health, closeness with disease, but the dis-ease of colonialism was unavoidable. Colonialists worried about the infections of the tropics, while Africans saw the colonialists as bringing infection. Kikuyu imagined the colonialists as bringing disease; colonialists saw themselves as gods.

The father of the Kikuyu family I lived with told me a paradigmatic story of men's disposition and feelings in regard to colonialism. He was usually a reticent and reserved man, whom I had been advised not to ask about his period of detention as a Mau Mau adherent for fear he would stop talking altogether. Not long after my husband and I began staying with his family, the father knocked loudly at the door of our rooms late one night after a beer party. He wanted me to get out my notebook; he understood that I was studying Kikuyu customs, but he had something more important to tell me. In mixed Swahili and English he began to tell me about the colonial period and, as he put it, "why we got *uhuru*," the Swahili word for freedom or independence. What he said was almost a poem, each stanza punctuated with "that's why we got *uhuru*." He explained to the sleepy anthropologist:

> The land that you see across the ridge over there, that land owned by *mzungu* [white person or European], that is my grandfather's land. I had to work on that land, my own family's land, for white people.
> That's why we got *uhuru*.
> If a white man drove past us in a car on a road, we had to stand at attention, holding our hats in our hands until he passed. Any white man could arrest us. Our word meant nothing against theirs.
> That's why we got *uhuru*.
> It was illegal for us to buy European beer. We could only drink traditional beer.
> That's why we got *uhuru*.
> A little white boy, no taller than my knee [indicated by a gesture, arm held straight down by his side, hand flexed] had to be called "master." That same

11

child could call a gray-haired old *mzee* [old man] "boy."
That's why we got *uhuru*.

The father of this prosperous postcolonial Kikuyu family was more concerned with enlightenment values—equality, liberty, fraternity, justice—in this outpost of Western civilization than were the colonialists or the colonial government. His first complaint, however, is alienation of the property that would have decided his estate and his demotion to serf from landowner. (He was never able to buy back his ancestral land, but did become a big landowner elsewhere.) The colonialist, the white man, in this portrait is arrogant, grasping, arbitrary, disrespectful, unjust; not paternalistic, hardworking, self-sacrificing. Are there undertones of the European as god that Dinesen speaks of? Perhaps. The colonialists represented themselves as and were perceived by Africans as powerful in and of themselves, as a powerful presence, like a brass serpent.

Not only were Europeans able to imbue their very bodies with authority and potency like brass serpents, but goods associated with them also were fetishized. European beer, as is evident in the father's speech, entered into this commodity fetishism. Bottled beer, brewed in the British style, easily transportable, always available, for some became a sign of the arbitrary power of the colonialists. Bottled beer was much sought after: it was a sign of European "scientific and mechanical progress" and paradoxically brought a temporary release from the burdens of colonialism.

Colonial Culture/Interculturality

A colonial culture, or colonial cultures, emerged in Kenya as white settlers and Africans created imagery of each other, and of themselves, as particular kinds of persons and political subjects. These images and representations, the products of discourses on race, class, gender, and sexuality, grew out of and shaped the patterns of interaction within and between communities.

Ideologies of class and race brought from Europe were amalgamated and transmuted into particular racist ideologies that differentiated among the African population in part according to their affinity with nature or their corruption by culture. The incorporation of the Kikuyu into the culture of the Europeans, especially the colonialist plantation system, led colonialists to create images of them as spiteful servants, while the "natural" nomadic Maasai remained noble savages.

Masculinist images of nomadic Africans contributed to European perception of sexual license in the African population, sealing differences between European populations of free-spirited aristocrats, flaunting metropolitan mores and envying Maasai masculinist privilege, and the loyal middle class, upholding metropolitan values as a part of their civilizing mission. This diversity in the European populations makes it impossible to speak of a single European point of view.

The African population was also diverse. Kikuyu took advantage of their position in the colonial setting to gain skills and resources needed in commerce, and Maasai "conservatism" unwittingly changed the nature of their society. The racial aesthetics of the colonialists celebrated the noble profile of the Maasai, but the Kikuyu and Maasai claimed cultural, not bodily, markers as most significant. The culture developed in the Kenya colony, with images and reflections of self and others, was based on the multiple articulations of partial societies.

Social Theory and the Colonial Encounter

Social Theory: A Personal Statement

Much of recent theory concentrates on the cultural, presented in its adjectival form to counter notions of essentialism and timelessness of culture. Culture is thought of as "contested, temporal, and emergent" (Clifford 1986: 11-19). I am interested in theories of the social that are congruent with recent interpretations of the cultural, and in playing back the cultural into recent social theories. Three interrelated streams influence my thinking: my own early training in British social anthropology, which led me to "processual anthropology"; feminist theory, which insists on the analysis of race, class, gender, and sexuality in order to understand women and society; and postmodernist critiques of Western society and scholarship. This voyage through recent social theory is a personal one: I show what I found intriguing in processual anthropology, feminist theory, and postmodern critiques, and lay out the theoretical synthesis I reached.

Africanist anthropology during the late colonial period, especially the British Manchester school, always contained a strain of scholarship that was not stereotypically focused on the little community—bounded and untouched by colonialism—but sought to elucidate the effects of the involvement of African populations in wider political and economic networks (Gluckman 1958, 1955; Epstein 1958, 1981, 1992; Swartz 1966), to reveal the variability and openness within African communities (Swartz 1960; Kapferer 1976; Turner 1957), and to assess structural and incidental change over time (Turner 1969; Mayer 1961). Such investigations of the permeability, mutability, and history of African communities do not jibe with Said's recent assimilation of Africanist scholarship to Orientalism—the creation of a tribal, vitalist, originary, and static Africa from Western percepts, for Western consumption. I am not the first to suggest that one of the problems Said has is his monolithic construction of "the West." In this case, the Manchester school's Marxist problematic led to queries about conflict, contradiction, dialectics, economic determination, and change—questions whose answers present a particular Africa for a particular West. These influences led me to a processual analysis of Kikuyu nineteenth-century political economy that recognizes the fluidity of interactional systems within and outside of the community (see chapter 2), and to a study of virginity that suggests that in Africa virginity is valued where it is included with other prestations used by kin groups in open competition for relative rank (see chapter 3). Processual analysis, while it focuses on the social system, deals with the relationship between structure and agency—the extant and emergent properties of social life—yielding a perspective of the social as temporal, contingent, and mutable.

The anthropology of women threw new variables into the mix. When I started my fieldwork in Kenya I was all set to see the positive and transformative effects of conflict and contradictions, to uncover economic and political inequities in the past and present social systems, and to explore the ways in which cultural understandings varied with status, situation, and resources. In short, I went to the field with a model that emphasized conflict, negotiations, and change, but I was unprepared for the social and cultural diversity that women represent. Thereafter, I conscientiously added gender differences to the issues I thought necessary to be evaluated to appreciate social and cultural dynamics, and I found to my liking work in the anthropology of women and feminist anthropology that combined historical materialism and gender analysis (especially Leacock 1978; Etienne and Leacock 1980; Sacks 1979; Rapp 1975; Ross and Rapp 1981; Mullings 1976; Sudarkasa 1973; J. Cole 1980).

Feminist anthropologists helped me grasp that it is the social construction of gender that is at stake in production and reproduction, and that gender, like kinship, emerges from an interactional field in which biology is just one of the constraining and empowering resources. Scholars in women's studies (e.g., Haraway 1988, 1989; Aptheker 1982; A. Davis 1983, 1989) underscored that woman, or more aptly women, must be apprehended through gender plus race, class, and, I insist, sexuality. Too often sexuality is understood as a subset of gender, obscuring the ways in which sexual categories and practices contravene notions of gender, and the role of sexuality itself in the social construction of the person. If the category "woman" is constructed with reference to race, class, gender, and sexuality, then is the coherence of the category, of any such category so multiply defined, lost? Anthropologists might contend that race, class, and sexuality are not a priori necessary to the definition of women, but that what must be considered are locally relevant social and political ideas and practices used in the construction of gender. Under the women's studies and the feminist anthropologists' conceptualizations of women, there is no essential woman. What is left are intersections, moments, instantiations, cross-cutting ties, mutual determinations, competing allegiances, ambivalent positionings, multivocality, and fragmentation. Feminist theory strengthened my inclination to look for economic considerations in the construction of the social, and it deepened my skepticism about the value of culture as a unifying concept.

Not only did my theoretical understanding of the multiplicity in women's lives lead me to reject the totalizing concept of culture, but my experiences as a black American have also caused me to worry about the political uses of the concept of culture. Rethinking culture in the United States prompted me to a more general reconceptionalization.

Deriving from the German *kultur*, the concept of culture linked together a people, a land, and a language in a coherent, integrated package, supporting both apartheid and multiculturalism. In the United States, behavior is blamed on culture. In mass media, and sometimes in government policy, culture is seen as the basis for deleterious socialization, psychological problems, and bad morals. Culture is used as a rallying cry for social action. In still unfinished research from the early 1980s, which I can allude to only briefly here, I examine the concept of culture in the study of black people, suggesting that an approach that ties culture to ongoing social processes is best for understanding the dilemmas and challenges of black people in the United States. When people interact, when they communicate, they use their cultural symbols, ideas, and beliefs to give meaning to action, to establish roles, to confirm or test the environment. Ideas, symbols, and beliefs that inform understandings or meanings people share are validated, modified, and created in the process of social interaction. Racism, social stratification, and economic oppression that are a part of domestic colonialism are major social forces affecting individuals who are carriers and creators of black culture. Established by social heritage, including African tradition, and modified through interaction, culture cannot be blamed for the social conditions of blacks, for culture does not exist as a separate entity outside of society. Maintaining as I do an analytical distinction between the social and the cultural, I value the use of diverse interpretive strategies to uncover meanings central to culture, but hold that these meanings are themselves contingent, invented.

There are varieties of black cultures in the United States; as black communities differ, so will black culture. The amazing similarities of blacks in the United States are as much a result of the impact of the social and cultural domination of whites as of the ethnic identity forged in those communities. Persisting throughout the variation of black cultures are crosscurrents of contradictory beliefs and ideas. In the study of black culture I examine closely two internally contradictory sets of ideas and beliefs. The first set includes the idea that education is the key to success, on the one hand, and the idea that racism overshadows education on the job market, on the other. The second set begins with the emphasis placed on the person, on the development of distinctive style and personal attributes (over the development of self through extension of occupational position, often achieved outside the black community), but is contrasted to the importance of positions achieved solely within the black community. In sum, because culture includes contradictions and tensions that are continually renegotiated and manipulated, I began to analyze culture as a part of social processes. By the 1980s, I could see that to the extent that the social was emergent, fragmentary, and multivocal, then so was culture. I was ready for postmodernism.

Postmodernism?

I am well aware of the vagaries let loose when I open the door to "postmodernism." Am I referring to a time period (mid-nineteenth century or late seventeenth century), to an epoch (late capitalism or early industrialism), to a philosophical school (nihilism, antihumanism, deconstruction, poststructuralism, post-Marxism), to continuities (spectacles, illusions, the recovery of local traditions), or to disjunctions (transgressions, alterity, the breakdown of grand theory and metanarratives)? Does postmodernism imply the impossibility of knowledge or the imbrication of power and knowledge? Is postmodernism apolitical, political aesthetics, reactionary, conservative, radical, liberating? Given the breadth of possibilities of what postmodernism is or can be, I was somewhat daunted to enter its corridors, fearing an attack from an unguarded corner. Yet I was compelled by my understanding of the social as historical, contested, and emergent to see how the cultural was being configured in explicitly postmodern scholarship, that is, to approach postmodernism as social and cultural critique, and to apply it to the production of scholarship on Africa.

One synthesis that makes orderly sense of the contradictions in postmodern scholarship is Pauline Marie Rosenau's *Post-modernism and the Social Sciences: Insights, Inroads, and Intrusions.* She envisions postmodernists as falling into two categories. Skeptical postmodernists, such as Baudrillard, "[offer] a pessimistic, negative, gloomy assessment, argue that the postmodern age is one of fragmentation, disintegration, malaise, meaninglessness, a vagueness or even absence of moral parameters and societal chaos" (1992: 15). Affirmative postmodernists, such as Spivak, are

> either open to positive political action (struggle and resistance) or content with the recognition of visionary, celebratory personal nondogmatic projects that range from New Age religion to New Wave life-styles and include a whole spectrum of post-modern social movements [New Age religions, liberation movements]. (1992: 15-16)

My personal synthesis is different. When I use *postmodernism,* I mean (1) a historical epoch encompassing late capitalism; (2) a post-Marxist political philosophy that incorporates interest groups, social movements, and identity politics with class relations to discern the power of ideology and culture in the production, maintenance, and transformation of relations of dominance and subordination; (3) a poststructuralist concern with the creation of the subject through discourse and the creation of discourse through alterity—engagement with an other; (4) the imbrication of power and knowledge such that power is implicated in all scholarship; (5) the collapse of unilinear time, creating disjunctures between the past and the present—the past shapes the future, and the future redeems the past; (6) a reflexive political aesthetic that questions the place of the author, the form, and the content of the text and the levels of meanings of the work; and (7) a potentially liberating politics open to renewal through struggle and resistance, destabilization and re-creation.

Working my way through the corridors of competing, contradictory, and ever-expanding characterizations of postmodernism leaves me secure in my sense that the social is temporal, mutable, contingent, fragmentary, localized, multivocal, the process and product of decentered selves. But this synthesis raises two more questions. The first, the topic of hot debate in some anthropological circles (cf. Appadurai 1991), has to do with the status and value of theory itself. Anthropologists' much-needed critique of realist ethnography (Marcus and Fischer 1986; Harrison 1991; Jordan 1991) and the concomitant rise in experimental ethnographies turned attention away from theory. By theory I mean articulable propositions or conjectures meant to explain or analyze particular phenomena, not master narratives from the West. Instead of reinvigorating theory, the critique of realist ethnography turned toward increased self-consciousness in discursive practices and emphasized anthropologists' acknowledgment of the collaboration of others in our writing about their lives. Theory, of course, is implicit in the style and content of writing, but more self-consciousness on the part of the writer about his or her positioning in regard to the particular theories would more honestly represent the anthropological enterprise. I agree with David Jacobson, who in his work on how to read ethnographies contends that "an ethnography constitutes an argument" (1991: 7). Out of the myriad observations in an ethnographic experience, particular observations are selected based on many factors, including the training and subjectivity of the anthropologist, and once again selected from based on the relevance of observations to the analytical or interpretive frame of the anthropologist. We cannot escape theory; there is a will to theory as basic as the differentiation between the word and the thing. I am attempting to self-consciously examine my own theory here, and in doing so I diffidently approach the second question raised by my statement on postmodernism: What is discourse?

Discourse

As I ease out of the back door of postmodernism, I am confronted with the thicket of discourse. In "Writing Against Culture," Lila Abu-Lughod (1991: 147) surveys the use of discourse as a shift away from the concept of culture, a concept "shadowed by coherence, timelessness, and discreetness" and compromised by the institutional and political power of its analysts. Very succinctly she captures the two central meanings of discourse for anthropology:

> In its Foucauldian derivation, as it relates to notions of discursive formations, apparatuses, and technologies, it is meant to refuse the distinction between ideas and practices or text and world that the culture concept too readily encourages. In its more sociolinguistic sense, it draws attention to the social uses by individuals of verbal resources. In either case, it allows for the possibility of recognizing within a social group the play of multiple, shifting, and competing statements with practical effects. (1991: 147-48)

In approaching discourse from the linguistic, or perhaps rhetorical, point of view, anthropologists have been concerned with the problems of translation of oral discourse into written, with the representation of indigenous discourse, with the stability of discourse, with discursive strategies and practices—dialogics, multivocality, reflexivity. While Foucauldian notions of discourse appear in the admonition that anthropologists should be concerned with the specifications of discourses in ethnography ("who speaks? who writes? when and where? with or to whom? under what institutional and historical constraints?" [Clifford 1986: 13]), full Foucauldian elaboration of discourse has been less readily taken up by anthropologists (cf. Feierman 1990 for a convincing discourse analysis using African material), and there are good reasons why. Foucault's meanings are slippery and hard to grasp. In his works, discourse desires, mechanisms and apparatuses move society; anthropologists concerned with rigorous analyses are appalled by these anthropomorphisms. Anthropologists who have restored human agency to a place of prominence in the determination of society are frustrated by his antihumanism. Anthropologists who believe in the power of stories to capture meaning in human life are turned off by his disdain for logic and narrative.

Setting out to do a discourse analysis of Foucault's work, Hayden White (1979), in an exceptional early overview of Foucault's philosophy and methods, identifies the theoretical and rhetorical problematic of Foucauldian discourse: "He [Foucault] cannot *say* anything directly. And this because he has no confidence in the power of words to represent either 'things' or 'thoughts'"

(1979: 92, emphasis in original). White's illuminating essay concentrates on Foucault's rhetorical strategies, showing how for Foucault authority is vested in style, "a certain constant manner of utterance" (Foucault quoted in White 1979: 86). In this section I attend to the aspects of discourse analysis most relevant to social and cultural theory. I do so reading Foucault through White, for White effectively brings together possibilities of Foucault's use of discourse as an analytical tool and discourse as rhetoric.

Foucault founds his philosophy on the idea of the arbitrariness of every rule and norm, especially the rules that assign meanings to words and relate those words to the world. Extending the precept of the arbitrariness of the relationship between the word and the world to the world itself, Foucault holds that the rules and norms upon which society is based—rules of exclusion and of hierarchichal order—are also arbitrary. Discourse fixes (though in the long run only temporarily) the relevant distinctions in society; society is created and held together by discourse. What we come to know as culture is the effects of the operations of power embedded in discourse. There is a tension between discourse and power: "Discourse wishes to 'speak the truth,' but in order to do this it must mask from itself its service to desire and power, must indeed mask from itself the fact that it is itself a manifestation of the operations of these two forces" (White 1979: 89). The dynamics among discourse, desire, and power establish the particularities of particular cultures:

> Like desire and power, discourse unfolds "in every society" within the context of external restraints which appear as "rules of exclusion," rules which determine what can be said and not said, who has the right to speak on a given subject, what will constitute reasonable and what "foolish" actions, what will count as "true" and what as "false." *These rules limit the conditions of discourse's existence in different ways in different times and places.* (White 1979: 89, emphasis added)

Foucault's intellectual project is the revelation and dissolution of power in discourse; that he also holds that power and discourse constitute each other throws his nihilism into fine relief. His goal is to restore arbitrariness and temporality to relationships, to make discourse into the free play of words and signs, to remove from discourse the duplicity and deception brought by restraints from the operations of power. The linguistic ontology of Foucault's schema is evident here—discourse, in this configuration, is as arbitrary as the relationship of sign to referent.

Discourse, however, is not solely about language. *Discourse* is the term under which Foucault collects the forms and categories of cultural life, including material elements, institutions, dispositions, technologies, practices, mechanisms, and modalities. The circularity of Foucauldian thought can be noted in the fact that all the forms and categories of cultural life gathered under discourse are in their particulars formed by discourse. Discourse is self-referential and dynamic: the elements of discourse are *events* (Foucauldian events included materials, technologies, practices, organizations, and attitudes) and functional segments that gradually come together to form a system. Discourse as event is therefore not grounded "in a subject (the author), an originating experience (such as writing or reading), or an activity (discourse conceived as mediation between perception and consciousness, or between consciousness and the world, as in philosophical or scientific theories of language)" (White 1979: 90).

The fragments of society are constituted in discourse through dominance and resistance and through the very creation of difference, and are linked in society and culture in discourse through rules of exclusion and hierarchy. The systematic and binding qualities of discourse derive from its being subsumed under the aegis of a constitutive episteme (for instance, the Classical age was under one episteme), which White defines as follows: "the total set of relations that unite, at a given period, the discursive practices that give rise to epistemological figures, sciences, and possibly formalized systems of knowledge" (1979: 92). In sum, I find discourse is a way of talking about social and cultural processes that link together, to use an older anthropological language, disparate ideas, resources, rules, persons, and institutions in an open interactional field, constituting the field, defining the elements of the field, the range of accepted behavior as well as the modes of resistance, and emphasizing the reality of power in the construction of what is and can be done and known.

Discourse analysis is the study of the processes having to do with the intersection of power and knowledge in the constitution of the person (subject), society, and culture. In *Discipline and Punish* (1979), Foucault states that "power and knowledge directly imply one another; that there is no power relation without the correlative constitution of a field of knowledge" (27). Power must have something to rule over; it creates its own dominion, does not simply impose itself on what is there. Power is manifest in dispositions, tactics, techniques, and functions; it is the outcome of practices that define the dominant and dominated—an outcome related to both the exertion of power and resistance to it. Power must be understood through localized, specific "whats and hows," mechanisms and modalities. Localized and specific mechanisms and modalities, however, affect the entire social/economic/political system.

The upshot of all this for me is that in using discourse I have a concept that will allow me to examine the widest range of ideas and practices for systematic interrelations, all the while recognizing that in discourse, knowledge of self, other, and society are created in and through the exercise of and resistance to power. A set of questions that I derived from my study of Foucault helps me see the possible interrelationships in an open field of discourse. Briefly, here are some of the questions—which I hope to develop further within this work—

stimulated by this form of analysis and an example of the insight on colonial Kenya this theoretical approach helped me reach:

* How and by what mechanism is the object of study produced? Mechanisms refer to social practices, cultural logic, technologies, and so forth, and the object of study includes these as well as persons, tasks, social relations, and so on. For example, I contrast the Kikuyu as deceitful servant to the Maasai as noble savage, suggesting that both subjects were created through British nostalgia for a preindustrial past, colonial labor policies and practices, and resistance and accommodation to the colonial state.

* How does the state establish and maintain its power, and how is that power expressed in the everyday? The emphasis here is on breaking down the distinctions between the state and everyday. For example, colonial laws confined Kikuyu land ownership to tribal reservations. The reservation system increased inequalities among the Kikuyu, drove the landless to tenant farming, and contributed to the pattern of domination between master and servant.

* How is it that the exact opposite from what is intended happens? How do mechanisms, technologies, strategies, semiotechniques turn back or reverse themselves in the play of power? For example, as whites attempted racial solidarity in Kenya, they also increased social and ethnic divisions among themselves.

* How is the same different and different the same? This suggests a series of related questions. What unintended equivalences are established by the distinctions discourse makes? One example is freedom-loving Maasai and freedom-seeking British aristocrats. What diverges from that which seems similar? For example, the subject African population is divided into noble savage and deceitful servant. What disjunctures occur in that which seems the same? For example, gender differences cause gaps within the racial hierarchy.

* What is the economy of the object of study—distribution, quantities, relationship, physical dimensions? For example, the economy of virginity would reveal both the role of virgins in political and economic exchange and the number and place of virgins in the moral economy—what should be, what is good, and how these are negotiated in society.

My most serious quarrels with Foucauldian discourse have to do with the disappearance of the individual as agent in shaping his or her own reality, the reification of abstract concepts and cumulative processes, and the postulation of the major overarching linkages as coming from the episteme. The exploration of the fit between my version of social theory and the cultural as configured in postmodernism helped me unravel three paradoxes related to my critique of Foucault. First, culture is extant and emergent: culture as temporal, mutable, and contingent is congruent with the notion of the social as a process of interpolation between structure and agency, the given and the negotiated reality. Second, the individual, the social agent, is a product of culture and produces culture: subjectivity, the sense of oneself as a social agent, is determined by that which one is subject to (laws, language, stories, etc.) and that which one is the subject of (personal decisions, actions, stories, etc.). For the third and final paradox, the question is, What holds together fragmentary culture and part societies? This question nags.

Taking up the fragmentation and integration of colonial part societies through the issue of epistemic unity, I find that the use of the concept of epistemic unity does indeed lead me to seek greater knowledge of the history of ideas of the colonial period. For instance, I am especially interested in understanding the role of eugenic theories and philosophies in the constitution of colonial power and knowledge. But whatever unity was achieved in the colonial period must have come about through various kinds of linkages and articulations. Surely, violence and coercion play a part in the maintenance of loosely integrated systems, as do hegemonic consent, media, communications technology, transportation systems, and social inertia. The state of the world's economy, military and trade alliances, wars and treaties, ecological and ethnic group movements can be forces for change and for conservatism. I submit that there are many different kinds of articulations, not all of them compatible, that pull together cultural fragments and partial societies; discourse analysis is but one method of finding connecting threads.

Interculturality/Local-Global

Fragmented planes of human interaction, posited by postmodernist or critical cultural theory, must in many different ways intersect with national and international economic and political systems. The theory that can capture this complexity of society and culture must include macro- as well as microlevels of social organization. State or national systems cannot circumscribe the domain of human social and cultural interaction; international communications, multinational corporations, fundamentalist religious movements, warfare, and refugee populations are among the forces that cross international borders. National or ethnic groups within states (and in earlier nonstate societies) also interrelate and codetermine one another. Through its peoples' resistance, accommodation, and transcendence of state hegemony, the state becomes a domain of cultural conservation and social continuity as well as social and cultural creativity and innovation. Local groups may develop local culture, but that culture and the nature and organization of the group are influenced by, among other things, other local groups, the state, multinational corporations, tourism, and other international agents and institutions. The accessibility of the cultural and social practices of one group to another allows for social interpenetration and interculturality.

Interculturality is somewhat like the invention of tradition that characterizes nation-states made up of diverse ethnic groups. National culture is constructed through itemization, fragmentation, and reshuffling of elements of preexisting cultures into new patterns.[7] The reorganization or recycling of customs, beliefs, values, attitudes, orientations, places, and things from different ethnic groups is never a free-form process. Centers of power, governmental or religious, with spiritual and material threats and rewards, discipline the population into recognition and acceptance of only certain combinations of ideas and items fragmented from various preexisting systems. But not only do individuals and local groups resist, subvert, accommodate, embrace, transform, or transcend the discourse, policies, and practices from the center, they also reach back into the past to bring forward other items and ideas for the mix and reconfigure the future through interpretations of past and present inventions and tradition.

The notion of interculturality recognizes the power differential between the colonizer and the colonized, but also recognizes that arrows of influence may be drawn from the colonized to the colonizers, and thus that interaction with the African people and landscape reshaped European ideas, attitudes, and practices. The instability of nation-states in Eastern Europe can be explained, in part, by looking at the intercultural processes of nationalism, but interculturality, intercultural processes of nationalism, also undergirds the institutionalization of national culture in Third World countries as well as tribalism and ethnic hostilities in those same countries.

Through interculturality, diverse groups, not circumscribed by the nation-state, share culture. Technologies of media, communication, and transportation allow worldwide sharing of events, entertainment, and interpretations; employees of multinational corporations worldwide lay the foundations for similarity of daily practices, and nation-states are themselves enmeshed in wider political and economic networks. The existence of many present-day nation-states resulted from the colonialism and imperialism of the late nineteenth and early twentieth century. Processes similar to colonialism and imperialism were instrumental in the extension of power and knowledge that formed the first European nation-states. Colonial encounters with distant others brought about changes in the social practices of local groups in the Third World and the metropole; new nations brought about others, and continuing neocolonial/capitalist relations even more. The approach to social theory that I use takes into account time, place, and interconnection of local groups in the partial societies that make up world systems.

Social Analysis: A Synthesis

From this discussion of social and cultural theory, I have come up with five guidelines for social analysis that I have tried to use in this study of colonialism and culture in Kenya. In some ways they are the scaffolding that allowed this work to be built. Seldom in the chapters that follow do I specifically refer to these imperatives, but many of the questions I raise and the paths of analyses I follow are based on them:

> *Put history first.* All phenomena of social life—individuals, groups, institutions, interests, ideas, and discourse—have histories that adumbrate the foundational elements, competing forces, and particular events constitutive of the time and place, the moment of study.

> *Analyze all units as parts of larger networks.* Individuals, local groups, institutions, states, and international organizations are variably influenced by their position in a hierarchy of needs, demands, interests, and resources. The exclusivity or permeability of the boundaries and borders that delineate social units must be established through analysis.

> *Examine race, class, gender, and sexuality* as conditions of social practice, belief, and discourse, and as conditioned by social practices, beliefs, and discourse. One might think that this list could be expanded, but I believe that the power of feminist analysis rests in the recognition of the primacy of race, class, and gender, and of their almost arbitrary relationship to one another. I have added sexuality to the central feminist analytic because too often sexuality is subsumed under gender and the social influence of sexuality ignored.

> *Deconstruct through poetry.* I do not mean this to be taken literally. Poetry requires that I look to the style, substance, and form of the text or event, that I decipher obvious and obscure codes, that I imagine myself within the context of the poem, and that I understand when the poem does not speak to my own experience. A poetic reading of the social, then, would legitimate different levels of knowledge, acknowledge situated knowledge, reflexively include the analyst, and press for compassion for the other.

Look for determinative changes everywhere. Changes in relations of productions most certainly influence social formations and ideology, but consciousness is not solely determined by class, and ideology shapes everyday practices. Lower classes embrace ruling-class ideas, but ruling classes also co-opt and appropriate the culture of those over whom they have power.

Culture and Colonialism in Kenya: The Book

Beginning in chapter 2, I focus on history to capture the understandings and conventions that emerged from everyday practices, and to underscore the constructed and negotiated quality of social and cultural life for late-nineteenth to early-twentieth-century Kikuyu. My research shows how women participated in the political economy and their roles in generating and decreasing inequality in local groups.

Europeans in the colonies and at home debated the topic of African sexual morality and the position of women. Chapter 3 deals with this debate. Kenyatta took up the topic in his ethnography, defending the virginity of unmarried women and the physical and psychological healthiness of Kikuyu sexual practices and attitudes. Leakey, having suffered through a very public divorce and having been brought up in a colonial community that condoned and contravened the metropolitan values, used the Kikuyu to attack metropolitan sexual mores. He championed Kikuyu practices of polygamy, institutionalized premarital sexual contact, and widow inheritance as evidence of women's power and autonomy. Neither man took up the issues of clitoridectomy as a constraint on female sexuality, though both wrote on the positive social functions of the practice as a part of female initiation and cultural continuity. Women were used by both ethnographers as allegories to speak of relations to the dominant powers. In an examination of the colonial discourse on women and race, I survey literature on clitoridectomy and suggest associations between it and certain social and sexual practices.

Chapter 4 begins with Louis Leakey's recollection of a trip he and Mary Leakey took to Angola in 1949. In his story Leakey brings out a number of the personal characteristics and motivations implicit in his other works. His is an adventure tale, not a confession, but the objects of his gaze and the quality of his stories tell much about his accommodation and resistance to colonialism, his science, and his self-promotion. Discussion of Leakey's representation of himself as "white African," as a Kikuyu, and the nature of his relationship to colonial Kenya and metropolitan Britain follow the Angolan adventure. These and other features of Leakey's biography help to determine his representation of the Kikuyu as egalitarian, rule-bound, and harmonious, a representation that Leakey maintains in spite of counterevidence contained in his own three-volume ethnography. I suggest that it was not insensitivity to his own data that compelled Leakey to write a Kikuyu pastoral, but his collaboration with the senior elders who for their own purposes painted a picture similar to that of Leakey's. His prime defense of Kikuyu men against accusations that they were lazy and that they abused and overworked "their" women was to show the ways in which Kikuyu women exercised legitimate authority and freedom of choice. Leakey's interpretation fit with his general view of Kikuyu as egalitarian, but does not jibe with other historical representations of Kikuyu as significantly divided in terms of ownership of productive property. I also show how macro-processes affected the local level, as the ethnography written during the depression of the 1930s shows the signs of contemporary economic and political forces. In the 1950s, Leakey's interpretation of Mau Mau was taken up by Western media and greatly influenced their representation of Jomo Kenyatta and the Kikuyu.

In chapter 5 I examine competing ideas about precolonial Kikuyu society, starting with a close examination of the conditions of production of Jomo Kenyatta's *Facing Mt. Kenya* (1938). Consumed by colonial politics and a politics of authenticity, Kenyatta came down firmly on the side of those who saw precolonial Kikuyu society as harmonious and egalitarian, as opposed to those who represented it as competitive and dominated by large landowning families. I suggest that neither side of this debate adequately captures Kikuyu social processes: structured inequality is not typical of Kikuyu society, nor is rule-governed egalitarianism. An ideology of achievement within an economy where low levels of accumulation of wealth were possible uneasily combined with ambivalent attitudes toward wealth and power, resulting in modulated competition within an open political field.

The debate over the nature of the Kikuyu-led Mau Mau movement in the 1950s harked back to earlier positions on the nature of Kikuyu. Leakey and others engaged in the fray called the Mau Mau movement a syncretistic religious movement gone bad, while Kenyatta and, in hindsight, noted historians, political scientists, and anthropologists called it a revolutionary struggle against colonialist oppressors.

When Mau Mau erupted onto the international scene, images of Jomo Kenyatta dominated popular media coverage of Kenya. Robert Ruark's (1955) best-selling novel *Something of Value* and the subsequent film (released in 1957) owe a considerable debt to Leakey's representation of Mau Mau as criminal and degenerate rather than anticolonial and political. American media portrayals of Kenyatta as a communist agitator competed with representations of him as a savage thug; the latter image won out. In chapter 6 I examine the representation of Kenyatta and the Mau Mau movement in the academic and popular press in the United States.

In chapter 7 I pay special attention to Elspeth Huxley's documentary novel *Red Strangers* (1939), her novel *Flame Trees of Thika* (1959), and her memoirs *Out in the Midday Sun* (1987), and to Karen Blixen's (Isak Dinesen's) *Out of Africa* (1937) as evidence of interculturality in colonial Kenya. European writers often contrast the horticultural Kikuyu with the pastoral Maasai, contrasting the autonomy and resistance of the herders to the stealth and accommodation of the farmers. These images of Africans accommodate European master narratives of progress and change. I argue that the representation of the Kikuyu and the Maasai as very different kinds of colonial subjects influenced land and labor practices toward them and, in turn, conditioned the differences in Maasai and Kikuyu responses to colonialization. The noble Maasai, whose faces—much appreciated by the colonialist—presented a classic profile, were protected and left in nature, though this protection required that they be removed from their homes. The darker, flat-featured Kikuyu, whose land was alienated by white settlers, lived among the Europeans, learned their ways, and were reviled for it. The colonial Maasai represented themselves as pragmatic and conservative, while the Kikuyu actively organized against colonialism. In addition to a colonialist racial aesthetic that praised Maasai beauty and bravery, Maasai sexual practices were admired, if not emulated, by the aristocratic denizens of Kenya's "Happy Valley." Unlike other British colonies in Africa, Kenya had a wide-ranging white population. As their numbers grew, whites enlisted class, ethnicity, national origin, and sexuality in a politics of whiteness in which European aristocrats appropriated Africanisms and African-born Afrikaners were scorned as brutish while the British middle class held the line against the darker races.

2

The Production of Women: Kikuyu Gender and Politics at the Beginning of the Colonial Era

A discourse of male dominance competed with a discourse of female power among the Kikuyu represented in colonial ethnographies. Although Kikuyu men and women jointly participated in some activities, and certain positions could be held by either men or women, Kikuyu conceived of their system as one in which women were excluded from political decision making. Colonial writers captured this ideology of male dominance in their reports and analyses of Kikuyu social and political structure, and they recorded many folktales and proverbs that repeat the same theme. I am interested in showing here, however, that a central ideology, even one congruent with an overt political structure, can exist in tensed opposition to alternative or counterhegemonic ideologies whether it is derived from a close study of social processes or as implicit knowledge in folklore.

Despite an ideology of male dominance pervasive in many kin relations and in an economy that valued livestock, generally under men's control, over vegetable produce, generally under women's control, Kikuyu women emerge in my reanalysis of colonial ethnographies as powerful political players. Women managed the distribution of food. In deciding to give food to work parties, which were important during the Kikuyus' expansionistic late nineteenth century, women at the same time, and by the same acts, recruited followers who added to their own power and prestige, and also made "big men" of their male kin. Kikuyu women's productivity and fertility underpinned male political success.

Early colonial ethnographers sought structure, positions, and authorities—systems to rule through—and failed to recognize social processes. Several ethnographers represented Kikuyu politics as a hierarchical system of councils (*kiama*) from family to district level. One identified *kiama* as a rank instead of a group of which a male elder could be a member (Routledge and Routledge 1910: 198). Instead of focusing on the statuses and structure of the political system, I ask when and how did *kiama* come into being, what was the distribution of power within the *kiama*, and what was the process by which power wielded in the *kiama* was achieved?

Knowing that women did not typically sit with men in the *kiama*, I try to assess women's roles in the Kikuyu political economy and to understand the interaction of power and gender in generating patterns of inequality. In my re-examination of colonial ethnographies with these new questions and points of view, I found evidence to support the interpretation that Kikuyu political relationships were an open field with variable alliances among villages and with influential men amassing power through their position on councils, in the kinship system, and through their stewardship of land. Women were crucial in turning land and its products into political resources. In their own councils, women could act independently of men and held sway over some men, but much of women's power came from their authoritative control over the production and distribution of food and beer.

Piecework: Constructing the Past

I must tease out information about turn-of-the-century Kikuyu from sources written during the colonial period and later. In her strong argument for the recognition and use of the work of our predecessors, and for acknowledgment of the interpretive aspects in our reading of the ethnographic literature, Larcom (1983) encouraged the kind of reading strategy I adopt here, a strategy that yields bits and pieces of old patterns and fabrics that I work together into new possibilities.[1]

Some of these writers, especially Leakey (1977) and Kenyatta (1938), wrote about an era that existed before they were born by interviewing old people, reflecting on stories of the past, and piecing together their own possibilities. Other sources, such as the early ethnographers W. Scoresby Routledge and Katherine Routledge, authors of *With a Prehistoric People: The Akikuyu of British East Africa* (1910), strategically displaced colonized Africans into a distant past, so that they could be brought into the present by British imperialism. These volumes must be read keeping in mind the conditions of their production and the ethics and methods of the writers. In chapters 4 and 5 of this volume, I devote considerable attention to Leakey's and Kenyatta's ethnographies, as well as to an invaluable history of the Kikuyu by Godfrey Muriuki. The other works I rely on heavily are Routledge and Routledge (1910) and Cagnolo (1933).

Routledge and Routledge, a husband and wife team, give us one of the oldest volumes on the Kikuyu. They were interested in the progress of "man," the expansion of knowledge, and the expansion of the British empire. Their volume, dedicated to one of the fathers of anthropology, Edward B. Tylor, takes up the challenge of the new field of anthropology to report on information "collected from a more purely scientific point of view" (1910: xviii). The goal of anthropology as they saw it was to further develop the story of "man's conquest over nature, the gradual development of his social powers, and his religious thought" (xvii). But they were also interested in guiding travelers, and, as W. Scoresby Routledge says on the first page of his preface, in gaining knowledge of the British "share in the general division of the African Continent between nations of Europe" (ix). Katherine Routledge echoes the same sentiment on the first page of her preface: "It is believed that some account of these thousands of our new fellow-subjects, whose destiny now lies in the hands of the British Parliament, may not be without interest to some at any rate of the British people" (xvii).

It is not just antiquarian knowledge of exotic people that should be of interest to the British people, but knowledge of how to subject the population. For instance, after a chapter on the initiation of boys and girls, including the circumcision of boys and clitoridectomy of girls, Katherine Routledge concludes with remarks on the deleterious effect of initiation on male servants:

> Young Kikuyu servants who have been entirely satisfactory till the time that
> they ask for temporary leave to go through these ceremonies, return, if they re-
> turn at all, entirely altered for the worse, and are frequently unable again to set-
> tle down to the routine of a European establishment. (167)

Ultimate observers, the Routledges tried to write about all they could see. They were self-conscious about their methods, but wanted so much to paint the perfect picture that they did not chase after contradictions. To fill in on what they did not see, they interviewed informants, and the two of them also captured images of many people and a wide array of everyday and ritual paraphernalia in photographs. They are meticulous in listing the names and places of origin of all their informants, "sources of information," and in indicating the informants' relationship to them; most were in their employ or were government-appointed chiefs and headmen or their family members. Interviews were conducted in Swahili or through non-Kikuyu interpreters. Information was often double-checked with other informants. I venture that it was their concern for the new science of anthropology that obliged them to be so painstaking in recounting their ethics, methods, and data base, and their concern for gaining knowledge to extend the empire that motivated the limited reflections they undertake in this "descriptive" work.

Starting their research in 1902, the Routledges found the Kikuyu already greatly changed by colonialism. Their writings show evidence of nostalgia for the golden past as reflected by both the Kikuyu and the British:

Though only some six years have elapsed since the English conquest, the new order has already laid its hand on the old. Young men are growing up unacquainted with the old regime; old men are apt unduly to glorify their own dignity in the past. The student looks sadly at the pages of his notebook, filled with information seriously given, about the power and position of the chief, when he realises that chieftainship itself in its present form is an English creation.

The reader of English history is taught that the strength of the Saxons lay in local government; also, that they fell before the Normans because they lacked cohesion.

Kikuyu polity is local government run mad. (195)

The nostalgia for a lost Anglo-Saxon past of equality and community is a theme that I will revisit in my discussion of Leakey's ethnography, written three decades after the Routledges', but the theme is already strongly figured in the Routledges' ethnography. This longing for a golden past destroyed by conquest or industrialization converged with the image of the Kikuyu as nonhierarchical and harmonious to shape particular settler and government discourses in colonial Kenya.

Where the Routledges devote several pages to detailing their methods and point of view, Italian missionary Father C. Cagnolo, in another major ethnography of the Kikuyu, boasts of the accomplishments of the missionaries, complains about government as opposed to missionary education, and laments the rise of Kikuyu independent churches and schools. (The particular role of *Italian* missionaries in a *British* colony also warrants scrutiny in his account.) *The Akikuyu: Their Customs, Traditions, and Folklore* was published in 1933, not long after the organization of the first interregional Kikuyu political party and its demand for greater political and economic participation in the colony, and for cultural autonomy, specifically the right to practice polygamy and clitoridectomy within Kikuyu-run Christian churches and schools. When the colonial government allowed the establishment of independent Christian churches and schools, the missionary deplored it. Father Cagnolo's unambiguously paternal position was also influenced by an anticommunist discourse:

We are observing the opening of independent schools, which the new Ordinance has rendered possible, real hot-beds of bolshevism rising here and there in the native reserve, with the ever increasing feeling of xenophoby and the childish pretence to be able and anxious to act by themselves. It was still more surprising recently to notice in a leading article in the local press how some responsible authority appears not to have grasped the true significance of such schools. (1933: 265)

Questions of the influence of international politics and the discourses on democracy, fascism, and communism at the beginning of World War II were explicit in some prewar ethnographies. I take up some of these issues in chapter 5, where I discuss the conditions of production of Jomo Kenyatta's ethnography, written about five years after Father Cagnolo's.

In his description of the Kikuyu, Father Cagnolo begins with a discussion of the land, the people, and the economy, and goes on to a second section on life cycle, law, medicine, superstition and beliefs, and manners and folklore. The final section deals with progress under colonialism, a brief history of his missionary order, the Consolata Mission in Kenya, and the improvement in the lives of women under missionary influence.

Father Cagnolo was fascinated by the everyday and tried in his ethnography to represent Kikuyu rules and patterns of living so that Europeans would understand them as exotic but not inscrutable, as knowable and therefore transformable. Because he felt that the missionaries were responsible for improving the lives of women, and because he was engaged in a battle to keep women in missionary schools and churches, Father Cagnolo devotes considerable space to explaining the imbalances in the Kikuyu gender system. The status of women and the relations between men and women are both played out against a backdrop of Western mores. Father Cagnolo also frequently recalls Orientalist discourse, as in his representation of "the Kikuyu husband" with its implied three-way contrasts between the unmarked categories of the civilized West, the barbarian Orient, and savage Africa:

> In Kikuyu the husband is not the absolute tyrant, the terror of the other members of the family, the master of life and death, such as we read in certain tribes of the far East, but he is the *moderator*, to the native mind, of every detail of the family routine, into which he admits no outside interference. (1933: 50)

Though their husbands did not have absolute power, wives and mothers in Father Cagnolo's representations are heavily taxed by burdensome domestic labor and often emotionally alienated from their husbands. Women in the Italian missionary's ethnography are in need of rescue from their hardships, but also from the freedoms they enjoy, which threaten Christian decency. Father Cagnolo finds the Kikuyu so corrupt as to openly institutionalize immoral practices. An instance of this is that "polygamy of the rich old men is nothing but a polyandry generally accepted by the persons concerned" (1933: 257).

Colonial ethnographies are useful to the extent that the data in the volumes are retrievable through their contextualization and recombinant in others. As a reader I must be aware of the construction of meaning by way of rhetoric and style, but the saving grace of ethnography may be our inadequacy as writers. Ethnographers struggle to tame masses of data and, as a result, their works often present much more than they know.

The Kikuyu

The following brief description of late-nineteenth-century to early-twentieth-century Kikuyu is based on my reading of the colonial ethnographies I have discussed and others (Hobley 1922; Beecher 1938; Middleton and Kershaw 1965). One of the major balancing forces in the countervailing representations in this literature is John Middleton and Greet Kershaw's contribution to the catalog of East African tribes. Compiled under the principles of structural functionalism, this work sought to identify structures, statuses, and authorities but also tasks, activities, and orientations productive of social relations. While not explicitly attending to them, this approach lays bare some of the behaviors, dispositions, and attitudes necessary in a processual analysis of society.

The Kikuyu are a Bantu-speaking people whose homeland is the foothills around Mount Kenya. Precolonially, they were a polygynous, patrilineal people with a predominant pattern of patrivirilocal residence (living with the husband's father), though patriuroxilocal residence (living with the wife's father) and tenancy with distant relatives or nonrelatives also was practiced. Kikuyu *matura* (*itura*, sing.; villages, groups of homesteads), scattered throughout the ridges of the highlands, were the homes of one or more of the localized *mbari* (subclan, family group), an exogamous group of families who trace some tie to the founding male ancestor. This populous tribe was divided into nine clans named after the daughters of the primordial couple, Gikuyu and Mumbi. The tribe is named after the father, Gikuyu, but Mumbi, the mother, is associated with the land, giving rise to powerful connections between land and kin. Clan ties, but more importantly the generation set and age grade system, provided the cross-cutting links that allowed members of different local groups to act co-operatively. Upon initiation, men—and women in some areas—became members of named age grades. Men in the junior age grade, warriors, were responsible for the defense of their territory, often went on cattle raids during wartime, and cleared roads and built bridges during more peaceful times. *Mũirĩtu* (Kikuyu for full-grown "circumcised" girl), young women after initiation, often worked together in their mothers' fields and organized and participated in dances with the warriors. As they married, had children, and paid the proper fees, warriors moved to elder status. Women, in some areas, also formed elder women's groups. Once every thirty to forty years there was an *ituĩka* ceremony, in which the "government" of the "country" (at best two or three districts consisting of perhaps hundreds of ridges and villages) would be transferred from the men who were senior elders to their sons, who by this time had also reached elder status. Outside of this rarely performed ceremony, the ad hoc councils of male elders—whose members were culled from different villages and/or ridges according to the issue or problem to be resolved—and influential prophets and diviners were the foci of political integration for the widest geographical expanse.

The nineteenth-century Kikuyu had a mixed economy in which women and girls performed the bulk of the horticultural and food processing activities, and men and boys were responsible for tending livestock—primarily goats and sheep, with many fewer cattle. Men and women sometimes engaged in the same productive activities. In fact, Kenyatta (1938: 178) characterizes Kikuyu agricultural labor as generally collective, with male and female workers recruited by kin and nonkin ties. Other observers (Leakey 1977: 170, 186; Cagnolo 1933: 32; Routledge and Routledge, 1910: 39-40) indicate that certain tasks, such as groundbreaking for planting in already cleared land and first weeding, were sometimes done jointly by men and women. They also concur with Kenyatta in listing sweet potatoes, sugar cane, and bananas as principally male crops, but note that responsibility for most of the day-to-day work in the fields fell on women. That women were primarily responsible for subsistence is underscored in a survey of Kikuyu society by Middleton and Kershaw (1965: 18-21), who list the following tasks in their discussion of the sexual division of labor:

Women's tasks
1) planting the staple crops—maize, beans and millet; hoeing, weeding and harvesting crops
2) storing and caring for the food supply; cooking, fetching water and firewood, grinding grain and pounding sugar cane for beer, tending hives and making honey.

Men's tasks
1) tending of cattle in all its aspects, and trading livestock
2) clearing fields, breaking up the surface for planting, cutting drains and water furrows, building roads and bridges
3) planting certain crops, bananas and sweet potatoes, scaring birds away, and uprooting and burning grain stalks

A provincial commissioner in colonial Kenya, Hobley, writing about the southern Kikuyu, saw men's participation in horticulture as minimal; he stated that women's "primary duty may be said to be the raising of food, be it in the form of grain, beans, bananas, sweet potatoes, etc." (1922: 277).

While men and boys occasionally worked in the fields with women and could take over women's tasks there without derogation (Middleton and Kershaw 1965: 18), they could not engage in cooking, washing utensils, or fetching firewood and water without, as Kenyatta puts it, "scandalising" the women (1938: 54). According to the literature, women did not engage in hunting and caring for livestock, although Kikuyu women did milk cows.

In other areas of social life, men and women were eligible for the same kind of positions. The Kikuyu believed that the gift of prophecy or clairvoyance could belong to either males or females, and acclaim was brought to the woman or man who achieved consistent accuracy in prediction. Both men and women could qualify as spiritual healers or diviners (*mundu mugo*), learning their lore after a dream or particular illness or affliction. The number of men in these positions far exceeded the number of women. Almost exclusively, men were the military leaders, ritual specialists, judicial elders, and political leaders. The great exception to this, Wangu Makeri, a female associate of the pro-British leader Karuri, was one of the first people to become a chief in Murang'a District, around 1900 (Muriuki 1974: 133, 161).

Most decisions that were considered binding for the group—the localized subclan, the village, or an amalgam of villages—were undertaken in the male-only council meetings. Routledge and Routledge (1910: 138) note that one "committee" whose task was to decide on the location of a "chief's" latest wife's house was composed of men and women. Hobley (1922: 274) mentions councils of women elders concerned with married life whose powers of witchcraft men feared. Kenyatta (1938: 111) emphasizes a parallelism in men's and women's groups, with women's councils concerned with the circumcision of girls, birth, and other religious duties. In areas where these women's councils were found, the Kikuyu could be said to have a limited dual-sex organization (see Okonjo 1976), limited in the sense that women's decisions were considered binding on women, while men's decisions bound the whole group, both men and women. Or, put another way, in order to implement their decision, men were bound to negotiate with women through their kin relationships, especially husband-wife, while many women's decisions affected only women and the resources they controlled.

Kikuyu ideology, represented in their oral tradition, gives evidence of a tension between male and female power through its concerted rationalization of male political dominance. According to their myth of matriarchy, men overthrew the tyrannical rule of the descendants of the daughters of the primordial couple when by male plot the women, all impregnated at the same time, were heavy with child and unable to quell the men's revolt (Kenyatta 1938: 7). Women's procreative duties also appear as an obstacle to their political activities in a folktale (Beecher 1938) in which women proved themselves unfit to rule when they, because they were ashamed, refused to dance nude (nudity is obligatory in some warrior dances). A meeting of women and men was convened to discuss this issue. The women left the meeting, which went on late into the night, because they feared for their children in the dark and the cold. With the women absent, the men decided that anyone who was both ashamed and afraid could not be a ruler. In both these examples of oral tradition, male democracy is opposed to women's rule or tyranny; thus, while justifying the "democratic" organization of male councils, they commend the containment of potentially uncontrollable female power.

Another folktale, which explains why women do not own such prestigious items as cattle, also speaks of women's cruelty and arrogance. Kenyatta relates that when he asked why his mother did not own cattle, he was told that women once owned cattle, but mistreated them. When asked about their cattle, they arrogantly told Ngai (the creator god) that women's cattle were theirs to do with as they pleased. Ngai took cattle away from women.

The procreative, horticultural, and cooking activities of women, however, were seen as benign and necessary for the survival of men. Two versions of the folktale "The Lost Sister," presented in full in the concluding sections of this chapter, indicate that without women, men would desperately devour their wealth in livestock and, left destitute, would need the bridewealth gained from a sister's marriage to prosper. Among the Kikuyu, men in many ways were and are responsible for the well-being of female members of their families: they made decisions for them, guided and protected them. Women's work in the gardens was necessary, not only for the physical survival of the family, but also for their husbands' achievement of social power and prestige.

The Political Economy of the Nineteenth-Century Kikuyu

In spite of the detailed evidence to the contrary, Godfrey Muriuki (1974), a Kikuyu historian whose description of one early Kikuyu political system is probably the best available, calls Kikuyu society highly egalitarian (110). Power and authority were diffuse, territorial organization ad hoc, and no single person or group controlled social and political institutions. As Muriuki puts it:

> Indeed, it was the duty and responsibility of each individual to safeguard that part of the society in which he was involved at any given time. Kikuyu society, therefore, was basically acephalous, with authority and power being widely diffused throughout its varied components. (110)

From a male point of view, the political system appeared democratic because every adult male was a member of the council appropriate to his age and, with marriage, the birth and initiation of his children, and the payment of specified fees (usually paid in *mburi*, goats), could advance to the level of senior elder. Senior elders had varied responsibilities; Muriuki concludes that sometimes individuals specialized in judicial matters, ceremonial affairs, or in general political concerns (132). A select group of senior elders formed a powerful inner council, *ndundu ya kiama*, and often a *muthamaki* (spokesman) for the group was chosen from this core. The rules for the formation of this system of councils were an important part of Kikuyu cultural beliefs—the understandings on which they organized their social life—though the councils themselves did not exist as enduring structures. Councils were organized on an ad hoc basis across clan and territorial lines.

A man who served as *muthamaki* for several important council meetings was likely to emerge as first among his peers, a candidate for "big man" status. Middleton and Kershaw succinctly summarize the qualities of a man most likely to be selected "spokesman" for a council as follows:

> Councils would seek to select a man who was known for his wisdom, a *muthamaki* [judge, spokesman], who could advise through his experience and command respect. These *athamaki* [plural] might in certain cases obtain renown far beyond their local councils and be sought after as arbiters in disputes within the *rugongo* (ridge [an important territorial division]) and even wider. If a *muthamaki* was moreover a senior member of the *mbari* [family group] with unused land at his disposal, then tenants would seek to come and live with him. He might thus be a very influential person, and also a very wealthy one. (1965: 31)

Surely big men or leaders did arise from this process. Before the colonial regime, the Kikuyu did not have chieftainships or any hereditary political positions or titles. The early reports on the Kikuyu abound with accounts of big men and leaders, many of whom were mistaken for chiefs and some of whom later became chiefs within the colonial system. On this point, Middleton and Kershaw make the following observation:

> Many of the writers on the Kikuyu mention chiefs, and the same names of chiefs occur in many different sources: at the beginning of the century there seem to have been some half dozen leaders who apparently held sway over very considerable areas. The names Karuri, Wangombe, Nduini, and Gakeri in the north, Kinyanui in Kiambu and Karuri in west Kikuyu often occur. It seems likely that these "chiefs" were important men in the indigenous system and were chosen by the early administrators or chiefs over large districts, their duties being to keep general law and order, provide carriers and so on. (1965: 31)

Wealth for the Kikuyu was measured in livestock, land, and people. Livestock were used for the many rituals and ceremonials that marked the yearly round of events, important stages in the life cycle, and special religious, judicial, and political events. More importantly for this discussion, livestock were used to increase the number of people belonging to the family group and the number of alliances available to the family. Through the exchange of livestock through bridewealth, marriages were legitimized, and women whose children increased the size of the group were incorporated into the family. These women put more land under cultivation and enabled the distribution of more foodstuff. Land, the symbol of Kikuyu unity—the mother of the tribe—was a political resource through its spiritual and economic value. The mobilization of wealth in the form of land, livestock, and people is a process that collapses the division between subsistence and political economy.

Land was a resource used by the head of a large *mbari* (family group, subclan) and potential member of the inner council of a *kiama* to recruit followers, men who could be called upon to support his voice in the council, and women who could put more land under cultivation. Such followers gave the landowners livestock for ritual occasions and a portion of each harvest (Leakey 1977: 117–18). The produce gotten from the land could be used in trade with Maasai, Kamba, and Arab traders in occasional large markets on the edge of Kikuyu territory; in hospitality through which alliances were kept alive; and to feed laborers who joined work parties to clear or prepare land for planting. A husband-wife team was the essential unit of recruitment, and wives within this setting still maintained the responsibility for judiciously allocating their harvests to take care of themselves and their families. The relationship between a big man and his followers is an example of a social relationship built on relations of production; that is, because of the necessity or an opportunity to acquire land, worked by women, some men entered into relationships with wealthy elders that provided them access to land, and provided the elder the resources that made him wealthy, powerful, and influential.

Necessity and opportunity were two forces that conditioned different types of relationships with wealthy landowners. The Kikuyu term *muhoi* (*ahoi*, plural), used to designate both types of relationships, means literally "one who asks for something." Through necessity, men whom Leakey calls "serfs," orphaned or left destitute, would leave their home area and travel to a different part of Kikuyuland to "beg" land from the head of a wealthy *mbari*. Some of these men entered into a matrilineal marriage with a daughter of the landowner's family, a widow under his guardianship, or an outsider for whom the landowner provided the bridewealth. Children from these unions belonged to the landowner's family. If, however, the "serf" was adopted by the landowner or through his own industry provided the bridewealth for the marriage, he could claim the children for his own patrilineal family. The followers who were seeking opportunities for expansion and diversification of land were called *ahoi*, tenants. They were generally warriors recruited through work parties, some of whom went to the frontier of Kikuyu territory to claim prized new land. Many of these men had the resources necessary to negotiate their own marriages and claim the children for their families. They lived on the elder's land for a few years until they themselves grew wealthy, or lived on their own family's land and considered the elder's land a valuable additional piece of land for cultivation.

By the middle of the nineteenth century the Kikuyu population had expanded north and south from Mukurue wa Gathanga in Murang'a District and was moving westward toward the Nyandura (Aberdares) Mountains.[2] According to Muriuki, "immigration southwards had been conducted along the traditional lines of small family groups spearheaded by individuals," but the westward expansion required greater defense from the Maasai, on whose territory they were again encroaching (1974: 71–79). It was around this time that it became essential to have groups of warriors to protect herds and defend the settlement, as well as to clear the land. Before this period, and in other areas of Kikuyuland, land was held, during his lifetime, to be the property of the individual who cleared it, and after his death to be *mbari* land. The westward expansion put a strain on this system. As more members of the *mbari* became active first in clearing and then in laying claim to the land, land became more quickly recognized as *mbari* land. The elder who was head of the *mbari* was responsible for allocating the land, and with the consent of the *mbari* could assign land to *athoni* (in-laws), and to serfs and tenants. None of these (*ahoi*) could inherit land, and their usufruct rights could be taken from them at will. Examining the process of individual acquisition and the warrior-tenant contribution, Muriuki gives the following summation:

> Having acquired land, an individual was normally followed by his relatives, or alternatively he *encouraged warriors to settle on the land* as *ahoi* to help with defence against possible attacks by the other *mbari* or the Maasai. The *ahoi* would also help in the arduous job of clearing the forest. They readily accepted such an invitation because the *rutere* (frontier) was regarded as the land of opportunity where an industrious person expected, sooner or later, to acquire wealth of his own to enable him to buy his own land. The frontiersman consequently built large *ihingo* (clusters of homesteads) capable of accommodating hundreds of people, some of whom were warriors under his patronage. (1974: 78, emphasis added)

Outside of frontier areas, working parties of young men assisted in clearing land, and could also become tenants-at-will. These men were encouraged through the possibility of women's presentation of cooked food and beer, a presentation that women did not solely control but that clearly entered into their realm of subsistence activities and domestic decision making. An *mbari* that could attract *ahoi* increased the chances of that *mbari* and its head becoming a powerful force in the community—which was defined by the range of members on particular councils.

A man became a leader by virtue of his position in the kinship network and age grade system, and through his achievement of wisdom and wealth. Wealth was transformed into political resources through its use in transactions that, minimally, affected the alignment of influential and powerful voices within the community. The formation of councils with particularly powerful spokesmen was essentially the manifestation of the ongoing political process. Livestock were circulated and land allocated in ways that maximized the leader's control over people and productive resources. Women did not compete with men for power in this domain, but did supply some of the resources used; and because as wives and mothers they were responsible for the allocation of harvest stored in their granaries, they had a say in the distribution of these resources.

Women's Contribution to the Political Economy

Even though I attempt to show that land and working the land in an extensive horticultural society were vital to the political economy, there is no gainsaying the fact that livestock were important measures of wealth used to consolidate alliances and to increase the number of followers. Cow's milk and meat were made available to warriors by rich men whose praise names were sung by members of the communities. Kenyatta makes the following statement on the importance of cattle and other livestock to wealth:

> To a Gikuyu the cattle in the first place are merely a display of wealth, for a man to be called rich he must own a number of cattle. Because, while every family has a number of sheep and goats, say, from one to hundreds, only a small minority own cattle, and therefore to own a cow or two is the first sign of being a wealthy man. (1938: 64)

The size of a family's herd of cattle and other livestock primarily grew by natural increase; cattle raids on neighboring groups—the Maasai on the frontier, and other Kikuyu, deeper into the Kikuyu homeland; receipt of bridewealth in the form of cattle, goats, and sheep; and gifts by *ahoi* to the *githaka* (estate) head.

Women also contributed to the size of the herds through their trade of vegetable produce for livestock. The Maasai were particularly anxious to get the flours, beans, maize, sugar cane, honey, tobacco, and pottery the Kikuyu women traded for skin cloaks, untanned skins, brass and copper wire, beads, *goats, sheep,* and *calves* (Leakey 1977: 480-83, emphasis added).

Women's trading expeditions may be characterized as long-distance trade. It would take several days to go to the edge of Kikuyu territory or into Maasai (or Kamba) territory and back. In some areas, especially along the northern and southern frontiers of Kikuyuland, extensive intermarriage between Kikuyu and Maasai resulted in an interculturality represented among the Kikuyu by the Maasai initiation guilds, lexical items, aspects of religion, and the organization and training of warriors (Muriuki 1974: 98-100; Lawren 1968a, 1968b). Even in areas and times where the relationship between Kikuyu and Maasai was more hostile, the women of the two groups carried on trade and reaffirmed the interdependence of the two groups. Leakey introduces his discussion of Kikuyu-Maasai trade with the following observations:

Between the Kikuyu and the Maasai there was a long-standing agreement that parties of women of either tribe could go into the territory of the other tribe unmolested, provided that they were on a trading expedition. In actual practice, this agreement meant that Kikuyu trading parties went continuously into Maasai country. (1977: 479)

Where hostilities were so great that trade could not be conducted and environmental conditions such that one group feared famine, they negotiated peace treaties to allow trade to continue; "such treaties were made exclusively in connection with trade requirements" (Leakey 1977: 491). Kikuyu women married to Maasai men usually accompanied them on such missions. The presence of women and girls at these negotiations and on trips into other neighboring tribes was a sign of peace.

Women's ability to carry on trade and to travel on various missions was not limited by their procreative duties, since older women—with at least one initiated daughter—usually undertook the journey. The daughter left at home would take care of the younger children while the mother went on a trading expedition organized and supervised by experienced women traders.

A woman kept the livestock brought back from Maasailand in her own house, and those animals could not be disposed of without consulting her. Other parts of the herd associated with a particular wife's house included a few sheep and goats given to her care at her marriage, and part of the bridewealth received at her daughter's marriage. These livestock would be used only as bridewealth in marriage transactions for full brothers of that particular daughter. The property also could not be separated from the mother's house at the death of her husband. In addition to the portion associated with his mother, following a matrifocal principle (Tanner 1974), the eldest son of each of a man's widows received a share of his father's herds for himself and his brothers.

If a man died without close male patrilineal kin and made a deathbed will to this effect, a widow might herself inherit a share of the herd. This, it should be noted, creates an option for autonomy in a society that practices widow inheritance. A widow of childbearing age who had inherited livestock might take a lover or lovers and have children who carry on her dead husband's name. If she were past childbearing age such a widow might marry a young woman in a woman-woman marriage (Leakey 1977: 800). The young woman was encouraged to take a married man as her lover because he would be eligible to participate in certain rituals for the children of the union. The female husband, however, was the legal father and participated in other ritual occasions. The names given the children and the kin terms used by them indicate, as Leakey carefully concludes, that the female husband was not marrying for her deceased hus-

41

band, but establishing a line for her future son(s). Leakey observes that woman-woman marriage "was not rare" (1977: 800-801).

Besides their activities in trade, which increased the number of livestock and maintained intercourse with neighboring groups, women's most consistent contribution to resources that were used in shaping the political economy was through the distribution of cooked food and beer to work parties from whom a pledge of reciprocal transaction was expected, or whose members stayed on as *ahoi* (tenants). The hospitality extended to others through the presentation of food and drink was one of the prime means through which a rich man manifested his wealth, and it bound others to him through a general expectation of reciprocity.

Food presentation and distribution have been little discussed as political resources in societies such as the Kikuyu in which livestock are major symbols of wealth, though this has been an important topic in the study of Melanesian societies where men are responsible for the distribution of some cooked food. Cattle can form a closed distributional system (Vincent 1971: 120–21, 222; Lancaster 1976: 550, passim), with only few examples of the transformation of vegetable products into livestock, such as was the case with Kikuyu women's Maasai trade. This tendency, however, should not obscure the realization that processes that mobilize signs and material, personnel, rules, and resources used to influence the formulation and implementation of political decisions are political. These processes occur in all domains of social life; their political import depends on the context in which they are viewed.

Food Presentation for Work Parties and for Hospitality

As I have said, Kikuyu women were responsible for most of the planting, day-to-day care, and harvesting of crops, while men did the heavy work of clearing and breaking the ground for first planting. Men's work was most often done in teams as work parties in a process the Kikuyu call *ngwatio*, sometimes translated as "communal labor," but which I see as a *reciprocal exchange of labor* among different task groups recruited by patrilineal and age grade ties. The work of clearing the land of virgin forest was the most difficult; it could take two men one day to fell a fairly large tree (Leakey 1977: 169). The job of clearing the land and establishing a new *githaka* (estate) could seldom be undertaken if a man could not provide food and beer for the work party. Young men labored for elders whose wives and daughters provided the beer and cooked food. Having participated in the first clearing, the young men were given an opportunity to settle as tenants on the elders' property. In this way any elder, who became the head of a large estate with still more unused land remaining, could expect to share in his tenants' successes and to increase the number of people who owed him allegiance.

Among the Kikuyu, as elsewhere, it seems the rich get richer, and the poor get dependent on them. *Mbari*(s) with several women cultivators were more likely to have the resources to support work parties, and eventually attract *ahoi* (tenants). Men who could entreat the women of their families to cook and distribute food and beer had a greater chance of expanding the *mbari*'s holdings and their own following.

Would it ever be to a woman's advantage to allocate a portion of her harvest for use in feeding work parties? Because a processual analysis of Kikuyu political economy has not been attempted before, the literature does not provide an unambiguous answer to this question. From my interpretation of this literature, it seems clear that women would benefit from an increase, to a certain limit, in the number of women attached to the *mbari* because of the greater possibilities for the formation of task groups such an increase would present. Even though each woman was responsible for her garden and its harvest, much of the weeding, thinning of plants, harvesting, and winnowing, as well as the fetching of firewood and water, was done by groups of coresident women and, in some areas, age mates. When a woman was ill, overwhelmed by "procreative duties," or otherwise confined, she turned to her co-wives or other women residing nearby for help. Women, of course, would like to ensure that this help would be forthcoming. The wives of tenants also could work cooperatively with the wives of landowners, though not as interdependently as co-wives, but without the divisive interests of their sons' inheritance and standing in the family.

It is not clear that a "big woman" might come from the processes of the political economy as did a "big man." Women's powers were often framed in terms of a religious or spiritual idiom—the mother's curse, fear of witchcraft of the elder women's council, or the importance of women in many groups' rituals. These areas are not deeply touched on by the processes outlined here and would be important within the family group regardless of the size or relative influence of the *mbari*.

Some women's rituals, such as the *Kūingata Mūrimū*—the ceremony to drive the evil spirits of disease out of Kikuyuland, which required that women work together across broad territorial lines—made it important for women to influence warriors to help them (Leakey 1977: 903–4). Among the southern Kikuyu, by the end of the nineteenth century, this ritual had fallen into the disfavor of the male elders, who would have nothing to do with it. "Occasionally the women enlisted the help of the warriors of their territory to make preliminary arrangements and to make sure that the women of the whole territory were aware that a day had been appointed for the ceremony," Leakey states

(1977: 903). Women, of course, used their kin relationships to ensure compliance. In this case it was primarily mother to son (warrior). Nonetheless, I believe that the women needed clout to organize this massive ritual and that the size and prestige of the initiating women's *mbari* worked to their advantage in gaining the warriors' assistance.

Because women often worked together, an increase in the number of followers could be advantageous. In situations where opposition could be expected, strength in numbers helped. This indicates enough evidence to answer in the affirmative. Yes, women could, at times, benefit from the processes that provided the dynamics of the Kikuyu political economy.

In times of ordinary harvests when a woman balanced feeding the family against making other allocations, the negotiations for use of the produce in the granaries must have involved some hard bargaining between husband and wife. Only in times of great surplus could a husband demand that a granary be put aside for purposes of his own (Leakey 1977: 280-81). Kenyatta lays the foundation for our understanding of the wife's rights and duties in regard to the produce from her fields:

> Each wife is held responsible for what she produces from the land, and can distribute it as she pleases, provided that she has reserved enough food for the use of herself and family until the next harvest. She can sell any surplus stock in the market and buy what she likes, or keep the proceeds for family purposes. (1938: 178)

Leakey likewise affirms the wife and mother's control over her crop:

> The seasonal crops which each woman planted in her garden were her own property, for the food supply of her own children, herself, and her husband. To a certain extent, she could do what she liked with this food. For instance, if she wished to buy any household article such as a winnowing tray, a cooking pot, a basket, or a gourd, she could barter for it with the food in her granaries without consulting her husband or anyone else. (1977: 280)

Husbands could not arbitrarily take the produce from their wives' granaries. Women would have to balance future gains against present needs. Perhaps they wanted to increase the number of women attached to the *mbari*, but were also concerned about providing sufficient food for their families. As wives and mothers, they were responsible for the management and distribution of the produce from their gardens, and also as wives they were expected to obey their husbands, who might have their own plans for the harvest. By no means is it clear that these decisions always had easy resolutions. It is clear that the women's power to make decisions in this context reverberated into other domains, including the alignment of power within the wider community.

Joan Vincent (1971: 187–208), in discussing the politics of agriculture of

Gondo, a community in modern Uganda, came to similar conclusions about the importance of women's subsistence activities in political processes that involve competition for work parties. In the economic system of Gondo, men are involved in fishing, keeping cattle, and growing cotton as a cash crop, while women take care of the subsistence crops, of which millet is a staple. Vincent states that "age, polygamy, and the working of the land [are] the three cornerstones of the prestige paradigm which forms the base of the pyramid of power in Gondo" (1971: 246). A man of sufficient age must have a large enough herd of cattle to give larger numbers than his coevals in marriage transactions, and to have more than two wives. He must use the alliances he has made through marriage and his own agnatic ties in forming work parties to plant and harvest the cash crop. Work parties may be rewarded with beer and reciprocity or with cash. Men try to maximize use of *eitai* (reciprocal transactions). According to Vincent, "the home that produces and is able to store a great deal of millet, not being obliged to sell it for cash as the hungry months proceed, can make most use of eitai organization, while poorer homes are rarely able to exploit it at all" (1971: 192). Beer is considered payment for these work parties, and women are necessary to cultivate the millet and brew the beer. Subsistence production influences the shape of the political economy, and women have recognized authority and negotiated power in making decisions about the use and distribution of these products.

Among the Kikuyu, beer and cooked food were also important in rewarding work parties of men who cleared away secondary bush and the groups of women who without men prepared the grass-covered land. A man and his family, joined by two or three of his friends, who expect him to reciprocate, might start to clear the bush. The next stage Leakey describes as follows:

> Having got thus far with the work, a man would arrange for a big working
> party for a single day, and make his wives cook a plentiful supply of food for
> them to eat while they worked, as well as beer to be drunk in the evening when
> the work was over. Twenty or thirty men would form such a working party and
> all their wives and womenfolk would come too. (1977: 170)

Leakey's use of the term *make* I interpret, in light of the conflicts the situation might present, as an active exchange between the husband and wife. In the work parties described, women harrowed while the men dug. The women worked with their female *mbari* members and friends, very likely age mates, where there were no bush or trees to be cleared. Food and refreshment were given to all groups.

Another way in which the food and drink prepared by Kikuyu women entered the extradomestic economy was through the hospitality by which a leader demonstrated, made manifest, his position. Men participated in the brewing of beer, but not in food preparation, save for rituals and meat feasts. Women's presentation of food to outsiders involved their judicious use of supplies; and by their choices, women set the tone for the interaction. Leacock, in a broader discussion of the status of women, provides apt illustrations of the public nature of such hospitality:

> Food presentation may be a "public" or political act or a private service, according to the structural setting. Among the Tor, as among the Iroquois of the past, women's dispensation of food to strangers is a public act; it set the stage for the reception of newcomers. The women's expressed attitude toward strangers coming into the villages determines how they will be received by the men. . . . By contrast, Bemba women dispense food as a family service that redounds to the husband's stature and enjoins obligations to him on the part of the recipients in the same way as does chiefly extending of hospitality. (1978: 254)

Women as Objects or Subjects in the Political Economy

Kikuyu women's power to exert control and authority to make decisions must be seen in conjunction with their limited autonomy within a system of male dominance. Within women's organizations and through their roles as wives and mothers, Kikuyu women had authority to make certain decisions, including allocation of the harvest. The power they had to make others comply was based on their spiritual powers, strength of character, ability to use kin lines of influence to their advantage, and knowledge of the indispensability of their household services. (One of the livelier topics of discussions that I engaged in with married couples while I was in the field concerned whether or not, and how much, a man would be punished if his wife refused to cook for him.)

On the question of autonomy—no one ever has freedom from control by others. Juniors are controlled by seniors, seniors by each other, some women by some men, and all of us by "the system." Among the Kikuyu, to continue with the husband-wife relationship, husbands are expected to consult with their wives, but wives are expected to obey their husbands. These cultural expectations or understandings do not determine behavior. Wives, of course, do not and did not always obey their husbands nor did they always exercise their right to make decisions. These sometimes conflicting expectations and the behavior they inform set up a paradox in which Kikuyu women are seen by some observers as oppressed and downtrodden and by others as opportunistic and aggressive.

Some women could opt for freedom from male authority as the female husband in a woman-woman marriage, or through the establishment of an independent household, as young widows who inherited livestock could do.[3] Most Kikuyu women, however, did not have these options. Nonetheless, most women could contribute to the political economy through the strategies they developed for maintenance and distribution of the resources over which they had control.

Part of the big man's power came from his focal position in the organization of labor and from the structural importance of his activities in reproducing certain ongoing relations of production. Women were vital in the processes by which power and influence, outside of council meetings, were consolidated.

Were Kikuyu women controllers of resources, or themselves resources controlled by men? Even though definite inequalities in relationships among people—juniors and seniors, men and women—abounded and were important in the Kikuyu political process, I contend that women were not primarily objects in the political economy. A Kikuyu wife and mother was expected to maintain a supply of food from one harvest to the next. At times it would be to her advantage to convert this produce into political resources used to recruit followers, essentially creating a husband-wife team. In other situations, such as when the harvest was scarce or if she were already a member of an extremely large *mbari*, a wife might be reluctant to use her granaries for this purpose. Except in times of overabundant harvests, these decisions were in the wife's hands. Her authority to make these decisions and ability to enforce them were tempered by her limited autonomy. The right to make decisions, the spiritual and economic power to enjoin compliance, and the expectation that wives obey their husbands together set up a dynamic of sometimes conflicting expectations that gave rise to decisions that at times affirmed women's control over resources, men's power over women, or women's power over men.

The Lost Sister

Broadly construed, the discourse of male dominance among the Kikuyu of the early colonial period was, in part, productive of the distinctions between men and women in Kikuyu culture. This discourse brought together the social practices, technologies, and dispositions that excluded women and placed men's concerns and authority hierarchically above women's. Yet this very creation of difference between men and women through men's dominance over women occurred within the context of an alternative discourse, a discourse of resistance, in which women's economic and spiritual practices, and dispositions to maintain management of the resources under their control, compete with ideas and practices constitutive of male dominance.

Kikuyu recognized separate spheres of influence for men and women, especially in the organization of men's and women's councils. But in this section I endeavor to show that the Kikuyu acknowledge the dynamic tension in the overlap of men's and women's spheres. The Kikuyu folktale "The Lost Sister," taken up in full here, illustrates Kikuyu narration of male dependence on female productivity. In the foregoing sections, I have argued that men manipulated kin ties, land, and livestock in order to achieve positions of authority within *kiama*(s), and that their ability to manipulate some of these resources was negotiated through women as daughters and wives, as managers of granaries, and as traders and spiritual leaders. "The Lost Sister" tells a more general story about men's dependence on women through depiction of the brother-sister relationship. Typically, brothers marry with the bridewealth given for their sisters, though *ahoi* or tenants might marry a female dependent of a landowner with or without the promise of future disbursement. For many Kikuyu men, the accumulation of bridewealth for marriage is the first step toward the establishment of a household and participation in ruling councils. The folktale illustrates brothers' dependence on sisters' bridewealth and productive labor for their well-being and prosperity.

I present "The Lost Sister" in detail as an example of Kikuyu gender ideology within the competing discourses of male dominance and female power. Folklore can be usefully viewed as a people's self-conscious exposition of their own society and culture, an overdetermined playground of signs and meanings. The juxtaposition of symbols, situations, and events strongly underscores understandings shared by members of society, and also portrays contradictions evident in basic cultural premises.

The two versions of this story were recorded by Katherine Routledge in different parts of northern Kikuyuland, probably between the years 1902 and 1909. Both versions of the folktale were presented only in English, so I have no way to check the translation of phrases such as "the price of his sister," "bought a wife," and "bought eight girls." I suspect that the effect of the colonial money economy influenced the choice of words, but the excessive and never-ending demands of a woman's family for goods in exchange for her marriage in the Kikuyu past and today easily assimilate to commercialized tone and language.

In her brief introduction to her chapter on folktales, Katherine Routledge calls on the Western reader to "deal tenderly with these romances of nature, these half-clad children of a sunnier clime" (1910: 286). Her concern is that taking the stories out of the context of their narration by mothers and elders to children sitting at noon under a sacred tree gazing out at the snowy peaks of Mount Kenya, or around a nighttime campfire with a hyena howling in the distance, loses the spirit that gave birth to the folktales (1910: 286). I am not at all certain that Katherine Routledge recorded the folktales under these circumstances; she reports only the name of the narrator at the beginning of each tale. The young man who tells the first version of the story worked for the Routledges for six months as their camera carrier. The Routledges' corpus of folktales contains only one story by this narrator.

The old woman Nagatuu, narrator of the second version, was apparently the wife of a chief—"Mother of one of the herds of the Chief N'Duini" (1910: 287)—near whose headquarters Katherine Routledge once resided. In addition to her version of "The Lost Sister," Nagatuu is responsible for three other stories in the Routledge corpus. Routledge puts in a separate category "The Tale of the Maiden Who Was Sacrificed by her Kin, and Whom her Lover Brought Back from Below," "A Tale Which Inculcates Kindness to Animals," and "The Girl and the Doves." All of Nagatuu's stories deal in one way or another with loss and restitution and with the divided loyalties between the natal family and "affines." "The Girl and the Doves" is the most allegorical. In this tale a cruel mother beats her daughter to death, but the daughter is revived by doves. When the mother refuses the demands for goods the doves make, the girl dies again. The girl can live only if she has no contact with her parents and refuses to help her sister, who has difficulties fetching water. Nagatuu's other stories end in a reconciliation accomplished by an exchange of bridewealth or other goods.

Both versions of "The Lost Sister" follow. Presented in the order published, the first is the young man's version; the second is the old woman's. In reprinting both here, I have left out the syllabization and nonstandard diacritical marks used in the text.

The Story as Told by NJarge, Son of the Chief Munge

A long time ago a young warrior and his sister lived together in a hut. They lived alone, for their parents had died when they were children, and the hut stood by itself; there were no other homesteads near. The name of the young man was Wagacharaibu, and the maiden was called Mweru. Wagacharaibu had beautiful hair which reached to his waist [footnote refers the reader to the photograph used as the frontispiece and to a discussion of hair dressing earlier in the volume], and all the young women admired him greatly, so that he often went away from home to a long distance to see his friends, and Mweru was left quite by herself.

Now one day when he came back after he had been thus away, Mweru said to him, "Three men came here last night when I was all alone, and each had a club and each had a spear, and if you go away and leave me all alone I know that they will come back and carry me off." But Wagacharaibu only said, "You talk nonsense," and he went away again as before. And the three men came back, as Mweru had said, with the three clubs and the three spears, and they took hold of the girl by the neck and by the legs and they lifted her up and they carried her away. When Wagacharaibu came home again he went to the house and found it quite empty, and as he went he heard a girl's voice crying from the opposite hillside, and the voice was the voice of his sister, and it said, "Wagacharaibu, men have come and carried me away. Go into the hut, you will find the gruel on the stool." And Wagacharaibu cried aloud and said, "Who will shave the front of my head now you are gone, for we have no neighbours?" And he plunged into the grass after Mweru, and the farther he went the farther she was carried away from him; and he heard her voice and she heard his voice, but they could not see one another; and he followed and followed for one month, and he became very hungry. And he wore a hat such as men used to wear in the old days; it was a piece of goatskin, and it had two holes cut in it and strings to tie under the chin, and the skin stood out over the forehead so that rain could not touch the face; and you may see such hats even now among the mountains where there are many trees and much rain, and among the Masai. So Wagacharaibu cut a piece of the leather and ate it, for he was very hungry, and he felt strong again; he went on and on a second month, and again a third month, till the hat was all finished; and then he took his garment of skin and he ate that, and so he went on a fourth month and a fifth month, until he had travelled one year and four months, and the cape was finished. Then being again hungry, when he came to a big homestead he went inside, and he saw a woman cooking food and he begged a little; and she gave him some, but she did not hand it to him in a nice vessel, but in a broken piece of an old pot. And that night he slept there, and the next morning he went out with the little son of the woman to scare the birds from the crops, for the grain was nearly ripe, and he took stones and threw them at the birds, and as he threw a stone he would say, "Fly away, fly away, little bird, like Mweru has flown away, never to be seen any more." And the little boy listened, and he went home, and when Wagacharaibu was not near, he told his mother the words the stranger had said, but she paid no attention to the tale of her son and did not listen to it, and the next day the same thing happened again, and the third day the woman went herself to the fields and she heard the words of Wagacharaibu, "Fly away, fly away little bird, like Mweru has flown away, never to be seen any more," and the woman's name was Mweru, and she said, "Why do you say those words to the birds?" And he said, "I once had a sister named Mweru, and she was lost, and I have followed her many months and years, but I have never seen her again." And the woman put her hand over her eyes and she wept, for she was indeed his sister, and she said, "Are you truly my brother?" for she had not known him, so changed was he by his long travels, and she said, "Truly your hair is unkempt and your clothes are not as they were, and I did not know you, but you shall be once more dressed as in time past, and I shall see if you are my very brother Wagacharaibu."

So she went to her husband, who had carried her away in the old days, and she got four sheep and three goats, and the four sheep were killed, and Wagacharaibu ate of the flesh and became big and strong once more, and his sister took of the fat and dressed his hair, and put it on his shoulders; and of the three goats two were black and one was white, and she made a cape, and she took a spear and gave it him, and it was the spear which her husband had carried when he came to the little hut when she was alone, and gave it to her brother. She put on his arms brass and iron armlets, and ornaments on his legs and round his neck, and then she said, "Now I see that you are indeed my brother Wagacharaibu." And the husband of Mweru loved Wagacharaibu dearly, and he gave him twenty goats and three oxen, which was much more than the price of his sister, but he gave it because of the affection he bore him, and he built him a hut in the homestead and gave him thirty goats to buy a wife. And Wagacharaibu bought a maiden and brought her to the hut, and the goats of Wagacharaibu increased and multiplied, and he took ten of the goats and his sister's husband gave him twenty goats and he bought a second wife, so that Wagacharaibu did not go back to his old life any more, but lived with the sister he had lost and with her husband.

The Story as Told by the Old Woman Nagatuu

Once upon a time there were a brother and sister who lived together, and the mother died leaving many goats, and the brother looked after the goats in the daytime, but in the evening he went away from home, for he was very beautiful, and had many friends. The name of the girl was Wachera, the name of the brother Wamwea. Now one day when the brother returned Wachera said to him, "Two men were here yesterday, and if you go away and leave me they will carry me off," but he said, "You talk nonsense," and she said, "I am speaking the truth, but when they take me I will bear with me a gourd full of sap which is like fat, and along the path I will let it drop, so that you can follow my trail."[4]

Now that night when Wamwea brought the goats home, Wachera made a great feast and gruel, but again he went away. And when Wamwea came back next morning he found the homestead empty, for his sister had been carried away as she said, but he saw the track where drop by drop she had let fall the sap which is like fat. And Wamwea followed over hill and down dale, and ever and again he heard her voice crying from the opposite hill side, "Follow after where you see the trail." The following day the sap began to take root, and to spring up into little plants, but his sister he saw not. And at last he returned to his home to herd the flock, and he took them out to feed, but he had no one to prepare food for him when he returned at night, and if he himself prepared the food there was no one to care for the flocks, so he slew a goat and ate it, and when it was finished he slew yet another, and so on till all the goats were finished. Then he killed and ate the oxen one by one, and they lasted him months and years for the flock was large, but at last they were all gone, and then he bethought him of his sister.

Now the plants which had sprung were by this time grown to trees, which marked the way she had gone, and so he journeyed on for one month and half a month, and at the end of that time he came to a stream, and by the stream were two children getting water, and he said to the younger, "Give me some water in your gourd," but the child refused; but the elder child spoke to the younger and said, "Give the stranger to drink, for our mother said if ever you see a stranger coming by the way of the trees he is my brother." So he and the children went up to the homestead, and he waited outside, and Wachera came out, and he knew her at once, but she did not know him, for he was not dressed as before with ochre and fat; and he came into her hut, and she gave him food, not in a good vessel, but in a potsherd, and he slept in the hut, but on the floor, not on the bed.

Now next day he went out with the children to drive away the birds from the crops, and as he threw a stone he would say, "Fly away, little bird, as

Wachera flew away and never came back any more," and another bird would come, and he would throw another stone and say the same words again, and this happened the next day and the next for a whole month; and the children heard, and so did others, and said, "Why does he say the name Wachera?" And they went and told their mother, and at last she came and waited among the grass and listened to his words, and said, "Surely this is my brother Wamwea," and she went back to the house and sent for a young man, and told him to go and fetch Wamwea to come to her, for she said, "He is my brother." And the young man went and told Wamwea the words of his sister, but he refused, for he said, "I have dwelt in the abode of my sister, and she has given me no cup for my food but a potsherd," and he would not go in. And the young man returned to Wachera, and told her the words of her brother, and she said, "Take ten goats and go again and bid him come to me," and the young man took ten goats and said, "Thy sister has sent these ten goats," but Wamwea refused, and the young man returned. And Wachera said, "Take ten oxen and give them to my brother," but Wamwea would not; and Wachera sent him ten cows, and again ten cows, and still Wamwea refused to come in. And Wachera told her husband how she had found her brother, and how he would not be reconciled to her, and her husband said, "Send him yet more beasts," so Wachera sent ten other cows and again ten more, till Wamwea had received forty cows besides the goats and the oxen which Wachera had sent at the first, and the heart of Wamwea relented, and he came into the house of his sister. And she killed a goat, and took the fat and dressed his hair and his shoulders, for she said, "I did not know you, for you were not adorned as before."

After Wamwea had been reconciled to his sister, he decided that eight wives should be given him, so the husband of Wachera sent to all his relations round about, and they brought in goats, and Wamwea bought eight girls, some for thirty goats, some for forty. Other relations all came and built eight huts for the wives near to the dwelling of Wachera, so Wamwea and his wives dwelt near the homestead of his sister. (Routledge and Routledge 1910: 290–96)

The two versions have several elements in common: isolation of the brother and sister, his leaving her alone after her warning, the sister's preparation of food for her brother and his helplessness without her, his searching for her and not being recognized when he finds her, the sister's child telling of her brother's presence, the reconciliation of brother and sister, the restoration of the brother to his former beauty by the sister, the brother's receiving livestock and goods from his sister's husband, and the brother's marrying and settling prosperously near the homestead of the sister's husband. The differences in the two versions highlight differences in men's and women's perception of their relationships—from the woman's point of view, the dutiful and caring sister versus the selfish and demanding brother, and from the man's point of view the bold and fearless brother versus the bountiful, lost sister.

These differences are significant. In the old woman's version, the sister's name means "cultivator," the brother's "the only one," setting up a specific contrast between the production of the woman and the status of the man. In the young man's version the sister is "brightness or whiteness" (qualities associated with the supreme being) and the brother is "the conceited one"; the contrast between man and woman here is even more stark. The sister possesses the qualities of greatness, while the brother only thinks he does. In the version told by a young man, the men who took the sister had clubs and spears, the sister did not cook a feast but left gruel for the brother to eat, the brother immediately went after his sister and while wandering in the forest ate his head covering and clothes; after the reconciliation the husband's spear is given to the brother, no livestock are given directly to the brother by the sister, but a more than generous bridewealth is given freely to the brother by his sister's husband.

Three important antecedent conditions set in this folktale are seldom found in Kikuyu society. First is women's ownership of herds of livestock. In both versions the scene is set by the statement that the mother has died, leaving large herds of animals. In the old woman's version, the sister, once she is married, seems to have control over many head of livestock, which she gives to her brother before consulting her husband. Among the Kikuyu, women did not usually own large herds of livestock, nor would widows typically inherit their husband's herds, which would, in most cases, be divided among the deceased man's sons, brothers, or patrilineal cousins. Second, finding a brother-sister pair of this age living in social isolation, not incorporated into some other homestead, would be exceptional: they would usually be affiliated with a father's brother or, failing that, more distantly related kin. Considerations other than descent also affected choice of residence—for example, a man would sometimes attach himself to matrilateral kin or become *muhoi* (tenant) of a particularly wealthy man. Yet even given the amount of variability in residence patterns, isolated sibling coresidence was uncommon.

The physical isolation of the brother and sister is the third anomalous antecedent condition. They were alone in that their household was not incorporated into a larger homestead, and in that their homestead had no nearby neighbors. Though homesteads were scattered throughout the hills and often separated by open fields and rivers, each homestead might contain several households. In keeping with Kikuyu practice, the brother-sister household should at least be a differentiated household within a larger homestead. At the end of both versions of the folktale, the brother builds his homestead adjacent to his sister's husband's, and some distance from his home territory, placing himself within a wider community. The singular isolation of the brother-sister pair in contradistinction to Kikuyu range of variation in residence indicates that the folktale "The Lost Sister" delves into existential male-female relationships and gender ideology as well as the specific nature of brother-sister relations in this patrilineal society.

Both versions of the folktale are multilayered, presenting several possible interpretations. Kikuyu writer Rose Gecau (1970: 9) maintains that in Kikuyu folktales "it was very rare to find tales the plot of which pointed to only one particular moral." Besides representing men's dependence on women's productivity, "The Lost Sister" can also be read as a man's coming of age story, and as a story of the transition from Kikuyu to Maasai. I will briefly review these two interpretations before turning to "The Lost Sister" as a story showing how turn-of-the-century Kikuyu commented on the men's dependency on women's productivity.

Sexuality and Age Grades

The sister's maturation into a sexually active, fertile, married woman is at the heart of both versions of the story. In neither story are we told the relative age of the sister. The primary indications that the sister was of marriageable age, had undergone initiation and clitoridectomy, are circumstantial—her resourcefulness in establishing a trail, her being prepared to be carried off, and her subsequent fertility.

Old women and men I interviewed in 1971 told me that without *irua*, the initiation ceremony that included clitoridectomy for women, girls would not be fertile, and they would not be intelligent. Jean Davison, in interviewing an older woman whom she calls a "traditional woman," fills in what it means to be intelligent:

> From *Irua* I learned what it meant to be grown-up, with more brains. This is because after circumcision, I began to listen to my mother's advice that moving about with men could easily make me become pregnant once I begin menstruating. Also from *Irua*, I learned what it means to be pure Mūgīkūyū—to have earned the stage of maturity when, being a circumcised person, one no longer moves about with those not yet circumcised.
>
> These things I am telling you, Nyina-wa-Stephen [mother of Stephen, referring to the interviewer], make my lips fearful to think of the way things have changed. Now, a girl misses something by not going through *Irua*—she does not know when she is talking nonsense in front of a grown person. (1989: 42)

"Talking nonsense" is just what the brother accuses his sister of when she complains that men will come to take her away.[5] Her intelligence in this instance is not measured by her abstinence from sexual intercourse, but by her knowledge of its inevitability and her preparation to maintain contact with her brother as representative of her natal family. In the old woman's version of the story, the sister shows her age and social status in knowing that she must leave her brother, in preparing the feast (a wedding feast?) for him, and in preparing a path for him to follow. The young man's version has an equally intelligent sister who leaves gruel for the brother and prepares the way for him to find her.

The sister is ready for marriage, yet still she protests. "The Lost Sister" narrates one of the last stages of the Kikuyu marriage ritual, the mock capture of the bride who cries when her husband's relatives come to fetch her, calling on her relatives to keep and protect her. (In recent years, mock capture may occur when the groom's men come to the bride's house to deliver her, already dressed in her wedding gown, to the church where the guests and minister await them.) The capture of the sister in both versions of "The Lost Sister" leads to her becoming a wife and mother. But in actuality, a woman would not have become a wife without the transfer of bridewealth in the form of beer, food, and livestock from the husband to the woman's patrilineal relatives or guardians. At one level, the folktale concerns the transformation of a woman from sister to wife through sexuality and childbirth, but denaturalizes this transition through the demands of the brother.[6]

While on the surface both versions of the tale suggest the brother's transition from carefree warrior days to elder status, married head of household, I propose that embedded in the story is another coming of age story that excites more interest among the Kikuyu—the transformation from boyhood to warriorhood. This is more distinctly implied in the young man's version. The brother whose sister is taken away by men with "clubs and spears" is in conflict with other men who have access to women, as is the uncircumcised boy with warriors. But in order for him to get a woman he must be born again, the transition through the forest ending in his transformed appearance, and he must lose his head covering (the foreskin of his penis)—be circumcised—thereby joining the warrior age grade. When he is reconciled with his sister, the brother receives the emblem of the warrior and of sexuality—the spear. Though he cannot have sex with his sister, he can with the wives provided by the bridewealth of the sister. The incest taboo makes it inevitable that a sister will leave her brother. The sister may provide for the brother, but in Kikuyu lore and general practice a productive, stable household cannot be sustained without a reproductive pair at its core.

How a Kikuyu Becomes a Maasai

An alternative reading of "The Lost Sister" is that it is the story of how a Kikuyu can become a Maasai. The pastoral Maasai, whose relationships to the Kikuyu ranged from kinship and alliance to competition and enmity, lived to the north, east, and southeast of the Kikuyu. Though no geographical directions are mentioned in the story, the social compass of the story points to increasing dependence on livestock and to the masculine ideal of the Maasai lifestyle. The brother in the old woman's version herds livestock, eats meat, and ignores horticulture (the sister's name means "cultivator"). His indulgence in meat feasts and avoidance of horticulture recall the Maasai in three ways: (1) Maasai men express disdain for people who "dig in the earth," especially neighboring horticultural peoples; (2) after initiation into warriorhood, the Maasai *moran* (warriors) gather in groups to feast off cows stolen from their fathers' or neighboring herds; and (3) the Maasai *moran* are especially antidomestic—they live outside of the homesteads occupied by married men and women, and neither cattle nor women "belong" to them (Llewelyn-Davies 1978: 206-37). The brother's social isolation, his rejection of cultivation, and his massive consumption of his herds pulls in the direction of the antidomestic Maasai warrior.

The brother becomes Maasai through his personal transformation, and by settling on the edge of the world with his sister. When the brother finally reaches his sister, it is clear that he is in a paradise rich in livestock, a pastoral Shangri-la. For many Kikuyu this lost horizon had a name, Maasailand, where Kikuyu rich in cattle could become Maasai. The brother is not recovering a sister taken during wartime hostilities, but rejoining an adult sister whose marriage affords him the resources to marry well and often.[7] The brother's acquisition of the spear, from his sister, underscores her role in the inauguration of the brother's married life.

Male Dependence on Female Productivity

Neither brother left on his own without his sister can increase his flock or his prosperity. In the old woman's version, the brother must live off his herd, for if he did the work of his sister, the "cultivator"—getting firewood, preparing and cooking food—he would jeopardize his herd. Only after the last of the herd is eaten do his thoughts turn to his lost sister: "Then he killed and ate the oxen one by one, and they lasted him months and years for the flock was large, but at last they were all gone, and then he bethought him of his sister." Arguably, the brother in the young man's version is worse off, for he is reduced to a state of nature as he eats his clothing while searching for his sister. In the young man's version, the brother, the "conceited one," cries, "Who will shave the front of my head?" when he learns that his sister is gone. The shaving of the brother's head is part of the sister's social production of the brother as warrior; he asks how he can maintain his position without his sister. In both versions the brother is reduced to great poverty and must find (or replace) his sister.

Sisters', or women's, labor is necessary for brothers, or men, to accumulate and enjoy their wealth. Women's control of vegetable products lead to cattle, as a line of trees leads the brother to his sister and her bridewealth. In the old woman's tale the sap, "sap which is like fat," from which the trees grow is an ambivalent substance. Fat, an animal product, is associated with men. It is a prized part of the diet—the wealthier the man, the more likely he is to "live off the fat of the land." But sap is vegetable, and associated here with women. Significantly, "sap which is like fat" encodes the sister's reproductive capacity, highlights her transformative powers, and also conjoins female productive abilities and male power and wealth.

The image of the spears and clubs in the young man's version is similar to the "sap which is like fat" in the old woman's version, emphasizing, I suggest, the differences in the young man's perception and evaluation of male courage and strength and the old woman's of female productivity and fertility. Phallic references here are obvious, and overdetermined, representing the sister's loss of virginity and marriage, the brother's sexual maturity and marriage, and the establishment of amicable relations between in-laws. When the brother and sister are reconciled at the end of the young man's story, the brother is given the husband's spear: enmity is changed to amity through marriage as the brother receives the spear that took his sister away from him.

The realizations that sisters must marry out and that brothers may profit from the marriage of a sister are major themes in "The Lost Sister." A brother should not be too thorough in protecting his sister from other men: the incest taboo prohibits sexual intercourse between the two of them; exogamy demands that she marry an outsider or nonfamily member. The brother must forfeit his responsibility in letting his sister marry, and she must marry in order for him to marry. Although the Kikuyu did not practice the custom of specifically cattle-linked siblings (in some African societies a brother and sister are paired such that he marries with the bridewealth gained from that particular sister's marriage), men did (and do) acknowledge that their sisters' marriages afforded them the wherewithal to marry.[8] The loss of his sister's labor reduces the brother to helplessness and causes him to destroy his wealth, but when brother and sister are reconciled, her bridewealth allows him to rebuild his herd, to marry, and live prosperously.

The nature of the exchange of bridewealth, freely given or extorted, is a critical difference in the two versions. In the old woman's version, the brother tortuously extracts an exorbitant amount of bridewealth from the sister and her husband, until finally the siblings are reconciled. After this the brother is provided with eight wives from the sister's husband's relatives. In the young man's version, we are told that

the husband of Mweru loved [her brother] dearly, and he gave him twenty goats and three oxen, which was much more than the price of his sister, but he gave it because of the affection he bore him, and he built him a hut in the homestead and gave him thirty goats to buy a wife.

This is an explicit statement of the dependence of brothers on the bridewealth gained from their sisters' marriage and an implicit recognition of his new guardianship and interest in the continuation of his sister's marriage: bridewealth or marriage insurance, as it is sometimes called, among the Kikuyu was returnable.

In "The Lost Sister," amicable relations between brother and sister's husband are also accomplished in two other ways: through the exchange of bridewealth, and through the mediation of the sister's son, who first befriends his mother's brother in both versions. Through his relationship to the child of a sister, a man establishes a relationship with his sister's husband's group. In both versions, the sister's child meets the brother at the end of his journey, and this child unravels the mystery of the identity of the stranger. The brother's acceptance of the bridewealth legitimizes the sister's marriage and the status of the child as a member of the husband's family. By this act the brother's social relations are expanded: he is now an in-law and an uncle or mother's brother with particular ritual and social obligations.

This interpretation of the folktale "The Lost Sister" adds to an understanding of cross-sibling relations, but more generally it is a commentary on gender dynamics. Some of the behavior evidenced by brother and sister in the tale is not typical of brother-sister relationships specifically, but is typical of men and women generally. For example, sisters do not have primary responsibility for providing vegetable foodstuff for their brothers, but in general women do for men. Brothers seldom settle down near their sisters, but in another sense men must "settle" with women, reconcile their differences and live with women. Brother and sister do not live in isolation but, in a real sense, men and women do. "The Lost Sister" counters the rationalizations of male dominance found in much of the rest of reported Kikuyu folklore.

Piecing It Together

The gender discourse of the early-twentieth-century Kikuyu linked together social processes in an open political field, creating differences and fixing relevant distinctions. The competition for pride of place among men was played out by landowning heads of household who could use their access to the elders' *kiama*, management of the family estate, and authority over kin to emerge as powerful big men. But men could not achieve prestigious position without the productive and reproductive contributions of women. Women's control over vegetable foodstuff was nearly inviolate: men had to negotiate with them for use of grain stores, and women had their own reasons for agreeing or disagreeing with men. In a situation that was not "separate but equal," but rather interdependent and interactive, the particularities of each gender's contribution to the social welfare weighed heavily.

Kikuyu ideology is ambivalent toward female power, reflecting the contradictions of male dominance and female power. A folktale of loss and restitution, "The Lost Sister" clarifies what men and women stand to gain and lose in the Kikuyu gender dynamic. In the folktale the brother loses beauty, wealth, and status, but regains them through the bridewealth and the productive and reproductive labor of the sister. The sister's situation is not a simple case of loss and gain, but of loss, transformation, and gain. Through the sister's transformation of vegetables into animals, relations between men are transformed, affinal relations between the brother and husband are established, the brother becomes mother's brother to his sister's son, and he becomes a married man among elders. She loses the protection of her brother, representing her natal family, and her virginity. But in giving in to the demands of the brother she gains legitimation of her marriage and children, and recognition as a married woman among women.

I have ventured three different interpretations of the folktale "The Lost Sister" as a coming of age story, as intertribal commentary, and as existential gender dynamic. These combine to make a particular representation of the Kikuyu during the early colonial period that I have pieced together from the colonial literature. When a Kikuyu boy becomes a man through the circumcision ritual, he turns his attention to extradomestic concerns, dancing, women, and cattle raiding. A favorite target of the raid is the Maasai, but Kikuyu and Maasai also intermarry. Gender relations negotiated at the Kikuyu-Maasai border often involved the transfer of livestock from Maasai to Kikuyu. Ironically, women are pivotal in the construction of the warrior's extradomestic domain, as male elders are to the creation of the domestic realm. Women's power, emanating from their vital role in reproduction and production, consists in their ability to transform energy and matter.

I now turn from an exploration of women's production and reproduction to colonial discourse on women and race, especially the representation of Kikuyu women's sexuality in the ethnographies of Louis Leakey and Jomo Kenyatta. In the next chapter, I reflect on Kikuyu sexual morality as represented by Kenyatta and Leakey and speculate on the meanings of clitoridectomy and female premarital virginity.

3

Kikuyu Women and Sexuality

Women as Allegory: Leakey

In his representation of Kikuyu women, Leakey, to paraphrase James Clifford (1986: 98), describes real cultural phenomena—the statuses, roles, powers, and autonomy of women's lives—and makes additional moral judgments regarding their goodness and rightness. The implicit questions or allegories that directed the representation of women in the ethnography led to a broad inclusion of women, yet did not allow women to be seen outside this particular frame of questions or moral concerns, but at the same time did challenge Western prejudices. Leakey does not present the individual voice of a woman negotiating her various roles and statuses, experimenting with implicit social knowledge. Predominating in the ethnography is the generic masculine of person and of culture—the culture seen as the invention and province of men, yielding such constructions as "Kikuyu women" contrasted not to "Kikuyu men" but rather to "the Kikuyu," and, of course, the Kikuyu and "their women." The major thrust of the discussions of women is the defense of Kikuyu men as the dominant force in a culture that employed women in backbreaking labor but allowed them social influence and "sexual freedom."

Leakey defends Kikuyu men against the accusation that the men are lazy and the women do all the work. This accusation derives from the concatenation of racist evolutionary and sexist thought: the state of evolution or advancement of a society was indicated by the position of the women in the society. The ideal Victorian woman—secluded, protected, pure, and maternal—was civilization's highest achievement. Elspeth Huxley, in an autobiographical novel set in colonial Kenya, evokes this ideology and colonial men's and women's different reactions to it in the following dialogue between an upper-middle-class British couple, Hereward and his unhappy wife, Lettice. The narrator's hardworking mother, Tilly, has the final word in this excerpt.

"I doubt if Hereward would like me to carry firewood about on my back with nothing on but some beads and a bit of greasy leather, and to share a hut with goats and hens."

"I have no wish for my wife to be a savage," Hereward agreed. Somehow one always got the impression that he was in uniform.

"This is a savage country, so perhaps it might be better. An ability to sketch in water-colour and sing German *Lieder* is not very useful if there is an outbreak of plague or a puff-adder has got into the kitchen."

"There is no need for the womenfolk to concern themselves with such things," Hereward replied.

"That is a very gallant attitude, but they do not always have men to do it for them. Whenever I look at a Kikuyu woman toiling up a hill with a baby and a load of produce on her back weighing about a hundred pounds, I feel guilty."

"How ridiculous!" Hereward exclaimed. "They are only natives. Do you expect to lower yourself to their level?"

"I sincerely hope I shall never have to try."

"Surely," Tilly put in, "the idea is that they should rise to ours." (1959: 119)

Earlier Hereward had castigated Kikuyu men for their laziness, suggesting a solution good for the colonial state:

Hereward's moustache bristled. "Young dogs should be made to work, if they won't do it voluntarily. No discipline, that's what's the trouble. This Government—" (114)

Leakey went on the offensive in his defense. Not only did he represent Kikuyu women as influential in their society, but in championing their sexual freedom he criticized the European ideal. Indeed, the ethnography is extremely valuable in its coverage of the range of statuses women held, women's influence in the domestic and public domains, and areas of female autonomy and choice. Leakey's debate with the West, however, does not involve, as it would today, a critical assessment of clitoridectomy or a study of rape. Clitoridectomy is deproblematized despite its importance in Kikuyu cultural nationalist struggles just a few years earlier. Regarding rape, Leakey records the laws in detail, but "ceremonial rape," which included physical abuse and forced heterosexual intercourse, is exempt from these laws and, in keeping with Leakey's general orientation, is not treated to special analysis or interpretation.[1]

Leakey explained Kikuyu women's carrying of heavy burdens by reference to their having been socialized to do this while they were children. About the division of labor by sex, Leakey states that men had their share of labor in cultivation, but

if the division of labour between the sexes seems, in spite of this, to be unfair, it has to be remembered that all young men had arduous and at times dangerous duties to perform as the protectors of the land, as well as being expected to enrich their families by raiding the Maasai. The older men, too, had public duties which took up much of their time, and had they been responsible for a bigger share of the labours of family life, they would have had to neglect their public duties. (1977: 11)

Leakey knew his opponents well and shared some interpretations with them. Even as he describes women in the "professional classes" as diviners, prophets, and spiritual healers and writes knowingly of the councils of elderly women and the district and territorial ceremonies organized by women, he lends authority to the association of males with the public and females with the domestic. I believe this association to be a part of Kikuyu ideology, and Leakey's position here could well be overdetermined. Ideology among the Kikuyu as elsewhere both represents and distorts reality, disguising social tensions and contradictions. The dynamics between those with power and little authority and those in positions to carry out their decisions, as with Kikuyu women and men, are often subsumed under such ideologies.

A great deal of Leakey's presentation of Kikuyu women takes place within the confines of his debate on sexual morality. For Europeans, female honor has been almost synonymous with women's control of their bodies and sexuality, with chastity and fidelity (see Haug 1984). In a move calculated to challenge these European sensibilities, Leakey reports that he questioned women about their engagement in sexual intercourse with men other than their husbands, which some rituals require,

> asking whether they objected to having men whom they did not care for perform such acts with them [they] replied, "Why should we mind when we know that such acts are as much for our benefit and the benefit of our children as for anybody else? These acts are sacrifices. Who minds about a sacrifice? It is not a personal matter." (1977: 796)

In reporting on extramarital relations and polygamy, Leakey records the categories and the conditions under which married men and women could legitimately engage in sexual intercourse with someone other than their spouses. The presumed naturalness of sexual jealousy is exploded in another reported dialogue with elderly Kikuyu women. He asked those who were first wives if they were jealous when their husbands slept with second wives in their presence. They said "that they never felt jealous . . . for he satisfied them first." Here Leakey makes another appeal to custom as an explanation:

> Their whole upbringing, including their lives as maidens (when a man often had two lovers with him simultaneously) had accustomed them to such a situation and they did not regard it as strange. (1977: 791)

Later, in a Herbert Spencer lecture at Oxford, Leakey praised what he saw as sexual freedom and openness among Kikuyu women. His biographer Sonia Cole criticizes his "missionary streak [which] sometimes tempted him to try to put the world to rights," when he asserted the superiority of African society and culture:

> He rightly argued that there were fundamental mental and psychological differences between Africans and Europeans, but he also implied that the former were superior in certain aspects of their social structure, customs, law, justice and religion. Before cultural contact with Western civilization, he said, Africans had no death penalty except for persistent murderers; *women had greater freedom, including sexual freedom, and had their own methods of birth control; there were no destitute widows and orphans, lonely spinsters, unmarried mothers or prostitutes.* (1975: 243–44, emphasis added)

Here there is no gainsaying the moral arguments Leakey employs in his "factual" representation of Kikuyu women. He uses statements about the lives of women to argue for the integrity of Kikuyu men, against Victorian moral codes, and for respect for Kikuyu culture as governed by law. Nonetheless, he has provided more information about the options and statuses of women than Kenyatta writing at the same time with different political incentives. Ironically, women, as objects in the domain controlled by the laws of men, emerge with a little more subjectivity than the men, whose honor is dependent on their following the laws. Yet a different set of allegories—implicit questions, in old-fashioned analysis—would have produced quite a different ethnography and different understandings about what it means to be a Kikuyu woman. Certain areas of women's lives are excluded or minimized because they are not relevant to the implicit questions and allegories. A perception of women that is different from, not defined in opposition to, the "West" is lost because of allegories and implicit questions that motivated Leakey. And an understanding of Kikuyu culture as active, dynamic, and generative in society and history is not possible given the ethnography's mission to transcribe the laws and to represent the Kikuyu as a democratic, harmonious, preindustrial idyll (see chapter 4).

Kenyatta on Women

Jomo Kenyatta's ethnography, *Facing Mt. Kenya* (1938), devotes considerably less attention to women, overall, and to sexual morality than does Leakey's, making women almost disappear except for the discussion of clitoridectomy and as their roles and statuses intersect with those of men. Twin pressures from politics and functionalism pushed Kenyatta to write in favor of the maintenance of the practice of clitoridectomy, more commonly called female circumcision (see chapter 5 for more on Kenyatta's ethnography).[2] The political organization, the Kikuyu Central Association (KCA), that supported Kenyatta during his long stays in London so that he might be an effective voice for change at the colonial office took a stand in opposition to the missionary-based Kikuyu who passed a resolution stating that the practice of clitoridectomy should be discontinued, that Christians who agreed with the practice should be suspended, and later called for teachers and mission employees who did not endorse the resolutions to be fired. Kenyatta ultimately brought his position in line with the KCA's stand in order to consolidate his political and economic position. But it was not until he was introduced to functionalism that he so proudly heralded clitoridectomy as the underpinning of Kikuyu society. Before both politics and functionalism began to work on him, Kenyatta had said that he was personally opposed to clitoridectomy, but also against the government and missionaries using threats and force to abolish the practice.

Kenyatta himself was circumcised within the mission with a surgical knife used by a Kikuyu hospital assistant (Murray-Brown 1972: 51). Going to live at the mission put Kenyatta among a small minority of his generation—he was born around 1894—who used missionaries to rebel against tribal constraints and parental authority, but these early converts did not completely defy tradition, as Kenyatta's participation in the male initiation rite attests. A sometimes uneasy combination of "traditional" and "modern" was the hallmark of Kenyatta's early politics, and of a number of Kikuyu activists, including Harry Thuku, a founder of the first Kikuyu political association who in the early 1920s led the fight against forced labor, alienation of land, and mandatory passbooks for Africans. Kenyatta emerged slowly as one of the leaders of the KCA, and was secretary of the activist group by 1928. In 1929 the KCA sent Kenyatta to London to present its grievances to the colonial office and to petition for change in the colonial regime. While he was in London, the question of ending or maintaining the practice of clitoridectomy became a heated issue in Kenya.

Protestant missionaries had long opposed clitoridectomy and put pressure on the colonial government to take an active stand against it. But the government took a laissez-faire attitude, hoping that with time and education the most brutal forms of the operation would desist. African members of churches working in Kikuyuland passed their own resolution that the "evil custom" should be abandoned by all Christians and that all Christians submitting to it should be suspended (Murray-Brown 1972: 136). The KCA took the opposite position. Campaigning for support throughout Kikuyuland, they argued that their lives as Kikuyu were threatened if this tradition were taken away. Meanwhile, Kenyatta in London had to deal with metropolitan outrage over violence that broke out among opposing factions, and over the genital mutilation and murder of an elderly American missionary in Kenya. Kenyatta responded by cooperating with his British benefactors to draft a letter in Kikuyu to the KCA explaining why the operation was unhealthy, and concluding that in due time "the Kikuyu people themselves would follow the lead of all the civilised nations throughout the world and discontinue the circumcision of their girls" (Murray-Brown 1972: 139). But Kenyatta did not sign the letter. He did, however, write the following statement to the colonial office:

> I would respectfully draw your attention to the fact that any attempt to coerce my people by "force majeure" will have the very opposite of the desired effect as it causes my people to attach accentuated importance to the maintenance of this custom. (Murray-Brown 1972: 140)

What was Kenyatta's early position on clitoridectomy? He was pro-choice. Historian and biographer Jeremy Murray-Brown maintains that Kenyatta was against the practice. Reporting on a meeting Kenyatta attended with KCA representatives and African and colonial missionaries, Murray-Brown found that Kenyatta contended "that for himself he was opposed to the practice but that the thing could only be done away with by education" (1972: 144). In a chapter of his ethnography entitled "Initiation of Boys and Girls," Kenyatta states his earlier position in the passive voice as follows:

> The writer was invited to attend the committee meeting and give the Gikuyu's point of view. It was then agreed that the best way to tackle the problem was through education and not by force of an enactment, and that the best way was to leave the people concerned free to choose what custom was best suited to their changing conditions. (1938: 131)

A gradualist, pro-choice position is quite different from the one Kenyatta actively promoted in *Facing Mt. Kenya*. By the time the ethnography was published, KCA-inspired Kikuyu independent churches and schools had taken root in Kenya, and were a major power base for Kenyatta and the KCA. Christians in these schools argued that since there were no biblical dictates against clitoridectomy and that polygamy was condoned in the Old Testament, they could practice Kikuyu customs without fear of damnation. Those opposed to clitoridectomy tended to be wealthier than those in favor of it, and were also better placed to take advantage of any opportunities colonialism offered.

Clitoridectomy, an operation on women's bodies, became a symbol for the "pure" or true Kikuyu. But it must be remembered that it was a symbol first used by Western-educated male leaders to stir their constituents against the discipline of the colonial state and its churches, and later became a rallying point for the Mau Mau rebellion. The promotion of clitoridectomy as a sign of ethnic purity and unity combines two moves not unusual in resistance to colonialism. First is the identification of the woman as the repository of tradition.

When men migrate to cities and industrial areas for work, many women remain in the countryside, maintaining their families' claim to land, managing property and family, and doing the rural labor of both men and women. This rural-urban divide, in the minds of colonialists and Africans, often is felt as "traditional" versus "modern," denying, of course, the substantial transformations of the countryside, that the colonial (and postcolonial) political economy brought. The second move common in intercultural colonial situations is the elaboration of ethnic or tribal differentiation within contexts where resources are allocated on tribal bases, and where ties to particular communities or networks give political or economic advantage.

Ethnic or tribal distinctions may be signified by clothing, adornment, hairstyle, tattoos, scarification, and clitoridectomy, all of which may also actively mark differences in wealth and power in colonial and postcolonial situations. Noting the role of female circumcision in the intersection of class and ethnicity in a multicultural African society, Gruenbaum (1988) points out that "the ideological use of female circumcision in the maintenance of ethnic identity has not received much attention" (314) and concludes that in the Sudan

> female circumcision [clitoridectomy and infibulation] is not merely a residual
> traditional practice, but is rather an important marker of privileged ethnic
> group status, used ideologically to exclude aspiring lower status groups, who are
> in turn tempted to adopt it as part of the cultural assimilation necessary to upward mobility. Thus individuals and groups that pursue strategies of assimilation tend to adopt circumcision as a critical cultural marker. Yet for those
> groups which have not been able or have not chosen to attempt to assimilate,
> their avoidance of this practice has in some cases become an element of their
> case for their own moral superiority over their dominators, reinforcing the cultural boundary from the other side. (316)

In Africa, female circumcision is used, as Kenyatta suggests, to bind a local group together; it is also used to draw lines between groups and to cross lines between groups.

Kenyatta's early position, that clitoridectomy would decline in the absence of colonial compulsion and with greater education, is reflected in the anticlitoridectomy stance taken by some African women today. The following is an excerpt of a newsletter entitled "Education and Female Circumcision" from a Nigerian women's group soliciting support in their struggle to end clitoridectomy:

> Indeed millions of adherents of traditional practices and beliefs in Nigeria
> today are illiterate. . . .
>   In a survey just conducted by our Women's Centre on the attitudes towards
> ending female genital mutilation, it was revealed that of the 100 women interviewed 55 women who favoured continuation were illiterate. They were the ar-

dent traditionalists who had willingly been circumcized and would be willing to see their daughters circumcized. But [except] for only 10 educated women with primary education who favoured continuation, but without compulsion; the remaining 35 respondents with college or university education favoured stopping the practice. They expressed shock at what happened to them on the day of circumcision; "it was not what they expected," they said. (Women's Centre, Akwa Ibom State, Nigeria, 1989)

Increasing inequalities based on class, income, and education and expressed through tribal and ethnic discourses do not portend well for education as the road to abolition of clitoridectomy. Kenyatta changed his view from a gradualist, pro-choice position to one in favor of clitoridectomy, not because he saw education as increasing differences among the Kikuyu, but because of political pressures and his adoption of Malinowskian functionalism.

Malinowskian Functionalism in Support of Clitoridectomy

Kenyatta mobilized Malinowskian functionalism to make Kikuyu "traditional" life understandable and rational to a European audience, and to protest to them the ravages brought by British colonialism. He articulated Kikuyu outrage over the colonial attack on Kikuyu culture, especially clitoridectomy, and the alienation of Kikuyu land. His major cultural nationalist accomplishment was the promotion of the interpretation of Mumbi, the mythical mother of the Kikuyu tribe, as symbolically associated with Kikuyu land and territory. Kikuyu protests over the land taken from them, phrased in terms of tribal rights and cultural identity (as descendants of Mumbi and Gikuyu—mother and father, land and spirit, of the tribe), quickened the nationalist movement.

In light of the European ideal, Kenyatta represents the Kikuyu as having strictly enforced their rules of premarital virginity for both young women and young men, but he deems the Kikuyu sexual practices healthier and more humane. Deriving his position from Freudian hydraulics—the need for release of sexual pressure—Kenyatta concluded that Kikuyu premarital sexual practices allowed adequate release and healthy pleasure. The sexual behavior condoned for the initiated "boys and girls" (girls were initiated just before menarche; boys were many years older than the girls) he considered "right and proper and the very foundation stone upon which to build a race morally, physically and mentally sound. For it safeguards the youth from nervous and psychic maladjustments" (1938: 155). Europeans who tried to keep unmarried couples separated or chaperoned, Kenyatta charged, could not understand the moral strength and restraint Kikuyu young people exercised (1938: 158-59).

Upon initiation, men, and women in some areas, became members of named age grades. The initiation ceremonies included circumcision of boys and clitoridectomy of girls (the operation varied: in one form the tip of the clitoris and sometimes parts of the labia majora were removed, at other times a more radical excision of the clitoris and labia minora was performed). Newly initiated men became warriors charged with the defense and maintenance of their villages and districts, with the expectation that they would raid cattle from neighboring groups to increase their own and their families' wealth. Cattle raids continued during the beginning of colonial occupation, but were curtailed with the active colonial subjugation of the area. Young women formed work groups for agricultural labor as well as for the production of the numerous dances they participated in before marrying. During this time, young people were expected to take lovers, but not to engage in intercourse.

As they married, had children, and paid the proper fees, men achieved elder status. Councils of senior men met to resolve political and judicial problems and to hold religious ceremonies. In some areas elderly women, too, formed councils with the responsibility of hearing cases regarding married women and carrying out some districtwide ceremonies (see chapter 2).

Clitoridectomy was the process by which girls were made into women, a key element in the initiation process in which women were taught their rules as wives and mothers, and a major moment in the structure of the age grade system. Kenyatta revisits the controversies from the late 1920s and early 1930s in his ethnography, finally settling for a recitation of Kikuyu opinion on clitoridectomy and an anthropological argument for it. Pointing out that "there is a strong community of educated Gikuyu opinion in defence of this custom" (1938: 132), he goes on to say that marriageability is determined by clitoridectomy; that adult sexual relations with an uncircumcised man or woman is taboo, requiring a cleansing ritual; and that parents will reject and disinherit a man who marries an uncircumcised woman. In his own words, here is how Jomo Kenyatta established the anthropological ground for his support of clitoridectomy:

In our short survey we have mentioned how the custom of clitoridectomy has been attacked on one side, and on the other how it has been defended. In view of these points *the important problem is an anthropological one:* it is unintelligent to discuss the emotional attitudes of either side, or to take violent sides in the question, without understanding *the reasons why the educated, intelligent Gikuyu still cling to this custom.*

The real argument lies not in the defence of the surgical operation or its details, but in the understanding of a very important fact in the *tribal psychology of the Gikuyu*—namely, that this operation is still regarded as the very essence of an institution which has enormous educational, social, moral, and religious implications, quite apart from the operation itself. For the present it is impossible for a member of the tribe to imagine an initiation without clitoridectomy.

Therefore the abolition of the surgical element in this custom means to the Gikuyu the abolition of the whole institution.

The real anthropological study, therefore, is to show that clitoridectomy, like Jewish circumcision, is a mere bodily mutilation which, however, is regarded as the *conditio sine qua non* of the whole teaching of tribal law, religion, and morality. (1938: 133, emphasis added)

For Kenyatta, doing the anthropology of his own people meant elucidating the social and psychological reasons for the continued practice of clitoridectomy and demonstrating the functional role of clitoridectomy in the maintenance of the whole of Kikuyu society. A nonfunctionalist anthropological study might conjoin two other notions of clitoridectomy: (1) the social and cultural production of gender and (2) clitoridectomy as bodily inscription. Kenyatta identifies circumcision and clitoridectomy as inscriptions in flesh in the following passage:

The *irua* [initiation ceremony that culminates in circumcision or clitoridectomy] marks the commencement of participation in various governing groups in the tribal administration, because the real age-groups begin from the day of the physical operation. . . . Without this custom a tribe which had no written records would not have been able to keep a record of important events and happenings in the life of the Gikuyu nation. (1938: 134–35)

The history of the tribe, and one's place in it, are written into the body through circumcision and clitoridectomy. The ritual teaches, the scar reminds.

Kenyatta is mute on the cultural production of gender through *irua*, concentrating instead on the passage into adulthood: "This signifies that the children have now been born again, not as the children of an individual, but of the whole tribe" (1938: 151). In my research, women told me that clitoridectomy made them "complete" women, and that without it they would not be fertile. Women believed that their reproductive capacities were activated by clitoridectomy, and with that activation they became women. Incorporating Kenyatta's idea of bodily inscription with what women told me, then clitoridectomy produced women whose scarred bodies reminded them of the importance of fertility, perhaps over sexuality, and of their place in tribal history.

A curious work by Alphonso Lingis, *Excesses: Eros and Culture*, a work itself given to excesses of imagination and interpretation, portrays clitoridectomy as an inscription productive of pain and gender. Lingis submits that neither history nor narrative is inscribed in the body through circumcision and clitoridectomy. Instead of history, what is inscribed is pain; pain creates intensive points that engrave into the flesh the law and the sentence much as a machine wrote the sentence into the prisoner's flesh in Kafka's *The Penal Colony.*

Such a machine, contrived in the bush, is circumcision and clitoridectomy. Their supremely public character is essential to them, and contrasts with the scarification, cicatrization and tattooing one warrior, one woman, does on another. They [circumcision and clitoridectomy] appear, we already noted, as the high-point of tribal self-celebration, and efforts to abolish them, by missionaries, shepherds of foreign herds, or by public health officials, are resisted vehemently, as though the very existence of the tribal bond were at stake. Circumcision and clitoridectomy, done at twelve to fourteen years, and without anaesthesia or hygiene, is a torture done by the public in one's most sensitive and pleasure-producing zone. This incision pronounces and inscribes the sentence by which the public disposes of the individual. It is at the same time the means by which law, the prohibition and the oppression that is the essence of the gregarious order, is made known and comes to exist. (Lingis 1983: 40)

The law Lingis refers to in the passage cited comprises the rules of exclusion between men and women—the creation of gender—and the production of men's and women's desire for each other. According to Lingis, the intensive points raised in bodily inscriptions cry out to be read, to be seen, to be touched: "They become marks for-another, they form the gaping cavities of demand, want, desire, hunger" (1983: 38). Through the inscription of gender distinctions, desire for the other is created. For women, then, clitoridectomy makes them not complete unto themselves, but completely open, desirous of the male to complete their fecundity.

Why have I presented this semiotic interpretation of clitoridectomy, conjecturing that clitoridectomy as a sign is read and remembered as the pain of gendering and the mark of the oppression of the social order? There are other nonfunctionalist anthropological interpretations of female circumcision that I could call on. The most notable is Boddy's (1982 and 1989) study of Sudanese infibulation, a form of female circumcision in which the external genitalia are removed or cut and the labia majora fused, leaving a small opening for urine and menses. Boddy elaborates the cultural equivalencies that give meaning and aesthetic power to infibulated genitals as womb—enclosed, smooth, clean, pure oasis. With clitoridectomy or excision the metaphors of enclosure do not fit; often a raised scar or rough scar tissue is left after the clitoris is cut away. The aesthetic, if you will, is different, and women must in some way adjust to their transformed bodies—celebrate, abhor, ignore, make peace with them. Alice Walker, in recent interviews and in the film with this title, likens these scars to "warrior marks"—the scars of the survivors of patriarchal wars.

I have brought Kenyatta into conversation with Lingis to propose that if clitoridectomy does indeed inscribe history, then it must be a history that is revisited every day, or that, in all likelihood, becomes a part of sexuality in societies practicing genital mutilation. Perhaps in the past, the history inscribed was the history of the tribe, as Kenyatta avers, but I doubt it. I speculate that circumcision and clitoridectomy for Kikuyu have always been about the *historical production of gendered bodies*, removing the female covering—the foreskin—from men and the phallic clitoris from women, marking bodies for the roles they will play.

Kenyatta's insistence on functionalist categories and cultural integration made it possible for European readers to find Kikuyu life intelligible but detracted from a presentation of Kikuyu life through indigenous cultural constructs and categories (this criticism has been applied more generally to Kenyatta's mentor, Malinowski; see Marcus and Fischer 1986: 187-88). Constrained by Malinowskian methods and orientations, and by the politics of double consciousness of the Western-educated African, Kenyatta presents Kikuyu customs by reference to comparable British ones without fully exploring the basis of similarity and difference. He follows this presentation with discussion of the ways colonialism changed or destroyed Kikuyu traditions. Drawing similarities between Kikuyu and Western beliefs and practices, Kenyatta often asserts that the Kikuyu, through their own mechanisms, lived up to the spirit of these valued traditions better than the British did.

Kikuyu Sexual Morality

Kenyatta and Leakey both found Kikuyu society worthy and honorable, but for different reasons, and each used his interpretation differently. Colonialism itself Kenyatta deemed reprehensible, but his fascination with the West and his defensiveness toward Western culture led him to define Kikuyu culture in terms of its achievement of Western goals and standards. Leakey was also defensive. With an aggression born of romanticism and opportunism, he went on the offensive against the industrialized and class-based West and defended his "tribe" against the derogation of the colonialists.

The attention devoted to Kikuyu sexual morality by both ethnographers is not insignificant. Leakey's representation of Kikuyu sexual morality is one of his many defenses of Kikuyu men against missionary and colonialist aspersions, in this instance against the charge that the men allow Kikuyu women only a low and degraded position in society (see Leakey 1977: 11). Leakey's ethnography, *The Southern Kikuyu before 1903*, also contains implicit criticism of the West through his holding up the mirror of the Kikuyu to reflect the ills of metropolitan and colonial society (see Cole 1975: 244). Kikuyu women, he suggests, had freedoms denied Western women (and men, especially legitimate extramarital sexual partners). Women's choice of dance partners (Leakey 1977: 417) and of lovers (418) and the necessity of their consent before marrying (750) or having sexual intercourse with someone other than their husbands (811) are presented as evidence of women's power and influence.

Both Kenyatta's and Leakey's interpretations of Kikuyu sexual morality were set in the context of colonial interculturality: colonial political and economic domination with concomitant submission, reinterpretation, and resistance of natives; colonial appropriation and fascination with native mores; and colonial dependence on nearby natives and on the distant metropole. For Kenyatta this resulted in an emphasis on the strict rules of enforcement of premarital virginity, countering the negative perceptions of colonialists and missionaries. But he also included an appeal to the more sophisticated metropolitan society by allowing that Kikuyu practices created "psychically" healthier individuals. Leakey was openly critical of colonial and metropolitan society, though he shared their belief in the possibility of just and fair colonial rule. His representation of Kikuyu sexual morality, emphasizing the number of legitimate nonmarital partners and the freedom of choice of men and women, was a judgment against the restriction of Western civilization.

Every ethnographer achieves only partial truths. Ethnographic truths must be understood as a creation growing out of the ethnographer's personal attitudes and orientations, his or her experience of the people and the culture, the social and political conditions at the time of fieldwork, the conventions of ethnographic writing, the institutional constraints of the academy, and the nature and specificity of the theoretical focus. Given the ways that Leakey and Kenyatta differed on many of these points, as I have tried to show, the similarity of their conclusions regarding Kikuyu sexual morality is striking. According to both Leakey and Kenyatta, among the Kikuyu premarital virginity was valued, a wide range of sexual activity was legitimate and encouraged, and choice and restraint marked individual behavior. In the next section I present the details, drawn from both ethnographers, upon which these conclusions are based.

The Conduct of Virginity

Kenyatta and Leakey agree that initiated young women and men were expected to engage in sexual play, but to stop short of intercourse. Such sexual activity typically followed a dance, where the partners chosen were often kept for the evening (for the sexual implications of dancing with members of the opposite sex, see Leakey 1977: 859, 861; Kenyatta 1938: 161). After the dance, according to the rules of *ngweko*, groups of young people paired off in the *thingira* (the men's or bachelors' house [Kenyatta 1968 [1938]: 157]) or the *kīrīrī* (girls' sleeping place [Leakey 1977: 740]). Leakey mentions that sometimes a young man had two young women as his partners for the evening (1977: 419). Before lying down, the young woman pulled her leather apron between her legs and secured the ends at the waist, making sure her genitals were covered. Neither partner was supposed to touch the other's genitals (Leakey 1977: 739). The couple lay facing each other and enjoyed restricted petting and caressing. Both Leakey and Kenyatta refer to this practice as "restricted intercourse," but do not specifically state the extent of sexual release typically achieved. Southall, writing broadly about this practice in East Africa, does:

> In East Africa, it is probably well-known that, among many of the peoples of Kenya, unmarried girls and boys slept communally. The boy lay between the legs of his sweetheart in such a manner as to secure sexual pleasure to himself, without conveying it, or its awkward consequences to her. (1960: 208)

An old woman I interviewed testified to the pleasure conveyed to the girls. In Central Province in Kenya, an old Kikuyu woman chided a much younger one about present-day sexual practices. "In my day," she said, "we shaved our heads, rubbed fat on our bodies, and lay with the warriors in *ngweko*. Today you comb your hair, put on a dress, and get pregnant." The old woman was referring to Kikuyu customs that valued premarital virginity but encouraged unmarried men and women to engage in formalized sexual activity within a group context. This she contrasted to the mores introduced by the Christian missionaries, which condemned sexual activity among unmarried partners in an effort to preserve virginity and spiritual purity. The old woman found the European traditions laughable: they deny unmarried people legitimate ways to express their sexuality, thus inviting trouble. Indeed, the young woman whom she chided, unmarried with her second pregnancy already showing, agreed.

The public nature of premarital sexual activity served as a brake to full sexual intercourse. If petting did lead to intercourse, the young man and woman both were ostracized by their age mates. Kenyatta emphasizes the self-control that was expected of both partners and the punishment that accompanied the pregnancy of an unmarried woman. The man had to pay a large fine in livestock to the council of elders and the woman was ridiculed and had to provide a feast for all the men and women in her age group (Kenyatta 1938: 160). The fear of ostracism, Kenyatta suggests, was a powerful form of social control. In another context he states:

> The stigma attached to the ostracism was far greater and very much worse than that attached to the European form of imprisonment. Many Gikuyu would prefer to go to jail rather than to be ostracised. The fear of this was one of the chief factors which prevented the people from committing crimes. (1938: 230)

Other legitimate sexual partners were denied unmarried men and women. While the rule of female premarital virginity was highly respected, young men more often bent another of the rules to allow themselves full sexual intercourse. Leakey reports that young men were told that they could not have sexual intercourse with any man's wife until they themselves were married (1977: 703). He later counters this, however, when he describes the "experience" of a newlywed couple on the day they would consummate their marriage:

> In the normal course of events the bride was still a virgin at this time. Her husband, on the other hand, had by now probably had full sexual intercourse once or twice with the wives of men belonging to his own initiation age-group, and knew the correct procedure connected with full intercourse, having been instructed by them in the art of love. (782)

Leakey sees fines and shame as consequences of breaking the rules of *ngweko* (Leakey uses the spelling *nguīko* for this practice), but in keeping with his promotion of sexual freedom suggests that the unwed mother's stigma was not so great. The worse situation was that of a young woman who would go off alone with a young man (Leakey 1977: 813). Such a young woman was much sought after, for it was believed that she would engage in full sexual intercourse. If she became pregnant, however, each of her partners would deny responsibility, and a civil case would ensue. In more typical cases of premarital pregnancy, where the woman could confidently identify the father of the child, marriage negotiations were rushed along, and the husband-to-be had to pay a fine of "a ram for causing increase" (Leakey 1977: 802). If marriage negotiations were not completed or even begun before the birth of the child, an unwed mother still had the possibility of getting married. In such instances the prospective husband was required to pay additional fees to claim the young woman's child as his (Leakey 1977: 802-3). If a woman had a second child out of wedlock, she could have become a "home daughter," living at her father's homestead with her lover and producing children who would legally be her father's (Leakey 1977: 535-36).

Leakey amasses evidence to show that the unwed mother could be incorporated into Kikuyu society, yet he concludes that the Kikuyu valued female premarital virginity and characterizes young women according to their accomplishment of this goal: a young woman who obeyed the rules of *ngweko* and married as a virgin was deemed a good or moral girl, *mūirītu mūthingu*, and "a girl who was known to allow young men more freedom than the law allowed was known as *mūirītu mwaganu* (a wicked or immoral girl)" (Leakey 1977: 813).

Despite the differences in their orientation toward the representation of Kikuyu sexual morality, especially in their discussion of the treatment of transgressors of the rules, both ethnographers represent the Kikuyu as a society that in the main honored its rule of female premarital virginity and that saw the maintenance of virginity as a challenge to young people, incontinence as failure, and family honor and fortune at stake in the process. In a father's standard speech to his newly initiated son, the young man was cautioned against engaging in intercourse, even with a young woman he intended to marry, because it might "involve your family in great shame, and considerable expense" (Leakey 1977: 703). Within this peroration, which Leakey transcribes as a list of rules, are several other interdictions and prescriptions that help to demarcate the context and meaning of virginity for the Kikuyu man. These rules placed virginity within a context that defined insiders versus outsiders and those to be obeyed versus those to be cautious of. They called for the protection and maintenance of one's family and honor against attack and stressed the control of emotions and the accumulation of wealth (Leakey 1977: 703-5).

The rules for proper behavior given by a mother to her newly initiated daughter (Leakey 1977: 705-6) correspond only in part to those given the young man, delimiting a narrower range of social interactions but underscoring the young woman's own role in the maintenance of her virginity. The young woman was exhorted to publicly denounce men who tried to cajole or force her into having sexual intercourse. She should immediately leave such a partner and deny him other partners through her public denunciation. As with the young man, the young woman was also charged with respecting and obeying patrilineal relatives, maintaining proper distance from senior age mates, and keeping solidarity with coinitiates. Moreover, the protection of her fertility (believed to have been secured, in part, by clitoridectomy) through the avoidance of the menstrual blood of others was paramount. Finally, she was told "be industrious and hardworking so that the good men may desire you as a wife" (Leakey 1977: 706). Female premarital virginity was achieved in the context of female solidarity and peer group pressure, but it also recognized the woman as an active agent in the maintenance of her virginity and her industry and strength of character as virtues.

In sum, virginity was not seen as a quality, a state of being, of a woman to be protected by the men of her family. Virginity was the woman's accomplishment—a woman showed her strength of character through the maintenance of her virginity in sexually charged situations. Because of her role in productive labor and trade as well as the expectations of her as an unmarried adult, the Kikuyu virgin was geographically mobile, socially visible, and sexually active. Young men, too, were challenged by Kikuyu society to maintain their virginity. Unmarried men were expected to control their emotions, to be in control of themselves, to bring wealth instead of shame and expense to their families. A double standard that allowed more freedom of sexual expression to men did exist. But young men were under pressure during this phase of their lives, the period with the greatest emphasis on individual achievement. This was the time when they were expected to show the character-management skills that would later bring them success as leaders among the elders. For unmarried Kikuyu young men and women, virginity was an achievement.

Clitoridectomy and Sexuality

This study has implications for an understanding of the way Kikuyu sexual practices fit with the practice of clitoridectomy. Anthropologists who place clitoridectomy within its cultural context have been accused of covering up women's pain, danger, and sexual debilitation, and anthropologists who publicly oppose it have been accused of cultural imperialism, the imposition of their values on the culture of others. Yet we cannot retreat to neutrality, for neutrality is as much a political stance as opposition and advocacy.

In a W. H. R. Rivers Prize essay, Daniel Gordon challenges medical anthropology to "develop an explanatory model that can integrate anthropological description, public health concerns, and our own cultural sensitivities" (1991: 13). Harriet Lyons went far in doing just that in an article published before Gordon's. In a richly nuanced review of anthropological treatments of genital mutilation, including a study of attitudes toward Jews and their circumcision of males, Lyons (1981) proposed a schema for discussing clitoridectomy that is "both morally acceptable and scientifically valid" (499). Starting with an acknowledgment of influences of racial hierarchies, evolutionary theories, and changing Western currents regarding sexuality on the production of anthropological theories and interpretations, Lyons goes on to propose investigative strategies that provide a standing place for anthropologists. The first is to admit that genital mutilation is about sex. As odd as that may sound, much of cultural anthropology's treatment of clitoridectomy and circumcision is not unlike Kenyatta's in that it presents functional explanations of the creation of social structure and promotion of social solidarity through rituals of genital operations, as though the genitals were not important, could be substituted for by other body parts. Still, Lyons cautions us that the degree to which sexuality is of significance in genital operations varies, cannot be assumed, must be investigated. The second investigative strategy, based on a conclusion Lyons reached in her research, is to separate the meanings associated with the male operations from those associated with the female operations. She ventures that among people who practice genital operations, female operations are more likely to be seen as involving sexuality and fertility and are more likely to be seen as "punitive and dystonic" than are male operations. To the extent that the generation of pain and limitation of sexual gratification are a part of genital mutilation, Lyons reminds the anthropological audience that

> it is important to realize that neither pain nor the limitation of sexual gratification can be regarded by anthropologists as *ipso facto* negative in its implications. The Sun Dance and the monastery are cases in point. (1981: 512)

76

Commitment to cultural relativity has not prohibited anthropologists from favoring the eradication of clitoridectomy and other forms of genital mutilation. Gruenbaum, also a winner of a W. H. R. Rivers Prize for an essay on female circumcision, directly addresses discourses on abolition of genital mutilation. The worst effect of campaigns for the eradication of operations on women's genitals has been the increase in such operations, as occurred in the colonial period in Kenya and the Sudan. Current abolition discourse emphasizes sexual gratification, health, and economic development. Gruenbaum finds fault with all three. The discourse on sexual gratification privileges the individual over the group, which is antithetical in many societies that practice female genital mutilation. On a public health strategy, Gruenbaum is adamant:

> It is not a matter of health education comparable to promoting immunisations. Rather, because of its ideological significance—tied up with concepts of gender, religion, ethnicity and ultimately the control of reproductive labour and its role in the capitalist economy—a more dramatic social change will be necessary. (1988: 322)

The more dramatic social change Gruenbaum calls for is not simply increased economic opportunities for women, though these would help (see A. Davis 1989 and my review of her book [Clark 1990]). Western critics of female genital mutilation, Gruenbaum demands, should see the interculturality of female circumcision, the local-global nexus of clitoridectomy, and assess the role of the West in maintaining these practices. Women critics from within societies that practice female genital mutilation often turn their attention to economic issues in assessing the conditions that would bring about an end to the practices, but many forswear the help of Western critics. Gruenbaum concludes:

> In fact, it is very likely that foreign criticism is viewed as a smokescreen, counter-productively blaming the victim while at the same time being unwilling to address the conditions of exploitation, inequality and economic crisis— and the role in them played by the same foreign powers anxious to help stamp out circumcision—which perpetuate conditions of underdevelopment. (1988: 318)

Despite the opposition set up between the haves and the have-nots in global politics, coalitions of Western feminists and African women have begun to develop, many spurred on by black American novelist Alice Walker's crusade against genital mutilation. Walker's work moves the discourse on genital mutilation in new directions. Not only does it evaluate the pro-female-circumcision position that the operation brings honor and maintains tradition and the by now standard anti-genital-mutilation criticism of the debilitating effects of the operation on women's health, fertility, and sexuality, it also incorporates African women into a discussion of genital mutilation as patriarchal oppression.

I would like to see the worldwide eradication of all forms of female circumcision. Having reached my opinion based on the past and present practice of clitoridectomy, I take my cue about how to present it from the debates over the operation going on in Kenya today. A prime concern of contemporary Kikuyu women who have spoken out against the operation is that fertility, which is supposed to be enhanced by clitoridectomy, can in fact be thwarted by infections from extensive excisions. Female circumcision may be a leading cause of infertility (Koso-Thomas 1987: 12). They also point to the problems with childbirth caused by inelastic scar tissue and other physical effects of female genital mutilation.

Arguments linking clitoridectomy to female oppression or to decreased sexual pleasure, often presented by European women, have not been of central importance to many African organizers. Studies of infibulation in Sudan (J. Kennedy 1978: 131; Boddy 1989: 55) contend that with infibulation or pharaonic circumcision, women achieve prestige and recognition and, most importantly, emphasize fertility over sexuality:

> By removing their external genitalia, female Hofriyati [a Sudanese group] seek not to diminish their own sexual pleasure—though this is an obvious effect—so much as to enhance their femininity. Pharaonic circumcision is a symbolic act which brings sharply into focus the fertility potential of women by dramatically deemphasizing their sexuality. In insisting upon circumcision for their daughters, women assert their social indispensability, an importance which is not as the sexual partners of their husbands [footnote 19], nor—in this highly segregated, overtly male authoritative society—as their servants, sexual or otherwise, but as the mothers of men. The ultimate social goal of a woman is to become, with her husband, the cofounder of a lineage section.
>
> Footnote 19: Women I spoke to did not object to their husbands' visiting brothels, so long as they did not spend too much money in such establishments. (Boddy 1989: 55)

Though some may think this obvious, I speculate that the renowned emotional and social distance between African husbands and wives may be related to the practice of female genital mutilation. Emotional investment in a sexual partner may be greater under conditions where fantasies of romantic love are fed by the expectation of intense sexual expression between husbands and wives. Whether or not I am right about this, it is clear from the Sudanese example, and others, that many African women have pursued a path that deemphasizes sexuality and marital intimacy. Yet from my study of the literature, I hold that where clitoridectomy and not infibulation is practiced, the question of women's participation in premarital sexuality, and the emotional involvement it brings, is open.

After clitoridectomy, Kikuyu virgins engaged in recreational sexual activity. Then as now, clitoridectomy no doubt changed the nature of women's sexual arousal and response, but it did not obliterate all sexual pleasure. The clitoris integrates and transforms sexual stimulation and elevates sexual tension (Masters and Johnson 1966: 45); the physical sensation without the clitoris is therefore likely to be less intense, more diffuse. Kikuyu sexual practices seem especially suited to polymorphous stimulation that provides diffuse and sustained arousal. *Ngweko* trained a woman to respond to a wide range of bodily sensations, and the period of socially sanctioned sexual activity allowed her time to appreciate her own body's responses. With *ngweko* as with extended foreplay and multiple sexual couplings within a single session, the woman may reach a high plateau of sexual excitement. Physiologically this is a result of the continued engorgement of the pelvic and genital blood vessels and stimulation of the nerve endings; psychologically it may be perceived as pleasurable. What is satisfying is learned; the mind trains the body as much as the body triggers the mind.

In a survey of more than 140 women in the west African nation of Sierra Leone, physician Olayinka Koso-Thomas (1987: 39-41) found that about 75 percent of the women who had been sexually active before genital mutilation (clitoridectomy and excision) experienced "mild" pleasure in sexual intercourse on a scale of "neutral," "mild," "intense," and about the same percentage reported that the nature of their sexual response was "excited" on a scale of "neutral," "excited," "orgasm." None of the women, whether they had been sexually active before their operations or not, reported intense pleasure or orgasm, and all of the women who had become sexually active only after a genital operation reported that their sexual response was "neutral," as opposed to "excited" or "orgasm." Overall, most women reported the lowest level of experience of sexual stimulation (58 percent said "neutral") and the lowest level of sexual response (77 percent said "neutral"). These figures, which I calculated from tables differently configured, point to the flattening of sexual stimulation and response as an effect of genital operations—though women report that they are more likely to feel stimulated than to feel a strong response—and to the importance of learning in sexual behavior. No differences were noted in the actual operations performed on women who had been sexually active before genital mutilation, yet their answers to the interview questions clearly indicate that they derive greater pleasure from sex. The implications for those who undergo clitoridectomy at an early age, as is the present trend, are dire.

Koso-Thomas, in examining the arguments in favor of female circumcision, debunks the view that female circumcision prevents promiscuity, submitting instead that because of the low level of satisfaction women gain from sex they might desperately go from partner to partner looking for fulfillment. Based on her work in a family planning clinic in the capital city, Freetown, Koso-Thomas concludes:

There is a feeling among circumcised women that there is a threshold of enjoyment which they are denied by their partners. Those who are able to speak freely about sex (and there are only a few in African societies) feel the urge to move from one male partner to another seeking sexual satisfaction. From interviews with 50 urban women who had sexual experience before circumcision I found that none had been able to reach the level of satisfaction they knew before circumcision—and were unaware, before the interview, that this deficiency was as a result of circumcision. During these interviews I was told of women who had striven to find the ideal partner through trial and error until they have lost their husbands and their homes. It seems ironical, therefore, that the operation intended to eliminate promiscuity in fact could have the opposite effect. (1987: 11)

The story of the woman who loses all in search of sexual satisfaction could be urban folklore. What I take from Koso-Thomas is that clitoridectomy lessens but does not deny women sexual pleasure, and that female circumcision does not necessarily beat women into submission and passivity; some women actively take control of their sex lives.

While the clitoridectomy operation is still widely performed, the social and cultural context of the operation has changed, as have the sexual morality and practices of the society in which it takes place. Socialization for sexuality is no longer a major part of the ceremony. In 1972 I conducted a survey of a small rural village in the Kenya highlands in which all heads of household were interviewed. Ninety-five percent of the respondents (about 66 percent of them were married women) said that they had had the operation and that their daughters had been or would be clitoridectomized. At that time, girls of ten or eleven years of age were initiated in groups of three to seven. Traditional songs praising the virtues of the female sex over the male were sung, and the girls became special friends. None of the traditional erotic arts were taught, and after clitoridectomy they adhered to, or tried to adhere to, Christian expectations of virgins. Since that time, girls have been initiated at younger and younger ages, often alone, and in a few instances by trained medical doctors. Marriageability is the primary reason women give for wanting their daughters to be clitoridectomized: without the operation, they believe, their daughters will not find husbands, and without husbands, they believe, their daughters' and their own life chances are diminished.

I have not done a study of the sexual behavior of contemporary Kikuyu young adults. If such a study were done it would be interesting to note the extent to which polymorphic stimulation is used, and what accommodations are made to the changed sexual arousal and response pattern of clitoridectomized women. Whatever the patterns of sexual practice, it is obvious that these practices exist today in an environment of multiple and conflicting sexual moralities. Beliefs in premarital virginity from Christianity, Islam, and Kikuyu custom must bump up against practices of sexual license as women and men negotiate paths of sexual pleasure and morality.

In interviews with Kikuyu in Murang'a District of central Kenya, I was told by older men and women that both circumcision and clitoridectomy promoted cleanliness among men and women, made both men and women intelligent, and made intercourse easier for men, and that clitoridectomy was necessary for female fertility. One old man, who had told me stories of the founding of the colonial headquarters in the district, began his discussion of circumcision by telling me that "one has to get circumcision so as to become a man or grown-up girl." I asked if there were other reasons for circumcision. The following is a translation of his response:

This is the custom of the Kikuyu tribe. We Kikuyu believe that if one happened to remain as a *kirigu* [large uncircumcised girl] or *kihii* [plural *ihi*; large uncircumcised boy], they would not be as intelligent as the person who was circumcised.

Also, when doing sexual intercourse, we do not want to struggle much. A *kirigu* has the clitoris in her vulva and a *kihii* has a skin that covers the penis. In the case of *ihii*, they have dirt [a whitish substance enclosed at the end of the penis by the skin]. Kikuyu women do not want to go with a *kihii* because of that dirt. Men also do find difficulties when they are doing sexual intercourse. That skin that is removed after circumcision gives trouble to a man during mating. The clitoris in the girl's vulva is not good when it touches the penis. When we are mating we like to do our work at once. Not a matter of troubling. When we mean mating we mean it.

Unfortunately, I had no follow-up questions then. Today I would have many.

Young men (nineteen to twenty-seven years old)—outside of the survey no young women were willing to talk about the practice—had a different view. They found clitoridectomy directly related to the control of female sexuality. I found the following passage in my notes from an interview with a young man: "The clitoris causes friction when walking and thus increases sexuality of the woman; therefore uncircumcised women have greater sexuality." Men, however, had to cope with circumcised women who would not be satisfied with one "contact per night." This man describes customary male circumcision as adapted to this situation as follows:

A part of the foreskin is left at the back and made hard while the person is healing from the operation. This is called *ngwati*. This hardened skin makes penetration easier and enables a man to participate in sexual intercourse longer and have several sexual contacts in one night.

It was believed that a woman would not be satisfied with only one contact per night, and men had to serve them, so that anything which could increase the number of contacts or which could increase desire was good. Women were supposed to just lie there, without working.

Kikuyu sexual beliefs and practices are ambivalent about female sexuality: women have desire, are to be pleased, should have lessened sexuality, should be passive sexual partners. Customary practices of *ngweko*, public petting, and *ngwati*-style circumcisions were adapted to accommodate the clitoridectomized body. Today the operations remain, but the accommodations are lost.

This study of precolonial Kikuyu sexual morality and practices has broad implications for an understanding of the social construction of sexuality and the history of sexuality. Contemporary European sexual morality, Foucault (1980: 36-49) posits, emerged with the creation of particular centralized medical, religious, educational, and political institutions and practices that defined norms (e.g., virginity, fidelity, heterosexuality) and simultaneously established peripheral, dissident sexualities and sexual practices. Individuals came to view sexuality as central to their identity, but around private sexual practices, secret sins and pleasures, developed many institutions that would seek to control the uses of body and of pleasure.

Kenyatta's and Leakey's ethnographies of the Kikuyu, in their different ways, reveal that the Kikuyu conceptualized sexuality as more open and social. Young people were constrained to engage in *ngweko* in public, and a range of extramarital relations was permitted both men and women. Surely Kikuyu interpretations of sexuality, even in "traditional" times, varied. In contradistinction to primary European conceptions, however, sexuality was generally conceived of as good, social, and pleasurable. Control of sexuality as a public activity was primarily invested in the individual (rather than confessors, doctors, teachers, or legal institutions). In this way, the Kikuyu seem similar to Foucault's (1986) rendering of the ancient Greeks, but the Kikuyu did not elaborate a philosophy of individualist moderation. Instead, individuals, always representatives of their kin, territorial, or age groups, were expected to manage themselves within challenging situations so as to exhibit strength of character and to reflect well on the group. The openness of the sexual situation and the sociality of individual conscience contributed to the construction of a Kikuyu sexual morality that held that virtue was achieved through the individual's control of the body in the social uses of pleasures.

Kikuyu Virginity within a Broader Context

The practice of female premarital virginity in sub-Saharan societies is shaped by discourses of inequality in which groups negotiate for relative standing through women. The meaning of virginity, intactness and inviolability, is often translated into political resources used by kin groups in their competition with each other. Virginity is a sign in two different ways. On the physical level virginity is an indexical sign, indicating a woman's physically inviolate or intact state, and on the sociocultural level virginity is an iconic sign, referring to the inviolability and intactness of the group the virgin represents. Virginity is about heterosexual intercourse, or rather the absence of heterosexual intercourse. Female virginity signifies intactness, the credibility of a woman's assertion of wholeness, the lack of penetration by the other. At another level of abstraction, the virginity of daughters and sisters represents in many societies the integrity of the family group or the group concerned with female fertility. The analysis offered here deals primarily with the politics of kinship, but should hold whenever the discourse on female premarital virginity mobilizes or is mobilized by organizations or institutions that (1) maintain interests in female fertility, (2) consciously construct themselves as bounded and enduring, and (3) enter competitively into the political arena. Some secret societies might meet these criteria, as well as other residential groupings. Virginity symbolizes the group's ability to maintain its own boundaries, and its prestige, in relation to like groups.

As a symbol of family prestige, value, or success, virginity is a political resource used in the competition between family groups. The virginity of a marriageable daughter or sister occasions the assertion of strength and integrity of the woman's family; it influences the amount of bridewealth or dowry; and it provides one more degree of prestige in the competition for prominence among family groups. In this study I concentrate on virginity in societies with officializing narratives of descent through the male line, and in which men authoritatively occupy a large proportion of political positions. Societies with predominant matrilineal organizing principles and egalitarian social systems appear less frequently in lists of societies that are highly restrictive in their control of female premarital and marital sexuality (cf. Ford and Beach 1951). Men who are heads of families in patriarchal societies that value female premarital virginity use female virginity to compete with other men. The avowed concerns are the virtue of women and the access of men to women, but equally salient are negotiations of relative rank and differential access to resources among political actors, male and female.

Virgins are not just objects in those transactions, though the tendency to objectify women is inherent in the institution of virginity. Women cooperate in maintaining their virginity for reasons of their own, including the attainment of many of the same political goals as men: power in affecting their own lives and the lives of others, and control of resources. A virgin may gain socially and materially from the marriage arranged for her; she may add to her family's social standing; and she may make possible prestigious marriages for her sisters and, later, her daughters.

While virginity in all contexts essentially has to do with the prestige and integrity of the woman and the group she stands for, the pattern of virginity varies greatly. Here my concern is with female premarital virginity in late-nineteenth- and early-twentieth-century sub-Saharan African societies, a reconstruction of the precolonial period.

Contradictory views of African women are prevalent in Western culture. The first and possibly the oldest is the racist-sexist image, projected from the libido of the Western mind, showing the African woman as sexual savage, barebreasted and undulating. Another image popular among many Western feminists is our wish fulfillment of woman as African matriarch—strong, competent, and independent. This view of the African woman is gradually being overshadowed by the ethnocentric and somatocentric construction of the oppressed African woman: one of many co-wives, beaten by her husband, subjected to genital mutilation. Discussions of virginity from each of those perspectives end quickly because it is believed that (1) Africa does not produce virgins, but natural fornicators, or (2) African women are too dominant to be seduced, or (3) African women do not seek sex because they get no pleasure from it. In truth, African virgins may have had sexual knowledge and experiences beyond that typical of virgins in late-nineteenth- and early-twentieth-century European and Asian societies. Moreover, the African woman herself was responsible for the maintenance of her virginity. And as to clitoridectomy, the most widely practiced genital operation south of the Sahara, it neither destroys a woman's sexual pleasure nor prevents intercourse.

Major anthropological interpretations of virginity in Europe and Asia, by their emphasis on female inheritance (Goody, 1971, 1973), hierarchical systems (Ortner 1978), and group boundaries (Schneider 1971), do not plumb the important correlates of virginity applicable to sub-Saharan Africa. South of the Sahara, women typically did not inherit property; virginity was valued in nonhierarchical societies; and, while the integrity of group boundaries remains a crucial consideration, the contexts in which transactions occurred differ significantly.

My study suggests that a discourse on virginity is most likely to link ideas, resources, rules, persons, and institutions in societies in which a group—usually but not exclusively a kin group—holds interests in female fertility and that group wields political power in the wider society, using kin relationships to gain or maintain its power. In particular, the political arena in which virginity is important is defined by the interplay of kinship and one or more of the following: degree of differential ownership of productive property, contractual and patron-client relations, membership in secret and age grade associations, and class and caste relations. If family and kin groups do not matter much in the wider society, then, whether or not they hold vested interest in fertility, virginity will not matter much. If family and kin groups matter, but there are few significant distinctions among groups, then virginity will not be very important. Societies in which kinship and politics are virtually the same, with no competing paradigms, societies in which kinship does not enter into the political arena, and societies in which kinship is of tertiary importance devalue virginity.

Wherever virginity is a custom, it brings prestige to the kin group. Prestige, the positive evaluation and esteem associated with the attainment of socially valued goods, events, or positions is an aspect of ideology, both representing and distorting reality. Ideologically, virginity is about women's virtue and men's access to women. The ideology represents the issue of men's access to women, but the emphasis on virtue hides the importance of men's competition for economic and political power and prestige, which I suggest is a crucial feature of societies in which female premarital virginity is highly valued.

A brief comparison of three African groups, the Igbo of Nigeria, the Kikuyu of Kenya, and the Maasai of Kenya and Tanzania, highlights the social structural difference associated with virginity in Africa. The Igbo and Kikuyu, who placed high value on female premarital virginity, had very different social structures, but were similar in the way that kinship shaped and defined political power. Individual achievement was highly valued in Igbo society: to be a leader of his community a man had to be an elder of his lineage, a member of the senior age grade in his village, a leader in a secret society, a good orator; and he had to use his resources to gain titles and host funerals. These multiple memberships and social identities intersected to define prestige and power for Igbo men. The Kikuyu were also achievement-oriented, but the patterns and processes of their social organization differed significantly from those of the Igbo. Patterns of clientship and other "big man–follower" relationships built around a core family group created Kikuyu wealth and power differentiation (I discuss women's role in Kikuyu power relations in chapter 2). The Kikuyu's neighbors and an immense influence on Kikuyu culture, the Maasai devalued female premarital virginity. Maasai social processes differed from the Kikuyu and Igbo in the temporality and relative importance of the kin group, the group concerned with female fertility, and the greater salience of age grade in defining the Maasai political arena.

Virginity and Clitoridectomy

There is no significant correlation between the practice of clitoridectomy and high value placed on female premarital virginity. Many more societies value clitoridectomy than value virginity; clitoridectomy is practiced in societies that do not rate female premarital virginity highly, and female premarital virginity is valued in societies that do not practice clitoridectomy. African women who have had clitoridectomies are among those who engage in socially approved premarital sexual activity, including heterosexual intercourse. A close study of the Coniagui of the Ivory Coast (Gessain 1963) answers those who postulate that clitoridectomy in itself is the underpinning of virginity and submissiveness in African women. In the early colonial period, among the matrilineal Coniagui, a girl was betrothed and sometimes married at or before her initiation rite, an important component of which was the clitoridectomy operation. In either case, she was not expected to settle down with her husband until she had taken many lovers and had had one or two children. The husbands and fiancés of these women wanted to affirm their adult status by having their wives settle down with them, but the young women, whose children belonged to their own lineages, wanted to stay "free" as long as possible. When she finally went to live with her husband, a woman was expected to remain faithful to him. Mothers in sympathy with their initiated daughters sometimes gave them medicines to bring about abortions in order to postpone the time when the daughters would become obedient wives. Other African women, such as Yoruba market women, noted for their strength and independence, undergo clitoridectomy (see Sudarkasa 1973). Clitoridectomy neither promotes submissiveness nor protects virginity.

Premarital virginity was not expected of Maasai girls where "it is believed that girls do not develop breasts until moran [the junior age set or warriors] have 'opened up the way' by having sexual relations with them" (Llewelyn-Davies 1978: 229). Once a girl went through the rite of clitoridectomy, she became a woman and married into the senior age set of elders soon afterward. Many married women, according to Llewelyn-Davies, continued to have affairs with members of the *moran* age set; their control of information regarding each other's adulteries was a major expression of women's solidarity (Llewelyn-Davies 1978: 230–36). Neighbors of the Maasai, the Kikuyu practiced clitoridectomy but expected unmarried women to stop short of heterosexual intercourse. The Igbo varied as to the practice of clitoridectomy, with some communities using fattening houses for female initiation, but generally valued female premarital virginity.

Male and female bodies are produced in culture, and cultural practices, modalities, and dispositions are learned to accompany those bodies. What, in any particular society, is attractive, erotic, and satisfying is learned. Many African sexual practices especially provided the diffuse and sustained arousal to accommodate the clitoridectomized body. Although the physiology of sexual response was not necessarily known or taught, education on sexual matters did traditionally accompany clitoridectomy. Not only was a girl taught what was expected of her as an adult member of the society, a woman among women, a mother, and a wife; erotic acts were explicitly detailed as a part of her wifely duties. To the extent that the operation has been removed from the education and ritual in which it was once set, the clitoris and the ways of finding pleasure in a clitoridectomized body both have been lost.

Sexual practices in sub-Saharan Africa were shaped within the context of the practice of clitoridectomy. Among the Kikuyu, initiated (circumcised and clitoridectomized) young men and women would go in a group to the warriors' house where they would pair off to pursue the pleasure of *ngweko*, prolonged fondling and caressing. *Ngweko* trained the woman's body to respond to nongenital stimulation and allowed time for her to recognize and perhaps savor her own bodily responses. Any discussion of African patterns of sexuality should not omit the sexualization of dance and the possibilities of overall bodily stimulation it brings. Interfemoral intercourse, mock intercourse with the penis inserted between the woman's thighs, a practice especially elaborated in Africa, also involves more diffuse sexual stimulation. In many African societies, a couple is expected to have intercourse more than once in any single session, helping the woman reach increasingly higher plateaus of sexual excitement.

Little of the traditional rites, which included sex education and activities aimed at developing loyalty and cooperation among women, remains. Even though clitoridectomy is now devoid of much of its social support, many women are scared to oppose genital mutilation because of the fear that they or their daughters will not be marriageable, because of the shame and dishonor it would bring to their families, and because, as Gruenbaum suggests for some groups in the Sudan, a chaste, pure woman without some form of female circumcision is unimaginable (1988: 312).

Yet today increasing numbers of courageous African women oppose the continuation of this custom as they disavow the belief that clitoridectomy makes a woman pure, as El Dareer (1982: 73) discusses for the Sudan; adult, as Llewelyn-Davies (1978: 216) discusses for the Maasai; more completely female, as for the Dogon interpreted by Ogotemmeli in Griaule (1975: 126); or fertile, as Kikuyu women told me. Their concern has been with the complications of childbirth, which many clitoridectomized women have, and with the infections that could lead to sterility. The rationalizations for genital mutilation go on. In her study of female circumcision in Sierra Leone, Koso-Thomas gives and refutes the following list of reasons proponents give for adopting and continuing the practice: (1) maintenance of cleanliness, (2) pursuance of aesthetics, (3) prevention of stillbirths in women giving birth to their first child, (4) promotion of social and political cohesion, (5) prevention of promiscuity, (6) improvement of male sexual performance and pleasure, (7) increase of matrimonial opportunities, (8) maintenance of good health, (9) preservation of virginity, and (10) enhancement of fertility (1987: 5).

The discourse of resistance to all forms of female circumcision has shifted to include African women's groups on the continent and in Europe who argue for increased education and economic opportunities for women, demand a greater range of sexual expression, and press to raise the consciousness of African women who are not aware of the reach of patriarchal oppression in their lives. At the United Nations conference on the Decade of Women in Denmark in 1975, African women addressed health issues associated with clitoridectomy but turned a deaf ear to Western women's concern about African women's right to sexual pleasure. Even as African women change their tactics, it would do well for us in the West to remember that in our recent discovery of the clitoris, we may have too much somatized and localized sexual response. Despite clitoridectomy, African women do seek and find pleasure in sexual intercourse.

The Achievement of Virginity

There is no unassailable proof of virginity. Periodic physical examination of a young unmarried woman's genitals, such as was traditionally done by the Shona of Zimbabwe, is rare in sub-Saharan Africa, and even this did not give unambiguous proof. There is a great deal of variation in thickness and elasticity of the hymen, the primary sign of intactness or virginity. Nawal El Saadawi, reporting on a forensic study done in Iraq between 1940 and 1970, states that about 16 percent of girls were born with a fine, easily torn hymen, while 42 percent had elastic membranes, most of which would allow penetration without tearing or bleeding, leaving the remaining 42 percent with the "normal" hymen, which tears and bleeds with penetration (1980: 26). The credibility of a woman's claim of virginity then depends on the propriety of her behavior and the lack of evidence, such as pregnancy, to the contrary.

The emphasis placed on virginity in societies valuing virginity and the expectation that young women actually remain virgins varied. Ford and Beach (1951: 178-92) divided the societies they surveyed into the following categories: restrictive, in which childhood and adolescent sexuality was strongly forbidden or punished; semirestrictive, in which female premarital virginity is a goal not expected to be reached; and permissive, in which there is no positive value placed on female premarital virginity. The Kikuyu and the Igbo were restrictive; they imposed negative sanctions against those who transgressed, and the Igbo also rewarded those who persevered. An examination of the written material on virginity is even more problematic than the physical examination of young women because it does not present evidence of the extent to which these cultural norms were heeded. In this study of secondary sources, I cannot differentiate between virgins and nonvirgins. I assume that a sizable proportion of postpubescent unmarried women who lived in a society that highly valued premarital virginity were virgins.

African virgins were not secluded. Unmarried women along with married women and children were crucial to traditional African economies. In most African horticultural societies, and especially in mixed horticultural-pastoral economies, women did and do most of the farm labor. In long-fallow horticultural systems several plots of land in different areas were typically set aside for the use of each wife. Women of all ages and young children often traveled to these plots, where they worked in groups composed of family and nonfamily members. In societies where women were not primarily responsible for farming, they engaged in trade and marketing. Market women had a wide radius of travel—twenty miles among the Yoruba of Nigeria. Women traders in some areas were granted immunity during tribal wars and were able to safely travel longer distances than many men (Sudarkasa 1973: 155-56). Virgins who worked in the marketplace used this time to flirt with and make assignations with young men (cf. LeVine 1959: 978 for a discussion of courting in a semirestrictive society with high sexual antagonism). In each of these instances of travel, women were thought of as able to protect themselves, if not through physical strength then through sharpness of wit and verbal ability. By the expectations placed on them as girls and women, African virgins were geographically mobile and socially visible.

As I have noted, African virgins legitimately engaged in controlled sexual activity with members of the opposite sex. As with the Kikuyu *ngweko*, they fondled and were fondled, but were expected to stop short of intercourse. If the petting led to intercourse, the unabstemious couple would be ostracized by their age mates, a grave exclusion in this age-graded society. Among the Igbo, a young couple traditionally found a deserted place to explore their sexuality, but from these encounters the young woman was expected to emerge victoriously intact. Thus virginity was not seen as a quality of a woman to be protected by the men of the family; it was the woman's accomplishment. As Isichei (1973), writing on the Asaba Igbo, put it, a woman showed her strength of character through the maintenance of her virginity in sexually charged situations. This was the achievement of virginity. Here I risk the generalization that because of her productive labor and commercial activities the sub-Saharan African virgin was geographically mobile and socially visible, could go about unchaperoned, and, even in more restrictive societies, was sexually active.

The African Contrast with Europe and Asia

In contrast to African ideals, chastity, purity, and the avoidance of thoughts, deeds, and situations that might lead to sexual intercourse were the ideals of the protected, secluded virgin in nineteenth- and early-twentieth-century Europe and Asia. Not all Asian and European women could attain or even aspired to that ideal. Young women at the top of the social scale often were secluded; some did not marry (because they were not matched with a person from the proper station); and they generally were chaperoned so that they would not by casual meeting fall in love with the wrong person. In these same societies, women at the very bottom of the scale had more leeway, or less chance to maintain the ideal of leisured seclusion. Lower-caste and lower-class European and Asian women, like African women, were more actively engaged in productive activities than women of the upper castes and classes. But since women's work in many Asian and European societies was confined to the domestic domain of the family, even lower-caste and -class European and Asian women did not have the same degree of social visibility and geographic mobility as African women. Primarily, women at the top who worked less had the social trappings necessary to this circumscribed life. They attained and represented the ideal of virginity.

Three major anthropological theories attempt to explain the social correlates of virginity in Europe and Asia. Goody (1973) and Jane Schneider (1971) center their discussion on property, either the possession and control of it by men in the family, or the competition for it among family members or competing families. The third (Ortner 1978) ultimately finds hierarchy itself a reflexive determinant of the value placed on virginity. Goody associates virginity with property, signified by the plow and the field. Men owned and operated the plow, but daughters as well as sons inherited the fields, the productive property. Usually such property went with the daughter as dowry at her marriage, to be used by her husband. The men of the women's natal family who maintained an interest in these fields were concerned that their sisters and daughters made a good match and that their property did not go to a no-account who might jeopardize it and the surrounding family property.

In her analysis of virginity in the circum-Mediterranean area, Jane Schneider too notes the importance of women's inheritance of property, but her main thesis is that brothers' interest in the honor and virtue of their sisters helped to establish the boundaries between family groups in an environment that lacked communitywide political integration, and in which families competed for very scarce resources. Brothers who otherwise might have competed with one another achieved solidarity in their assertion and protection of family honor as represented by the virginity and virtue of women.

Sherry Ortner's position has changed from her earlier work, "The Virgin and the State" (1978), to her concluding contribution to *Sexual Meanings*, "Gender and Sexuality in Hierarchical Societies: The Case of Polynesia and Some Comparative Implications" (1981). Hypergamy, the practice of marrying up, marrying into a higher social stratum, was the crucial feature that Ortner surmises maintained the practice of female premarital virginity in stratified state societies. In prestate societies, she noted, following Mary Douglas (1966), women are "dangerous and polluting," while in state societies they are "in danger and pure." Ortner associated this transformation with the increasing level of purity in state societies, as much represented by celibate priests as by virgins. In societies where purity is valued, women collude in denying themselves sexual pleasure so that they might marry into a higher social level, thereby gaining access to more resources of various kinds and adding to the prestige of their natal families. Virgins by this formulation represent the very qualities, exclusivity and eliteness, for which hierarchical societies strive.

Ortner's later work takes a different tack, but shares the essential feature of emphasizing the state systems themselves. Criticizing and refining Goody's discussion of female inheritance, Ortner separates systems with dowry, where property goes with the woman at marriage, from those with female inheritance, in which women inherit property in their own right, not associated with marriage. Along with dowry goes patriliny, exogamy, hypergamy (marrying up), and the wife as the dominant female symbol. Female inheritance is associated with bilateral kinship, endogamy, uxorilocality, higher divorce rates, and the sister as the dominant female symbol. According to Ortner, because virginity is highly valued both in dowry systems where hypergamy is present and in female inheritance systems where it is not, hypergamy cannot be a defining feature of virginity. Ortner concludes:

> Based on the discussions of the present essay, I would now suggest that the concern for the virginity of daughters in hierarchical societies, across the dowry/female inheritance divide, relates more to the argument made earlier concerning the general elevation in status of women in such systems. That is, "stratification" by nongender-based principles places women in each "stratum" on a more equal footing with men, raising them toward equivalence with men at any given level. In this sense, I argued, women's status tends to be higher in such societies than in simpler societies in which gender itself is often a dominant principle of social ranking. (1981: 400-401)

Ortner sees virginity as a form of positive evaluation of women in hierarchical societies—a recognition of women's higher status in such societies. My examination of virginity in nonhierarchical societies negates the thesis that hierarchy is necessary to valuing virginity, but does not answer the assertion that there is a general elevation of women's status in hierarchical systems. Eleanor Leacock (1981) writes convincingly of egalitarianism in band-level societies in which women's participation was public and autonomous, and of the social evolution of women's oppression in more complex societies. Along with Leacock, I believe that in more complex societies the multiplicity of principles of social ranking does not subordinate gender ranking, but rather transforms and deepens gender distinctions. The debate over whether increasing differentiations among men in more stratified societies result in increasing oppression of women, while crucial, does not have to be resolved before some general statements can be made about social correlates of virginity.

Ortner recognizes that virginity expresses continuity of male dominance within class and caste systems. She also believes that because virginity downplays the uniquely feminine capacity for penetration leading to birth, "a virgin is still a generic kinsperson; a non-virgin is downgraded to mere womanhood" (1981: 401). What is needed, Ortner suggests, is more culture-specific analyses to determine in each case whether virginity is really oriented to marriage, as is the case in hypergamous systems, or is about the importance of a woman to her kin group, as in systems with female inheritance.

Each of these theories—Goody's, Schneider's, and Ortner's—makes a contribution to my understanding of virginity in sub-Saharan Africa, but none of them actually matches my reading. Goody's (1973) concentration on the association between dowry and virginity would eliminate much of Africa where bridewealth, property going from the husband's family to the bride's family, is the typical marriage payment. But I keep the emphasis on the ownership and management of property as an integrating process. Schneider (1971) concludes that the virginity of daughters is a means of establishing group boundaries and common interests in societies where property individuates rather than binds. I find her analysis of the relationship between the internal dynamics of kin groups and their external political relations extremely valuable.

Ortner's work is most problematic. I believe that she is wrong in some of her conclusions: that women in stratified societies are "more equal" to their male cohorts than women in simpler societies, and the corollary that because some women are at the top, the status of all women is raised; that the evaluation of women is determined by the dominant female symbol in the society; and that female sexuality causes women as wives to be considered lower than women as sisters. Too many everyday and ethnographic examples contradict the first point. These include the situation of most women in well-documented systems of slavery, the great differences between the high-caste minority and lower-caste majority women in India, and the general status of women in Elizabethan and Thatcherian England. Likewise, the ethnographic literature on Africa shows that women at the top may exploit women below them: powerful Mende women used dependent women and girls for political gain (Hoffer 1974), women attempted to keep adult daughters and sons subordinate and obedient among the Kpelle (Bledsoe 1976), and economically independent Akan women deferred to their brothers and tried to control their younger sisters, daughters, and cousins (Oppong 1974). It is not the sex of the person in high position that is most crucial, but the nature of the political process—the overriding ideology, the available resources, and the processes by which power is gained—that most influences whether having a woman at the top improves the lot of women generally in the society. As to dominant symbols of womanhood, in some societies women may be seen primarily as sisters, in others as wives, and in still others as mothers; but in all wives, sisters, and mothers are women. Women, individually and as a category, have to mediate the difference. That is the crucial social dynamic in most women's lives.

Ortner's analysis seems ultimately to rest on the idea that if a man can legitimately have sex with a woman, then she will be beneath him, not only literally but figuratively as well. A man penetrates a woman, and her animal nature may be made manifest through a resulting pregnancy, birth, and lactation. In truth, the meaning of heterosexual intercourse varies from society to society, as do the positions couples assume and the meanings associated with particular arrangements of body parts. From vagina dentata to the debilitating she-devils of the Mediterranean and the Arabian Peninsula to sexual intercourse as art form in Polynesia, we have enough evidence to suggest an absence of universals in cultural perceptions and conceptualizations of female sexuality and heterosexual intercourse. Sex does not necessarily disempower women.

While I have quarreled with Ortner's later formulations, I found much of her work most insightful and important in helping me identify essential processes in African societies where virginity is valued. Virginity, the African material clearly illustrates, is valued outside of state and clearly hierarchical systems. It is not the structure of hierarchy or nonhierarchy that is crucial, but the processes, practices, and negotiations by which virginity is noted as a social value. In an open competitive political field in which kin groups use their control over women as well as other social relations to gain political power, marrying up becomes an important political strategy. Through the virginity of its daughters and sisters, the kin group asserts its strength and unity, its position in society, and its desire to gain greater renown. Female sexual expression may be controlled by the expectation that through marriage women can bring prestige and access to resources and power to themselves or their families. By their marriages, women improve the relative ranking of their families—this must be the essential definition of "marrying up," hypergamy, which can exist in the absence of the state.

Both the conduct of virginity and the social structures correlated with the practice differ between Africa and Europe and Asia. The interpretations of virginity in Europe and Asia, when they are divorced from their structural constraints, do shed light on significant elements: men's concern with women's reproduction as property rights, kin group competition within an open political field, and the transactions by which prestige is negotiated. Virginity is an idiom used to represent the social relations between kin groups competing in the political arena.

In this chapter, I have dealt with the contemporary politics of clitoridectomy, competing theories of female premarital virginity, and Jomo Kenyatta's and Louis Leakey's colonial discourses on Kikuyu women's sexuality. The next chapter takes up Louis Leakey's representations of the Kikuyu as egalitarian, rule-bound, and harmonious and the role of Kikuyu elders in this construction of Kikuyu culture and society. Important in the production of his colonial discourse was Leakey's promotion of himself as "white African," colonialist, and ethnographer.

4

Louis Leakey and the Kikuyu

The Excursion

In 1947 Louis and Mary Leakey went to Angola to study deposits for a diamond mining company to determine whether certain quantities and configu-
rations of artifacts could consistently be found in association with diamond deposits. To this trip Leakey devotes one chapter in the last installment of his
memoirs, *By the Evidence, 1932-1951*. His recollection of an evening with an anthropologist there shows the prominence given to his consideration of traditional African customs and his uneasy relationship with established academic
and colonial conventions. I have tried to keep Leakey's tone in the following
summary of that evening.

At a dinner party at the home of a leading Portuguese anthropologist who
had lived and worked in Angola for thirty years, Leakey asked the host if he
knew whether any of the Angolan tribes made string figures. His host said that
he had never seen any evidence of string figures or string tricks. After dinner
Mary and Louis began to show the host and guests some string figures from
different countries. When the African servant came in to serve coffee and
found them so engaged, he left abruptly without completing his task. Leakey
noted the man's consternation and read his mind as he reports, "A white man,
a white man, doing string figures!" Assuring his host that the servant should
not be reprimanded, Leakey explained that the man had just suffered a terrible
shock and should be left alone. Later the servant, joined by his wife and others
of the household staff, began to peer through the doorway. Leakey asked if
they could be invited in; his host acceded. Soon they were showing Leakey new
figures, and his host, the renowned anthropologist, finally relaxed the blank
mask he had been hiding behind and began to question his staff in their own
language. The evening ended with the party sitting on the drawing-room floor
doing string figures.

The structure of this story is as important as its content. Leakey introduced

Angolan Africans by way of this story, which simultaneously demonstrates his knowledge of African customs and his flouting of colonial mores, and, more than coincidentally, embarrasses the anthropological expert. Leakey was and considered himself to be an academic outsider. He fought hard for scholarly recognition, opportunistically used his knowledge of Africa and its history, and uneasily confronted colonial privilege and destructiveness. This chapter on his excursion to Angola, more than anything else Leakey wrote about himself, puts me in touch with him as a person. It is part of his last retrospective; the first was published in 1937 when he was thirty-four, while this one was completed just days before he died at sixty-nine in 1972. Everything is in this chapter—his academic bravado, his identification with Africans and his distance from them, his quest for money, and his desire to build something for himself in Kenya. I believe that the narrative structure or ordering of elements in this story in which Leakey presents himself as a visitor to Africa contains a key to his vision and ethics, to his representation of himself as a white African and as an ethnographer.

In the following brief outline of the Angola chapter (1974: 211–21), look at when and where Africans come in and what is said about them, how money and research figure in, and how Leakey takes account of the colonial and physical environments: Leakey introduces the geologist who invited them to Angola, sets up the problem for the mining company, describes what he and Mary were asked to do, comments on this use of prehistory in mining as a first, recounts his flight to Angola, comments on the financial generosity of the mining company, reports the association of the diamond gravel with Sangoan culture, relates how Mary, who smoked and wore trousers, was introduced as Mr. Leakey in order not to inspire the wives of the Portuguese to such liberties, tells the dinner-party story about the string figures, reviews some of the literature on string figures, raves about the Dundo museum, which included a "folk village" where representatives of different tribes actually "lived their normal lives," contributes an observation of women doing competitive "dust figures," assesses the wildlife of the country, comments on the deplorable condition of the Africans in the mines and towns, cites the publications that came from the trip, and ends with a description of his efforts to get the museum trustees in Nairobi to expand the museum and his plans for fund-raising for that purpose.

Africans are mentioned, first of all, in relation to their traditional customs. Leakey contributes to the worldwide survey of string figures and compares Angolan dust figures to those practiced in Melanesia. For this his anthropological and colonialist sensibilities work in concert: a student of A. C. Haddon, Leakey was concerned with the distribution and coherence of cultural traits, and as an adherent of the colonial pastoral he was interested in the mainte-

Fig. 1. Cover of By the Evidence: Memoirs 1932-1951, *Louis Leakey*

nance of traditional culture in the face of the corrupting influence of the West. Perhaps that is why Leakey was not aghast at the sight of Africans in a living museum. It would be going too far to say that many ethnographers and some colonialists in the first half of the twentieth century wanted all of Africa to be a living museum, but the truth lurks nearby. Only in the final paragraphs of the chapter does Leakey decry the conditions of Angolan Africans—illiterate, poor, "treated almost as slaves." But before reporting on living conditions of the natives, he conveys his regret that he had such few sightings of supposedly abundant wildlife.

Publications and fund-raising for his museum in Nairobi in the end command his attention. Throughout his life Louis Leakey wrote popular books for money to support himself and his scientific expeditions; he never had a permanent, full-time academic appointment. Making new discoveries kept him in business. Angola, like Kenya, represented adventure, scientific exploration, profit, and appropriation.

Leakey's journal of his excursion to Angola lays out before me his compassion and insensitivity as a white African, and his arrogance and competitiveness as an ethnographer. Though he was never properly trained, Leakey believed that his insight into the African mind, by virtue of his "being" Kikuyu, gave him greater authority than anthropological experts had. When I first read portions of the *Southern Kikuyu before 1903* manuscript in 1971, before it was published, I was struck by how unengaged and stiff it was—rather like an old-fashioned etiquette manual, I thought then. Returning the manuscript to Dr. Leakey, I mentioned that he might get a social anthropologist to edit it for him. He answered that a very famous Africanist anthropologist had offered to do so, and he had refused the offer. He liked the book just as it was, though he had failed to get it published in thirty-four years. In the Angola story, Leakey bests the expert by knowing more about "his" people and by breaking down the hierarchy set up in the household. Leakey's authority was based on his friendship and identity with Africans. But *white* is more than just a modifier of *African*. In his self-definition as a white African, Leakey expected, and often received, praise and adulation from Africans for his patronage, knowledge, and competence. Returning to Kenya for the rest of this chapter, I closely examine Leakey's ethnography of the Kikuyu, his claim to be Kikuyu, and the social and political conditions under which the ethnography was written.

Leakey described *The Southern Kikuyu before 1903* as "the most detailed anthropological study that had ever been written on an African or any other primitive tribe anywhere in the world" (1974: 109). But he also wrote that "it is not without fear of being accused of false modesty that I state that I am fully aware that this book is both wholly inadequate and incomplete" (1977: xiv). The second statement appears in the preface of the ethnography, completed in 1939 but published posthumously in 1977. The first, written in the final installment of his memoirs, was part of a long-term effort to promote the publication of the ethnography and was also published posthumously, in 1974. The praise recalls the details of Kikuyu history, patterns of production, exchange and consumption, arts and crafts, the life cycle of men and women, religion, and social organization, checked and rechecked. The disclaimer, more than anthropological convention, covers Leakey's concern that it was not his experience of the culture—he called himself a member of the Kikuyu tribe—but reliance on information gathered from committees of Kikuyu elders (about an epoch ending in the year of his birth) that formed the basis for his ethnography. Lack of details on a major rite of passage also caused Leakey sincere regret about the in-

Fig. 2. Cover of The Southern Kikuyu before 1903, *Louis Leakey*

completeness of his ethnography. The tones of the quotations—self-congratu-
latory, regretful, and positivistic (in its confidence in the answers complete
evidence would give)—reveal glimpses of the complexity of the person Louis
Leakey was and highlight the problem of the assessment of an ethnography so
praised and so qualified by its author.

In studying Leakey's biographies and autobiographies, I weigh both
Leakey's claim to be Kikuyu and the quality of his ethnography of the Kikuyu.
I take seriously Leakey's claim to be Kikuyu, which he often presented as his
major credential for ethnographic authority, and try to see on what this claim
is based. Leakey's accomplishment as an ethnographer is examined in the light

of questions raised by recent critiques of ethnography: Is this an ethnographic pastoral (Rosaldo 1986; Clifford 1986)? Was this a collaborative effort (Marcus and Fischer 1986; Tyler 1986)? To what extent did Leakey as ethnographer infuse his writing on Kikuyu culture with moral statements or allegories (Clifford 1986)? I will argue that the ethnography was a cooperative effort by Leakey and the Kikuyu elders, each using history, implicit social knowledge (Taussig 1987), and each other, for their own purposes.

The details do not make this a good ethnography, but it is a useful one. Several scholars have gleaned information from its thousand pages or referred to it in their works on Kenyan history and culture (cf. Ambler 1989; MacKenzie 1986; Krymkowski and Middleton 1987). But perhaps more important than its content on precolonial customs is what the ethnography, in combination with Leakey's other writings on the Kikuyu, presents of the social history of colonial Kenya at the time of the production of the ethnography. Leakey's collaboration with the Kikuyu elders involved both parties in the construction of a Kikuyu past, shaped by their different positions in and perceptions of the then current Kenyan politics and economics, and their desires for the future. It is what Leakey lamented as the inadequacy of the ethnography—its dependence on informants' statements rather than participant observation—and the incompleteness resulting from the refusal of the elders to give particular information that redeems this detailed work and makes it a valuable study of colonial encounters and social history.

Louis Seymour Bazette Leakey

"Born and Bred among the Kikuyu"

Leakey and writers about Leakey uncritically repeat his claim to have been a member of the Kikuyu tribe, to have been not only white African, but white Kikuyu. More than a decade after his death, Mary Leakey writes, "Louis, it must never be forgotten, thought of himself as a Kikuyu" (1984: 111). Sonia Cole, in a very patronizing view of Africans, describes the "essentially African qualities in his make-up" and more dispassionately mentions the Kikuyu as Leakey's "adopted tribe" (1975: 20). I am convinced by what I read of Leakey's own statements that he made this claim without irony, though not without an eye to his own self-interest. In this overview of Leakey's life I want to examine critically his identification with the Kikuyu, a claim that obscures the colonial domination of the Kikuyu by the British and disguises race, gender, and class privileges.

Louis Leakey was born in 1903 to missionary parents living on the Kikuyu reserve in central Kenya. He spent one-quarter of his first sixteen years outside of Kenya, and while he was in Kenya his parents strove to impress upon him not only European languages and sciences but also European morals and customs. He and his brother and sisters had tutors and governesses from Britain and South Africa. In their play, Leakey and his older sisters transformed local waterfalls not into African fantasies, but into imaginary monarchies, each with its own prime minister. At the age of sixteen he began formal schooling in England, and he entered Cambridge in 1922.

Leakey does not regale the reader of his memoirs with first-person stories of lessons learned from his life among the Kikuyu, or even with lavish description of the African landscape. Instead he places himself in a universe with his family and household servants at the center, followed by the circle of mission converts and their families. Other colonists, as individuals or in the ubiquitous and powerful collective settler organizations or clubs, figure little in the story he tells. Just outside of range of the missionaries and colonists is the supposed "traditional" Kikuyu society and also the science and mysteries of metropolitan Britain.

Leakey's position as son of the missionaries afforded him the privilege to participate in, observe, and intrude upon Kikuyu life. The location of the mission station, a difficult day's travel to the colonial capital of Nairobi, limited Leakey's playmates to his siblings and the Kikuyu children living on the reserve. As a child he listened to the folktales told by his Kikuyu nurse, and he was trained in hunting and tracking by another African employee of his parents. As a preadolescent and adolescent he played with Kikuyu boys, visited their villages, and shared the privileges of Kikuyu males. Leakey participated in the Kikuyu ceremony of initiation into adulthood, a major part of which is the circumcision of boys and the clitoridectomy of girls, but he did not undergo the operation at that time. After he was married, he paid the fees to be accepted as an elder and eventually became "a second grade elder" (Leakey 1977: xii). He expressed his Kikuyu identity in his competence in Kikuyu lore and language, and later in life he used that knowledge for his own and what he perceived as the tribe's and the country's benefit.

In contrast to the acceptance and joy he felt among his Kikuyu age mates, Leakey writes of his loneliness and frustration in public school and university in England. At school he was treated as a boy, with dress codes, prefects, and study hours, when at sixteen he felt quite grown-up:

> I had, after all, built myself a three-roomed house and lived in it for over two years. I had employed labour of my own and earned money by trapping in order to buy materials for my house. I had helped my father in the teaching work at the Kabete school and had run and organised the Kabete football club. (1937: 83-84)

Leakey's biographer describes his years in public school as the most traumatic experience of his life (Cole 1975: 38). The uneasy composite of his identities as student, missionary teacher, employer, archaeologist, and Kikuyu age mate presage Cole's conclusion that "throughout most of his career Louis found himself a misfit" (1975: 14). The identities changed as he grew older, but were always of these diverse origins. I suggest that Leakey wore his personae several at a time, each influencing the others. Like the telltale legs of the African masked dancers who are supposed to embody the spirit of the masks they don, something of his other identities always shone through. What he presented of his various social personalities varied with time and circumstance. Leakey could mix Kikuyu conservatism, British nonconformity, and colonial outrage, or Kikuyu opportunism, British loyalty, and colonial paternalism.

In sum, Leakey's claim to being Kikuyu had much to do with his sense of being an outsider in British society, the feelings of belonging and freedom he had as a child at the mission on the Kikuyu reserve, and the pride he derived from his privileged position among his Kikuyu contemporaries. These sentiments spring from the relationship between the colony and the metropole as much as from the relationship between the colonizers and the colonized. As a colonialist Leakey desired the respect of metropolitan Britain and sought after its rewards. But, also as a colonialist, he found freedom from metropolitan conventions and the possibility of a return to the ideals of the preclass, preindustrial world.

His life history shows that Leakey called on and used his mediating identity as white Kikuyu often. His books on the Kikuyu, written during times of personal and international economic depression or political turmoil, are primarily addressed to a British audience that he tries to convince of the dignity and integrity of precolonial Kikuyu life or for whom he puts in perspective the violent uprisings against colonial rule. He was an advocate for Kikuyu land rights, for better housing and higher wages for Africans, and he wrote in favor of abolition of the color bar in public establishments and jobs.

Louis Leakey as Colonialist

Certainly Leakey's relationship to the Kikuyu was longer-lasting and more intimate than that of many whites. But an identification with the Kikuyu, though not of the same etiology as Leakey's, was not unusual among colonial officials. Leakey's perception of "traditional" precolonial society as especially democratic, orderly, and organic was shared, I believe, more widely by local-level colonial administrators than by the Kikuyu. Even as Leakey tried to present the image of Kikuyu society before 1903 as cooperative, democratic, and rule-governed, the life history of an elder transcribed in his ethnography counters it with its emphasis on individual achievement, economic differentiation, and envy. My research on late-nineteenth-century and early-twentieth-century Kikuyu political economy reiterates the importance of democratic structures such as the councils of senior male elders but underscores the differences in power and influence among the men on the councils resulting from the large landholders' economic and political benefits from the labor and loyalty of their tenants (see chapter 2).

Leakey, as the son of missionaries living among the Kikuyu, like local-level colonial administrators moving among those in their charge, saw the political and economic discord within the contemporary Kikuyu community but chose to discount its relevance in defining Kikuyu culture by identifying with the more "traditional" elements. Both represented Kikuyu society as an ideal little community that would be torn apart by individuality, greed, and "politics." I call this fiction of the organic, rule-governed, preindustrial community the colonial pastoral. In a following section I will show the extent to which the elders' representation of Kikuyu society accommodated the colonialists' interpretations. The pastoral both was imposed upon and grew out of an interpretation that the Kikuyu elders held of their society.

In their preface to his Kikuyu ethnography, the editors summarize Leakey's central themes as follows:

> Within the tribe, so long as it kept to itself, everyone was provided for in one way or another. Individuality was discouraged. There were rules and regulations governing every aspect of life and the rules had to be obeyed. . . .
> The detailed rules of behaviour are set out in this book. . . . The overall picture is of people going about their business in a community that provided everyone with a place and an occupation, and that made use of the natural resources at its disposal. (1977: vii)[1]

This summary of the life of a tribe that no longer "kept to itself" encapsulates the ethnographic pastoral, the anthropologists' nostalgic depiction of a time just past (Clifford 1986). Here I suggest that the appearance of this pastoral in Leakey's ethnography derives in large part from an interpretation of reality he shared with a class of colonial officials.

Rosaldo's retrospective on Evans-Pritchard (and Ladurie's medieval interrogator in Montaillou) best approaches my understanding of the political uses of the pastoral in his conclusion that the pastoral "permits a polite tenderness that more direct ways of acknowledging inequality could inhibit" (1986: 97). I would underscore, however, that the pastoral is often a part of the implicit social knowledge shared and used by members of a society, and thus a part of the culture itself. In *Shamanism, Colonialism, and the Wild Man: A Study in Terror and Healing*, Taussig describes implicit social knowledge in several ways. In one place it is "what moves people without their knowing quite why or quite how" and "what makes ethical distinctions politically powerful" (1987: 366). On the following page he states, "I take implicit social knowledge to be an essentially inarticulable and imageric nondiscursive knowing of social relationality" (367). Overall, he sees it as active experimentation in interpreting the possibilities and near impossibilities of social discourse and the various shades of meaning in social situations (393-94). Taussig uses the concept of implicit social knowledge to describe the way historical events in Columbia, especially those of conquest and colonialism, become objectified and empowered with magic used by shamans in relieving misfortune (367). I use it here to describe the parceling out of and reinterpretation of information and perceptions by colonialists in their interactions with the colonized, perceptions and interpretations used in the domination of others.

The image of Kikuyu society represented by Leakey in the Kikuyu ethnography, and the image evoked by his identifications with the Kikuyu tribe, is captured by a description of the ethos of the administrators who believed in the possibility of fair and just colonial rule:

> Central to this system of attitudes and values was an image of society as an integrated organic community characterized by stability and harmony. Change was regarded as disruptive unless it took the form of a gradual organic evolution that preserved essential continuity and order. These ideas were coupled with an emphasis on the value of tradition, a romanticized image of rural society (notably the English country village of some ill-defined golden past) and an insistence on loyalty and a sense of duty toward the community or group ("team spirit"). Colonial administrators deeply distrusted economic individualism, urbanization and industrialization as threats to the organic unity of society. (Berman 1976: 151)

Leakey seems to fit the pattern of the paternalistic, fair-minded local-level official who fought to maintain the integrity of the little community against the exactions of the central government, the disrespect of the settlers, and the individualizing politics of the African educated elite. These officers in the prefectorial system shared an orientation and interpretation that was the "anti-rationalist, anti-urban, anti-materialist and anti-bourgeois response of the traditional landed ruling class to the development of modern industrial society" (Berman 1976: 151).

Colonial officials and others who saw in Africa the possibility of return to a simpler society and the road to prosperity denied the inherent contradictions within African society and, most importantly, did not acknowledge the psychological and social violence they inflicted as a part of colonial domination. The social knowledge of these early-twentieth-century colonizers, used inarticulately and implicitly to envision a colonizable Africa, included ideas of the inferiority of blacks and the nobility of their nonclass society and of the superiority of Western technology and the self-sufficiency, even abundance, of simpler societies. From this contradictory mix have come many shadings on the image of the African. The interpretations and images that Leakey used (and that were shared, used, and reshaped by colonial administrators) pictured the Kikuyu as an integrated, organic community capable of redeeming modern industrial society and at the same time needing to be led by representatives of that society to higher moral, political, and economic development.

This interpretation of Kikuyu society helps explain the intensity of Leakey's response to Mau Mau: adherents of Mau Mau, as he saw them, were semieducated gangster politicians who exaggerated legitimate grievances, distorted traditional customs, undermined colonial improvement schemes, manipulated the beliefs of a religious people, and intimidated the people of the little community into going along with them (see chapter 6 for more on Mau Mau).

This reaction was paternalistic in its protection of the interests of the little community, conservative in its denunciation of the misuse and distortion of Kikuyu customs, and liberal in its design for increased social welfare and civil rights for Africans. Like most colonialists of the time, Leakey did not envision black rule.

Leakey's Luck: The Search for Money

In Leakey's case the politics of research funding became a part of the colonial encounter, and his identity as a Kikuyu salvaged his career in East African prehistory. The motive force throughout most of Leakey's life was his compulsion to examine, to know, the physical evidence of the human past. Living Africans were sometimes seen as representatives of that past, their customs to be preserved, their lives to be exhibited. Money to support his research in prehistory and human evolution was difficult to come by until the National Geographic Foundation began funding his work at Olduvai in 1960 and the Leakey Foundation was established in 1968 (Mary Leakey 1984: 122, 156, passim). The politics of the subdiscipline of physical anthropology is still such that the major grants go to the scientists who make the new discoveries, not necessarily to the laboratory scientist or those who find further examples (Ferrell 1987; Cole 1975: 16). Leakey was an entrepreneur of prehistory who never held a regular academic position. Royalties from his memoirs and popular books contributed to his subsistence as did, later, his position at the National Museum in Nairobi. Still he was continually under pressure to find new species and thereby to secure funds to support his work. While marveling at Leakey's ability to do so much research with so little money, his biographer dramatically captures what I see as the interactive layering of the Leakey persona, evoking Leakey as Kikuyu, colonialist, ethnographer, and prehistorian:

There came a nasty moment when it seemed that he might have to abandon prehistory and—worse—abandon East Africa. Instead he benefited from his unique knowledge of the Kikuyu, and spent nearly two years collecting an enormous amount of information on their customs. Circumstances then forced him to deviate once again from prehistory, and during the second world war he did intelligence work (as he did also during the Mau Mau emergency in the 1950s); this satisfied his love of intrigue and interest in all kinds of people. (Cole 1975: 17)

It was at this "nasty moment," when the expected funds for an expedition were not forthcoming, that Leakey was asked to do a study of the Kikuyu. As Leakey puts it, anthropologists at Oxford suggested that "since [he] had been born and bred among the Kikuyu, and claimed to speak their language better than English, [he] really should devote some time to writing a complete, detailed study of the tribe" (Leakey 1974: 74). A few months after this suggestion, the Rhodes Trust made him an offer of salary and expenses for a minimum of two years to complete a detailed study of the Kikuyu. Leakey accepted.

Louis Leakey's Ethnography of the Kikuyu

The Elders

Deciding to concentrate his study on the southern Kikuyu, Leakey asked a senior chief who was his longtime acquaintance to arrange a meeting with the senior elders of the district. At this meeting, Leakey reports, he argued the need for such a study by likening the Kikuyu's situation to that of the ancient Britons at the time of Roman conquest, emphasizing the present-day Britons' ignorance of their previous customs. Leakey summarizes his argument in the preface to the ethnography:

> I stressed that their own descendants would be in much the same position of ignorance if a detailed account of Kikuyu law and custom was not prepared now, while there were still elders living who could describe the position as it was at the end of the nineteenth century, when European influence first began to make itself felt. I urged that for the sake of their own descendants, if not for any other reason, I should be allowed to have information which, as a white man, and as one who was only a second grade elder, I was not really entitled to receive. I further asked to be allowed to prepare this information in book form. (Leakey 1977: xii)

The elders agreed.

The methodology Leakey used involved eliciting information, based on his prior knowledge, from a large group of Kikuyu elders, checking that information with a smaller group, writing in concert with two senior elders, and checking his draft with another large group of senior elders that did not include members of the first (Leakey 1977: xii). The chapter on magic was written with information obtained from a committee of eight specialists. No women are noted as being among the senior elders, though Leakey mentions conversations with women in the text. One reviewer derisively describes Leakey's accomplishment as his having "painstakingly consulted a series of Kikuyu editorial committees mobilized by Chief Koinange. The work deserves therefore to be set alongside the Kikuyu evidence to the Kenya Land Commission and the complaints of the political associations as a major source for Kikuyu thought in the 1930s" (Lonsdale 1979: 570). I do not disagree with this conclusion, but rather would change the tone of it through an examination that shows how Leakey's personal history and interpretations he shared with colonialists combined with the interpretations and interests of the Kikuyu elders to result in particular constructions of the Kikuyu past and the production of the ethnography.

While I suggest that this was a cooperative effort between the Kikuyu elders and Leakey, the methodology and the resulting ethnography do not fit the current model of fieldwork and ethnography as communication and collaboration between anthropologist and the native. I have not rediscovered Leakey's ethnography as a little-noted precursor of the postmodern ethnography. I raise the question of postmodern ethnography because *The Southern Kikuyu before 1903* is so clearly collaborative that it is important to know in what ways this collaboration fits and does not fit current models. Within this domain of discourse, it is modern (cf. Strathern 1987) in its attempts to represent Kikuyu culture and society as an organic, integrated whole, but bears traces of pre-modern (pre-Malinowskian) "survivals" in its use of survivals and moralistic comparisons. In addition, it falls short of postmodern ethnographic dimensions on two crucial counts. First, it is not dialogic. According to Marcus and Fischer:

> Dialogue has become the imagery for expressing the way anthropologists (and by extension their readers) must engage in an active communicative process with another culture. It is a two-way and two-dimensional exchange, interpretive processes being necessary both for communication internally within a cultural system and externally between systems of meaning. (1986: 30)

Sophisticated as opposed to simplistic dialogue, as they explain it, presents a "balanced, full-bodied representation of communication" (1986: 30) through the juxtaposition of concepts from the culture studied with those shared by anthropologists and their readers. Recognizing the influence of global political structures and economic power, the postmodern ethnographer strives to maintain cultural diversity in the face of anthropological generalizations and universalizing Western values. Leakey, in contradistinction, does little to directly interpret Kikuyu practices and beliefs; he does not usually present the native's point of view, nor does he seriously compare Western and Kikuyu points of view. It is sufficient in most cases for him to explain behavior by saying that it is "age-long" and rule-governed. Disagreements among his informants or between his informants and himself are put down to regional variations, faulty memory, or inadequate information. Places where the ethnography does permit dialogue of the more simplistic kind, dealing with communication between himself and his informants, find Leakey arguing with Kikuyu men about information he wants to record, or addressing the reader and Kikuyu women about the position of women. The ethnography's treatment of women, which I take up in chapter 3, does involve Leakey in explicit and implicit comparisons of what he sees as his readers' values and practices and Kikuyu values and practices. But this comparison does not qualify as "juxtaposition" because of Leakey's lack of self-consciousness and reflexivity in the use of Western concepts, and because the comparisons are often based on moral statements, in this case praising the Kikuyu and criticizing Western civilization.

Second, Leakey's ethnography falls far short of the stringent antirepresentational requirements of the postmodern ethnography as Tyler has defined it. Few ethnographies and probably none so far written could fit Tyler's definition:

A post-modern ethnography is a cooperatively evolved text consisting of fragments of discourse intended to evoke in the minds of both reader and writer an emergent fantasy of a possible world of commonsense reality, and thus to provoke an aesthetic integration that will have a therapeutic effect. (1986: 125)

Tyler envisions ethnography as poetry; Leakey's ethnography is more encyclopedia, the representation of Kikuyu life and the transcription of what Leakey saw as the already existing text of Kikuyu culture. Leakey intended it to be holistic rather than fragmentary, though he does not consistently accomplish this. As to the issue of therapy, it is clear from Leakey's other writings that he intended this ethnography to be used in bettering relations between colonialists and the Kikuyu (Leakey 1952: vii), and he wanted to hold it up as a mirror so that Western civilization might better see itself (Leakey 1961). It is not clear that this is what Tyler meant by "therapeutic." What this study shows is that a collaborationist or cooperative ethnography need not be confined to postmodernist strictures and that collaboration itself does not increase the "truths of cultural accounts" (Clifford 1986: 25).

From my reading of the ethnography and the times, I find that the Kikuyu elders were concerned with consolidating and asserting their power as elders in a changing political and economic environment. The writing of the ethnography was a political act that provided them a stage. The elders collaborated in the production of this ethnography in an attempt to define and maintain their rights and authority.

The ethnography is structured around Kikuyu rites of passage, and throughout the three volumes Leakey recites the many ceremonies and rituals requiring the participation of elders and the fees and fines to be paid to them. In focusing on the many ceremonies, rituals, fees, and fines, Kikuyu culture and society are represented as especially rule-governed and orderly. Few activities take place without the consent, supervision, or other participation of the elders. The many rules recorded in the ethnography were not infrequently broken in the course of everyday life, bringing ritual uncleanliness to the perpetrator and his or her family. The elders possessed the knowledge and paraphernalia necessary to remove the uncleanliness and restore order. The interpretation of Kikuyu society reached through Leakey's consultation with the elders is of a community run by a democratic council of senior male elders, integrated by religious precepts, and made manifest in the instances of ceremonies and ritual. The elders' ambitions accommodated—or, more strongly worded, were codetermined by—forces that promoted the colonial interpretation of the little community.

At the time when Leakey began this research, Kenya was experiencing its version of the Great Depression (this historical overview follows Ranger 1985). With the collapse of the prices of agricultural products on the world market during the Depression, not only the peasant and commercial farmers were hard hit; the Kenya government found it difficult to pay the interest on its debts to Great Britain. The colonial state, under pressure to increase revenue, encouraged African production of certain export crops. This was a time of increased social and economic differentiation of the African population, especially among the centrally located Kikuyu. In the reserves, Kikuyu of means bought out the poorer farmers, extending and transforming, under new economic conditions, the older pattern of large landholders and landless tenants. The traditional elders' councils were pitted against the new elites of wealth and colonial position, the poor against the landed gentry, and the Africans against the colonialists.

By the 1930s the Kikuyu had "colonized" (Ranger's term) the colonial infrastructure, turning to their own uses the roads, communication systems, markets, and schools set up by the British; Kikuyu nationalism was also an important social force. In the late 1920s Kikuyu nationalists had fought missionaries over the maintenance of clitoridectomy as a part of the female initiation ceremony, and against the intransigence of the European missionaries, independent Kikuyu Christian churches and schools that allowed clitoridectomy and polygamy had been formed (cf. Kenyatta 1938 and chapter 5 of this volume). Protests against the alienation of Kikuyu land to the settlers had resulted in land commissions to study and resolve the question of Kikuyu borders and compensations for land taken by the government. (Leakey was an advocate for the Kikuyu in one of them.) With the 1932 Carter Land Commission the area of the Kikuyu reserve was finally established, but the Kikuyu never accepted this and continued to protest the limited land allotted to them. Land pressure from insufficient land, overgrazing, and increased population made cash cropping and even subsistence difficult for the average Kikuyu farmer. As small farmers went under, many left for work in the cities or on European farms, and more and more land in the reserves was in the hands of fewer wealthy Kikuyu, primarily government chiefs, large landholders, traders, and other entrepreneurs.

This social and economic differentiation also had its political counterpart and helped determine the dynamics of colonial politics. Already a hierarchical system of government chiefs and headmen was in place, taking away political power from the council of elders. Native courts, subsidiary under British law, were presided over by three senior elders and dealt with a limited range of civil cases. These positions were used to accumulate wealth. Wealthy Kikuyu outside of these institutions were also powerful in controlling access to vital resources, in setting the conditions and content of social relations, and in shaping and implementing decisions within Kikuyu communities. Colonialism penetrated the very core of the communities, leaving the elders with little political, economic, and moral authority.

Certainly the charge put to the elders of providing the customs and rules for future generations engaged them in a political act that shaped the entire ethnographic enterprise. On the whole, they gave and withheld information with a collective eye on the centrality of their position. In the final chapter of the ethnography Leakey describes what I see as the senior elders' bid to regain some of the power and rewards of elder status: they withheld from Leakey, but most importantly from the wealthy younger elders, the details of the *ituīka* ceremony, the ceremony through which the leadership of the country—religious, judicial, political, and educational—passed from elders in one generation to those in the next. The elders refused to reveal the details of the ceremony until all members of the younger generation had paid their fees for the ceremony. Leakey states that that would have come to the equivalent of 150,000 pounds sterling in 1939 valuations, the retirement pensions to be divided among 7,000 to 8,000 elders (1977: 1284). In addition to the elders' reneging on their collaboration in the Kikuyu ethnography, younger men questioned Leakey's right to be given the information. Consequently, in the final chapter of the ethnography on precolonial life, Leakey is confronted by the problems of modern-day Kikuyu: not only did the elders promote the *ituīka* as a political token, but also a group of young Kikuyu men objected to the elders' giving information to a

European and threatened to withhold payment of fees if Leakey were told the details of the ceremony.

Although real politics called a halt to it, the Kikuyu elders collaborated in the construction of a Kikuyu past that put them at the apex of political and judicial power and the center of the system of redistribution. This interpretation by the Kikuyu elders is congruent with what I see as the implicit social knowledge of the colonial pastoral, the fiction of the organic, harmonious, rule-governed little community. As a "possible" interpretation of social relations of the southern Kikuyu before 1903, the Kikuyu elders' representation is quite reasonable. But it is at odds with the perception of Kikuyu society gained from Kikuyu social history and the discordant voice from an elder's life history included in the ethnography, presented in chapter 5 of this volume.

While Kabetŭ's story recalls the importance of the warriors' individual achievement and the relationship between property ownership and power in an interpretation that counters Leakey's, Kabetŭ also joined with the other elders in asserting the rights and centrality of elders. The *ituĩka* ceremony is again the focus. In his story, Kabetŭ seems to answer a question concerning the *ituĩka* ceremony. Katebŭ explains:

> The meaning of and reasons for the *ituĩka* ceremonies are as follows. Both long ago, and even until now [1936], the Kikuyu had certain ceremonies which they could participate in only by paying fees to those of the senior grades. . . .
>
> The present day generation is no longer concerned with such matters, but in the olden days the generation that had not been through the *ituĩka* ceremonies did not have the right to initiate their children unless they paid special fees to the ruling generation. Similarly, a man who was not of the ruling generation had no right to claim either the skin or the breast of an animal slaughtered in connection with legal cases, and in the days when raiding parties were the order of the day, the generation that was not in power could not participate in a raid, or in its proceeds, without first paying special fees to those in power.
>
> We, the *Mwangi* generation, had our *ituĩka* a very long time ago, and since the new *Maina* generation has never "redeemed the land" from us, we are still in power to this day. (Leakey 1977: 29)

The younger generation never paid the fees to claim rulership of the land. The elders did not succeed in changing the political arena, though this tension between the generations seems to haunt more conservative interpretations of the Mau Mau movement, which followed a decade or so later. Through his story Kabetŭ gives intimations of Kikuyu experimentation with implicit social knowledge, actively interpreting the possibilities and near impossibilities of particular social discourses. This interpretation contrasts with the colonial pastoral that Leakey brought to his study of the Kikuyu, but does not deny the collaboration of Leakey and the elders where they had mutual interests. Their interests intersected at the point where the colonizer's vision of the little community met the elders' dream of power and wealth.

Leakey used the pattern of Kabetũ's life, especially the rituals and ceremonies reported, as the exemplar for the ethnography. Yet the social climate in which the ethnography was produced led him and the elders to downplay the contradictions of differential wealth and democracy in Kabetũ's story and to play up the harmony of following the rules.

The Uses of the Past

Louis Leakey undertook the study of the Kikuyu because he believed himself to be the best person to do it because of his identification with and connections among the tribe, because he felt he could help the Kikuyu through providing information about their customs to the colonial administration, and because the research funds provided transportation to East Africa and a means to get back to research on prehistory. Although he stood in opposition to many colonial practices, he shared in ambivalent feelings that colonists had toward the metropole and toward the colonized. His view of Kikuyu society and culture focused on the qualities of democracy, harmony, and integration lost to class-ridden, industrialized Britain. He argued against piecemeal missionary education as not providing the relevant moral education, and for an interpretation of Kikuyu culture as similar to the laws of the Old Testament. He broke with colonial and metropolitan conventions regarding love and marriage, and held up the Kikuyu sexual morality as a model for the British. Leakey believed the plenitude of Kikuyu society lost during colonialism could be restored through colonial improvement schemes and fair housing and employment codes. Leakey wanted gradual change and multiracial rule in Kenya, and he saw his employment by the colonial establishment as an attempt to bring this about. With his knowledge of Kikuyu language and culture and sensitivity to colonial practices, he wrote books (an important source of income for him) designed to draw respect for Kikuyu customs and to influence colonial policy toward the Kikuyu. He was outraged by the abuse of Kikuyu customs and the violence that was a part of Mau Mau. He became a citizen of independent Kenya, made peace with his former enemy, President Jomo Kenyatta, and to the end was struggling for more money for his research in human evolution and prehistory.

The ethnography, *The Southern Kikuyu before 1903*, is an attempt to describe the late-nineteenth-century customs of the Kikuyu. It accomplishes this through a transcription of the laws of the society as understood by "committees" of senior elders and through a representation of the Kikuyu in the various ceremonies and rituals they performed. Even though a different perspective may be gleaned from the singular story of an elder's life, the ethnography is successful overall in representing generic masculine Kikuyu culture as rule-governed, democratic, and orderly. The ethnography also captures the present or emergent culture that was a part of the colonial encounter. Kikuyu elders collaborated in an interpretation of their society as especially democratic, harmonious, and integrated that would secure their important political and economic positions. The production of the ethnography itself became a part of Kikuyu culture as the senior elders used it to reassert the need for the long-abandoned *ituīka* ceremony, and younger men used the writing of the ethnography and the senior elders' revival of the *ituīka* ceremony as an occasion to proclaim Kikuyu opposition to whites. Particular colonial events of the 1930s—increasing nationalism and increasing social and economic differentiation among the Kikuyu—are reflected in both these battles.

Using Clifford's notion of ethnographic allegory (1986), this ethnography, produced in 1937-39 about the late nineteenth century, is an example of the "redemptive Western allegory." Presenting the "facts" of another culture and at the same time structuring moral and ideological statements about them constitutes what Clifford, historian and critic of anthropology, calls ethnographic allegories. According to Clifford, ethnography cannot escape allegory—all ethnography is allegorical. Ethnographies are allegorical in that they are written reports that

> describe real cultural events and make additional, moral, ideological, and even cosmological statements. Ethnographic writing is allegorical at the level both of its content (what it says about cultures and their histories) and of its form (what is implied by its mode of textualization). (1986: 98)

The term *allegory* carries a negative valence, implying that ethnographers write about one thing but convey a second meaning. Seldom are ethnographers aware of their second meanings: few intend to write "morally charged stories," as Clifford calls ethnographies (1986: 100). In his loosest characterization of allegory, Clifford includes the presence of theory in ethnographies as being on an allegorical level—theory uses actual cultural events to define abstract relations and systems. Even success at making other cultures understandable implies allegory:

> Strange behavior is portrayed as meaningful within a common network of symbols—a common ground of understandable activity valid for both observer and observed, and by implication for all human groups. Thus ethnography's narrative of specific differences presupposes, and always refers to, an abstract plane of similarity. (Clifford 1986: 101)

The breadth of this application makes the identification of an allegorical level of an ethnography less profound, though nonetheless insightful and innovative. Noting that ethnography cannot escape allegory (by his usage, could any speakers and writers of human language be free of allegory?), Clifford calls for a heroic examination of the allegories most common to anthropological thought. Ethnographers and readers of ethnography should identify those allegories that are canon and those that are emergent and be cognizant of historical and political influences in our science and art. Despite my criticisms, I believe Clifford offers a way of "hearing" ethnography that is especially sensitive to the social and political conditions of its production. The different "voices" or "registers" used by Leakey in the construction of the Kikuyu ethnography and the moral and ideological statements resonating in it were sounded out with an ear to Clifford's sensibilities.

In Leakey's retelling of why he undertook the study, in the preface of the ethnography and in his discussion of methodology, Leakey states his mission of salvaging or redeeming "traditional" Kikuyu culture, to write it down before it dies with the senior elders. The "redemptive Western allegory" is one form of the ethnographic pastoral, revealing the ethnographer's emphasis on a society's past culture and a "critical nostalgia," an escape from the corruption and disorientation of the present into the past as an alternative reality. Clifford suggests that the concern with the past and the disregard of or even escapism from the present is also evidence of an attitude of predeterminism toward the future. The "progress" and devastation of Western civilization, of science, of capitalism is believed to be destined to prevail in the societies they encounter. In this view, the future is set, the present is corrupt, and only the past holds interest.

A focus on the past, I have tried to show here in a discussion of colonial mentality, is one of the ways colonialists make the colonized knowable, accessible, and domitable. The colonized are assimilated to an earlier, more primitive time in British culture, a time attractive in its ideals, but that must give way to the superiority of the present. Colonialists look to the image of African society that they have constructed to redeem or save them, and at the same time they undermine its integrity with their imperialist mission. Leakey's incorporation of this secondary level of meanings into the ethnography may be seen as allegory (despite its power, I am uncomfortable with the term), but it is equally a "fact" of the culture of colonial Kenya. I suggest that the focus on the past ensues from particularities of the colonial enterprise in Kenya, especially the conflicts among the various constituencies of colonialists—central government, local-level administrators, missionaries, and settlers—and the efforts of segments of the Kikuyu population, not just senior elders, to arrive at a positive definition of themselves in relation to the colonialists. This aspect of colonial culture resulted in colonialists' interpretations of Kikuyu culture as noble, savage, and domitable, and it contributed to Kikuyu perceptions of themselves as strong, capable, and oppressed. These perceptions and interpretations were a part of the Kikuyu and colonialist culture of the 1930s. The ethnography and the testimony of the elders who helped produce it were also a part of a culture shared by some, contested by others, that emerged out of the political and economic conditions of the period. Clifford has argued that the ethnographer's emphasis on the past defines culture as fragile and essential (1986: 112), as an object to be described (19): "Culture is contested, temporal, and emergent. Representation and explanation—both by insiders and outsiders—is implicated in this emergence" (19). I suggest that Leakey's emphasis on the past conveyed those very qualities. The past, or more properly interpretations of or constructions of the past, is a part of the present culture.

Similarly, the convergence of Leakey's biblical allegory and the elders' list of rules and ceremonies suggests that both may have been using extant Christian imagery and ideology. Kikuyu independent churches had been established by then, and the argument that Kikuyu customs were not proscribed, and some were practiced and prescribed, in the Old Testament was a part of implicit social knowledge. What seems to be Leakey's most archaic allegory may be an embedding of his ethnography in contested, but very influential, thought of the time. I believe that ethnographers learn or hear at different levels, that perhaps we apprehend the paralinguistic and contextual messages of a society and play them back without our conscious awareness. This would explain why Geertz's theory of human evolution (1973) seems particularly Balinese in its conceptions of time and integration and why Ortner's theory of nature and culture (1974 and 1981) fits the symbolic divisions of Nepalese dwellings, but not much of African thought. Perhaps the Kikuyu communicated the universe in which their thoughts nested in a way that conveyed and obscured their secondary meanings. Within the existing or emerging culture of the Kikuyu in the 1930s were ideas regarding the Kikuyu and the Bible that could have been included in Leakey's ethnography and could be perceived by readers today as Leakey's second meanings or allegory.

An idea widely held in sub-Saharan Africa is that the past and future coexist within the present. It may be because of my unconscious learning of that bit of African lore that I am wary of the univalent conception that an emphasis on the past denies the present and relinquishes the future, and why I am so open to the interpretation that the past may be used to redeem the future. I see in Leakey's and the Kikuyu elders' uses of the ethnographic past neither a repudiation of the present nor a surrender of the future. I think that it is conceivable that they were both engaged in "redemptive criticism," the present employment of the past in the hopes of reshaping the future. Taussig, following philosopher Walter Benjamin, has suggested that there are times when the myths of history and the objects of mass culture are used to break out of the bounds of the present and to "animate images of the past in the hope of a better future" (1987: 166). Benjamin was concerned with the stultifying effects of materialist thought on Marxist praxis—the reluctance of materialists to use the power of historical myths and religious images in bringing about changes in consciousness and in social relations. Taussig masterfully demonstrates the ways in which Columbian myths of the lowland Indians were involved in colonial domination and resistance to that domination and are presently involved in healing and terror. More broadly, he suggests that the magical quality of reality and myths of history and objects of mass culture have been used in the establishment of fascism in Europe, the church in Latin America, and race relations in the United States, providing "the very fantasia through which class domination permeates the political unconscious" (1987: 166-67). What I take from these two provocative thinkers for my analysis of Leakey's Kikuyu ethnography is the realization that the interpretations of the Kikuyu past can become objects set in contradiction to a present reality (interpretation) and used as a talisman for or guide to the future.

Leakey's redemptive act, his interviews, his sitting before the elders with notebook and pen, undertaken for sentimental and monetary reasons, also contained the hope that the ethnography would affect the future of the Kikuyu through its influence on the colonial administration. Leakey believed that "it is impossible to study and understand the present day problems in the Kikuyu tribe without a knowledge of what their laws and customs were before the impact of European civilisation" (Leakey 1977: xv). With characteristic arrogance, he protested that Mau Mau could have been avoided if he had been successful in his attempts to "make the government open its eyes to the realities of the situation" and change the old colonial regime (Leakey 1974: 237-38). Mau Mau to him represented the failure of his work, but the images of the past stirred up by the production of the ethnography might also have influenced Mau Mau as an assertion of the power of past—the warriors and the oaths—to change the future. The elders' use of the past to shape their future (the promotion of the *ituīka* ceremony in their bid for power), too, seems to have been stirred by the production of the ethnography. Indeed, the *ituīka* ceremony, long lost to the Kikuyu by the time Leakey began his study, was retrieved and reformulated as a political weapon to ensure the elders' present and future well-being. Myths, heroes, and interpretations of the past, some written in Leakey's ethnographic pastoral, were actively employed in wresting the future from the hands of the colonialists. The violence of colonialism, the surrealism of colonialism, impelled both the colonized and the colonialists backward and forward in search of the means to redeem and transform themselves.

In this chapter, I have shown how the fantasy of a harmonious, egalitarian Kikuyu past, produced by Louis Leakey from his multiple subjectivities as white African, colonialist, and ethnographer, emerged from and contributed to a colonialist pastoral and Kikuyu opportunism. In the next chapter, I take a similar look at Kenya's premier native son, Jomo Kenyatta. In contrast to Leakey as white African, colonialist, and ethnographer, Kenyatta was authentic African, colonized, and ethnographer, but Kenyatta's identities were equally as contested and ironic as Leakey's. During his seventeen years in Europe and after, Kenyatta self-consciously manipulated his image as "authentic" African. He was colonized and cosmopolitan, and his ethnography of his own people was strongly influenced by international politics and the development of modernist anthropology. Jomo Kenyatta agreed with Louis Leakey's redemptive political grammar, which coded the past, perfect, and future tense, but, in his present, Kenyatta imagined and presided over black rule in Kenya.

5

The Ethnographic Past:
Jomo Kenyatta and Friends

Jomo Kenyatta and Louis Leakey were on the same side in the debate over the nature of precolonial Kikuyu social life—egalitarian or structured inequalities?—though they squared off against each other when the Kikuyu-based Mau Mau moved against colonialists and the colonial power structure. Their ethnographies emphasize egalitarianism among Kikuyu men and portray precolonial Kikuyu society as based on incontestable moral precepts and the rule of law. Here I would like to investigate the representation of the Kikuyu in both their works, setting them off against recent historical works on precolonial Kikuyu society, turning finally to Mau Mau itself and the part these two native sons played in it. This study reveals the indebtedness both Kenyatta's and Leakey's Kikuyu ethnographies owe to particular colonial discourses, which in turn shaped the authors' later imaging of Mau Mau. The historians whose work I discuss have the advantage of having written their work fully aware of postcolonial society and looking back through the Mau Mau period, while the ethnographers could only anticipate changes. The ethnographers were especially interested in shaping the future through their portrayals of the past. In fact, both Louis Leakey and Jomo Kenyatta, and to a lesser extent their works, provided the underpinnings for particular interpretations of the 1950s Mau Mau movement.

The Ethnographic Past

Historians, especially Muriuki (1974), Kitching (1980), Ranger (1985), and Lonsdale (1982), looking at precolonial Kikuyu find large landowners exploiting the labor of younger and poorer men and powerful "big men" being "more equal" than their fellow elders. They pose a structurally differentiated society on its way to becoming a capitalist amalgam of petite bourgeoisie and proletariat against the ethnographers' egalitarian, functionally integrated society being destroyed by colonialism, economic exploitation, and racism. Following on my analysis of women's work for late-nineteenth-century Kikuyu, I suggest that the findings of these historians and the ethnographers are not as far apart as they seem. The presumption of structured inequality among the precolonial Kikuyu is faulty, though there is no denying that men, and sometimes women, distinguished themselves as wealthier and more powerful than their contemporaries. Part of the big man's power came from his focal position in the organization of labor and from the importance of his activities in reproducing the relations of production. But there is little evidence that this differentiation was structured and conventionalized, or that the positions, before the divisive influence of colonialism, were permanent or long term. Before that time the vicissitudes of weather, disease, stock management, and human birth and death, along with intra- and intertribal warfare and cultural contradictions, contributed significantly to the determination of patterns of inequality among the Kikuyu. Social relations among men in a political field that was competitive and egalitarian and that placed cultural brakes on accumulation are unlikely to yield structured patterns of haves and have-nots. Rather, the ideology of achievement along with the possibility of acquisition set against the immediacy of power and seniority present a picture of individual movement through the modulated highs and lows of society, a scenario of flux as the normal state.

The social historians' renditions of late-nineteenth- and early-twentieth-century Kikuyu do not note ambivalent attitudes toward property and power among the Kikuyu. Historians emphasize the inequality of the relationship between the landowners and the landless, foreshadowing later internal divisions and exposing the fertile ground from which a Kikuyu bureaucratic elite grew. A brief overview of two important works, Muriuki's *A History of the Kikuyu, 1500 to 1900* (1974) and Kitching's *Class and Economic Change in Kenya: The Making of an African Petite-Bourgeoisie* (1980), illustrates their positions.

According to Kikuyu historian Godfrey Muriuki, by the middle of the nineteenth century the Kikuyu population had expanded from its homeland in the Central Highlands and was moving west toward the Rift Valley. The organization of labor that made possible this expansion required the cooperation of kinsmen and -women, warriors, and land-hungry elders for the acquisition of new land. Groups of these people would help in clearing the forest at the behest of a lineage head, and often they would be encouraged to settle on the recently cleared land as tenants of the landowner. Outside of the frontier areas, such cooperative labor, especially work parties, also redounded to the benefit of the landowning families (see chapter 2). In both instances, the landowner commanded the labor of others.

The cover of Muriuki's 1974 book (fig. 3) heralds his emphasis on oral history. In three different places the same picture of a Kikuyu elder appears. Photographed around 1900, the seated elder is clad in a blanket and holds a large

Fig. 3. Cover of A History of the Kikuyu, 1500 to 1900, *Godfrey Muriuki*

stoppered gourd. On the front cover the elder is superimposed over a photo of himself in the yard of a compound, with children off to one side and women in the background. On the back cover, where one might expect to see the picture of the author, the elder reappears. While he consulted numerous written sources—Leakey's then unpublished ethnography is included as a primary source—Muriuki privileges the interviews, many of them one-on-one, that he conducted with young and old Kikuyu men across a wide range of Kikuyu territory in the late 1960s. He intended this work to counter origin myths and legends about the Kikuyu past, to highlight the agency of Africans in shaping their own lives, and to put into perspective the relatively short period of colonial rule.

Muriuki explicitly tackles one of the myths recounted by Kenyatta, who was president of Kenya at the time of his research and publication: the myth of the Kikuyu Garden of Eden. He disregards Kenyatta's myth of the king of the Kikuyu, accepts his myth of matriarchy, and dismisses the myth of kinship among the Kikuyu, Maasai, Kamba, and Athi, a myth not mentioned by Kenyatta. Using detailed archaeological reports, other scholarly works, and official and unofficial colonial documents, Muriuki shows the pattern of migration of diverse peoples into the Mount Kenya area and the consolidation of the core of Kikuyu customs from practices brought with them and borrowed from people already living in the area. By the middle of the eighteenth century these traits had already been consolidated in an area south and east of Mukurue wa Gathanga, the professed Kikuyu Garden of Eden, decreed by God as the home of Gikuyu and Mumbi, the founders of the tribe, when he allocated the land of ravines, rivers, and game around Mount Kenya to them (1974: 58). Muriuki suggests that the actual Garden of Eden for the Kikuyu was elsewhere, the place where Kikuyu pioneers turned from hunting and pastoralism when they began smelting iron to make axes with which to transform forests into farms. This place, to the south and east, could be the actual primary point of dispersal into the foothills of Mount Kenya of people now differentiated from others as Kikuyu, but Muriuki's research shows that there are several major dispersal points. His concern to find a Garden of Eden is but one indication of how difficult it is to write a history of a people about whom the very powerful president of the country wrote.

Even as he criticizes the use of myth and legend to capture African history, Muriuki fails to actually assess the meaning and value of the myths as opposed to history. Myths, as Lévi-Strauss told us, are good to think. The myths Muriuki mentions tell us how the Kikuyu think about themselves in different contexts. The Garden of Eden establishes the Kikuyu ecological niche, the myth of matriarchy recognizes the ongoing struggle between men's authority and women's power, the myth that a tyrannical king was overthrown legitimates the democracy of the elders' councils, and the myth of the four sons illustrates the linkages among neighboring ethnic groups or tribes.

Muriuki's research was begun in 1966, three years after Kenya's independence from British rule. It was written against what he considered to be the "bad reputation" of the Kikuyu and against accusations of "tribalism" in Kenya. Muriuki's study of the migration of Mount Kenya peoples shows the cooperative interaction of many groups over a period of four hundred years and the gradual differentiation of these people into present-day tribal or ethnic groups.

Explaining that the Maasai and the Kikuyu both played at warfare, "jousts and tournaments," and fought within their own groups as much as against each other, Muriuki deduces that "the Maasai and the Kikuyu were not implacable enemies, and there was no chronic tension and confrontation between them" (1974: 95). He contends that the increasing competition for trade partnerships and trade routes for caravans in the late nineteenth century encouraged the Kamba people, the most prominent middlemen, to represent the Maasai as fierce and the Kikuyu as untrustworthy. Muriuki concludes:

Thus the popular stories about the hostility and depredations of the Maasai against their neighbours have been very much exaggerated. The alleged bad reputation between the Maasai and Kikuyu can be attributed to the stories spread by the Kamba traders about them. These traders, anxious to retain their monopoly of the interior trade, were quick in spreading weird stories not only of the fierceness of the Maasai, but also of the "thievish and treacherous" nature of the Kikuyu. (1974: 96)

Muriuki describes Kikuyu men as individualistic and competitive, and Kikuyu society as economically and socially interdependent with other Bantu-speaking groups and with the Maasai of the surrounding area. Inequalities did exist among men in Kikuyu society in that not all adult men owned or controlled land. The *mbari* or family group owned land, but in some areas, especially along the frontier, *ahoi*, tenants, were a large part of the labor pool: "The *ahoi*, or those given rights of cultivation such as friends and *athoni* [in-laws], could not inherit such land outright and their continued use of it rested solely with the *mbari* owners who could terminate such rights at will" (Muriuki 1974: 77). Colonialism accommodated already existing divisions within Kikuyu society and created ever more exploitative relations among Kikuyu men.

Gavin Kitching investigated the political economy of the Kikuyu through a vast array of archival material, travelers' reports, and statistical analyses. His book describes two classes of men among precolonial Kikuyu, the landowners and the landless. Detailed reports on the resources and conduct of wealthy men insinuate their greater political power. Early colonialists encountered and made deals with Kikuyu "big men" who owned or managed impressive quantities of land, and who held sway among the councils of elders. These men made deals with the European traders and settlers through which the roads were made safe, goods were exchanged, porters were hired, and armies were recruited. Eventually colonial officials appointed chiefs from among these "big men," and the differences between the landed and the landless were exacerbated by the privileges and power accorded the chiefs. Wealthy landowners grew richer and more powerful as more men left the land to engage in the wage labor extorted from them by the colonial government. The social advantages of wealthy landowners, chiefs, and their families and retainers created the basis for development of the Kikuyu petite bourgeoisie and, with their greater access to European education and jobs, a bureaucratic elite.

The theoretical orientation that drives social historians like Kitching to investigate social and political differentiation and the role of family and labor in organizing everyday life yields a representation of assured inequality among the precolonial Kikuyu. Yet this work seems dangerously close to constructing a past that stresses those elements that lead to the present. What is to be explained is why the Kikuyu more than any other ethnic group in modern Kenya make up such a large proportion of the merchant classes and are so well ensconced among the technical and bureaucratic elite. The historian asks what features of Kikuyu society and which of the particularities of their colonial experience led to their ability to adapt to and transform capitalist society. The answer lies in precolonial social relations whose contradictions were similar to those of feudal society and in the Kikuyu's access to the infrastructure built for colonial markets and colonial well-being. Kitching, following the conventions of social history, represents a continuous dialectical process where as ethnographers Kenyatta and Leakey portray destruction and disjuncture.

Jomo Kenyatta: Author, Authentic Native

Kenyatta's construction of traditional Kikuyu life, or rather his perception of what was lost with colonialism, is as much influenced by his understanding of international politics, his resistance to colonialism and attraction to socialism, as by his experience and memory of Kikuyu life at the turn of the twentieth century. In England, even among his Pan-Africanist friends, Kenyatta represented the authentic native (see Paul Robeson's biography, Duberman 1988: 179), but in actuality, from the first, his life was shaped by the presence of European colonialists in central Kenya. Kenyatta's ethnography of the Kikuyu, *Facing Mt. Kenya* (1938), was written against British colonialism in the light of the battles between capitalism and communism, and democracy and fascism. The author had firsthand knowledge of all these systems, moving freely (if at times exoticized and eroticized) among different classes and social groups in Europe.

Jomo Kenyatta was born around 1894 to Kikuyu farmers in the Central Highlands of Kenya, in a riverine site not far from the Maasai plains and the Kikuyu forests. By the time of Kenyatta's birth, Kikuyu in his part of the Central Highlands were already feeling the effects of the presence of Europeans. Kenyatta biographer Jeremy Murray-Brown contends that as Kenyatta's father and his brother, among others, took "advantage of the white man's arrival and the discomfiture this occasioned the Masai, they would leave some of their number to safeguard the lands they already cultivated, while others pushed on to the frontier" (1972: 37). Orphaned while still a herd boy, probably around ten years old, Kenyatta spent a great deal of time with his paternal grandfather, a Kikuyu medicine man or spiritual healer, traveling with him and learning his lore. But the stories he heard around this time were also of the whites on the coast, the wealth of Nairobi, and the power of the train and railway (Kenyatta 1966).

When he went to live at the Church of Scotland Mission (Presbyterian) in 1909, Kenyatta joined other boys for the gospel, industrial training, and strong doses of discipline sweetened with Western education in liberalism. What

Ranger found generally to be true of British colonialists in Africa is specifically true for mission schools: "They drew upon European invented traditions both to define and to justify their roles, and also to provide models of subservience into which it was sometimes possible to draw Africans" (1983: 211). Africans in missionary schools were fitted for work in the bureaucracy and the service traditions of the army, church, schools, and commerce. They also learned of the triumph of freedom over tyranny in the study of Western civilization, and of the virtue of obedience in the master-servant relationship of colonialism.

By the age of nineteen, Kenyatta was aswirl in colonial contradictions— learning of freedom and living obedience, turning away from Kikuyu identities and undertaking employment no African had done before. He went through the Kikuyu male initiation ceremony, circumcision, at a river with other mission boys, the operation performed by a hospital surgical assistant. A year later he was baptized in the church. Kenyatta did not distinguish himself as a scholar or a devout Christian; he was not groomed to be an evangelist or a teacher. Instead he trained as an apprentice carpenter. He soon tired of this and left the school around 1916, working briefly handling money and men for a British engineer. As the East African campaign of World War I heated up, many young Kikuyu men were forced into the army, mostly serving as porters, but Kenyatta avoided conscription by living with his Maasai relatives. After the war, he went to work in Nairobi as a clerk and interpreter, marrying the first of at least three wives in 1920.

Kenya officially became a colony in 1920, having been a part of the Imperial British East Africa Protectorate from 1888. By the time of establishment of the Crown Colony of Kenya, British settlers had fought and won wars of conquest, often using African tribes against one another, fanning old animosities and creating new ones. With the cessation of military operations against Africans came the Pax Britannica, and with it Africans waged legal battles over land, wielded petitions against the government and strikes against employers, and opposed one another in accommodationist and reformist political associations.

In the capital city, Nairobi, around 1922, Kenyatta became active in the East African Association. Founded by Harry Thuku in 1921, the East African Association had members from several tribes and received material backing from progressive Indians in the colony. The association resisted the proposed colonial increase in hut taxes levied on African men, the change in currency, decreases in wages paid to Africans, and the alienation of land from Africans; it encouraged the establishment of independent African churches and schools. When colonial soldiers in Nairobi fired into a crowd of strikers organized by the East African Association, twenty-one men and women were killed. Thuku was later arrested and imprisoned. In this environment of political unrest and open resistance, Kenyatta got to know Nairobi.

Nairobi was politically exciting, but it was also "bright lights, big city." In Nairobi, Kenyatta was a man about town, enjoying drinking and the company of old friends (Murray-Brown 1972: 91). Photographs of Kenyatta from these years show him in neat Western garb, almost meticulous in his appearance—a far cry from the leopard skin he wears on the cover of *Facing Mt. Kenya* (fig. 4). Biographer Murray-Brown characterizes Kenyatta's photographic history of this period as follows: "While in the photographer's studio the raffish character in safari outfit gave way to a family man in plus-fours and sun helmet, for all the world one of the tweedy sort at the local golf club" (1972: 95). Still, no matter how attractive the city nightlife or how demanding the duties of domesticity, Kenyatta was drawn to the politics of resistance to the colonial regime, and that politics took him to the even greater attractions of London.

Kenyatta went to London as an envoy to the colonial office for the Kikuyu Central Association (KCA), the political party that grew in the space created by the demise of the East African Association. He spent about seventeen years in Europe, from 1929 to 1946, returning only once during that time. Supported by stipends from the KCA, British patrons, and work in the phonetics department of University College at London University, Kenyatta spent his time taking petitions and writing letters to the colonial office and calling attention to the colonial question in newspapers and other publications. He also affiliated with labor and left politicians, married an English woman, organized with other Africans in the metropole, attended anthropology classes, wrote his ethnography of the Kikuyu, traveled in the Soviet Union, and participated in Pan-Africanist conferences.

Kenyatta went to London in 1929 with the KCA demands for more land and secure land tenure, more schools, no hut tax for women, African representation in the colonial legislature, and freedom to follow Kikuyu tradition. He stayed to demand self-determination and full independence for the African majority of Kenya. Certainly changing politics in Kenya influenced Kenyatta's new stance, but his vision of the future was also shaped by his contact with left-wing intellectuals, radical thinkers and activists, among them many Africans and African Americans he met in London. His conversations with labor, socialist, and communist thinkers in London encouraged his visits to the Soviet Union, to Moscow in 1929, and wider travels in 1932; he stayed the second time for about a year. Kenyatta has written little about his experiences in the Soviet Union. An overview of his life and collection of his speeches, *Suffering without Bitterness* (1968), holds these few lines on his experience in the Soviet Union:

> He toured Russia briefly in 1929, and went there again—this time across as far as Siberia—in 1932. Many people had tried to persuade Jomo Kenyatta that

Fig. 4. Cover of Facing Mt. Kenya, *Jomo Kenyatta*

Russian techniques in dealing with backward areas could have useful application in Africa, and he wanted to see for himself. (33)

He seemed more impressed with farming cooperatives in Scandinavia than collectives in Siberia, as we learn in the paragraph following his description of his experience in the Soviet Union: "In 1936, Kenyatta toured Denmark, Sweden, and Norway, where he was so impressed by the farming co-operatives that he made special reference to them (more than a quarter of a century later) in an early Parliamentary speech" (34). In his travels across the Soviet Union to Siberia, we do not know whether he was exposed to the massive famines of collectivization or took "an official tour, like those Westerners were treated to, to see Magnitogorsk, the city of steel behind the Urals, or Dnieprostroi, the giant new hydro-electric works in the Ukraine" (Murray-Brown 1972: 168). Very likely he attended the KUTV (Communist University for Toilers from the East) begun in Moscow in 1921 to build Third World revolutionaries (see Wilson 1974: 124) where the Comintern (Communist International) philosophy was taught. The revolutionary philosophy that Kenyatta was exposed to was probably established at the 1928 Comintern Congress and lasted through the high point of Comintern concern with African colonialism, roughly 1928–35. The Sixth Comintern Congress in 1928 marked the beginning of a new activist era: "Essentially it involved a shift away from reliance upon bourgeois nationalists for revolutionary leadership in favor of a 'fighting front' led by the proletariat with the peasantry at its side" (Wilson 1974: 160).

Away from Moscow, he had great help in understanding the nature of revolution from George Padmore, Pan Africanist and West Indian communist who was Kenyatta's friend and would-be mentor. (Despite Kenyatta's study of Marxist-Leninist philosophies and his exposure to communist thinkers, he never sustained a practical revolutionary politics based on these precepts.) In a history of the relations between Russia and Africa, Wilson sums up Padmore's influence on African nationalism as follows:

> If it would be too much to assert with C. L. R. James that "up to 1945 there was hardly a single African leader still active who had not passed through the school of thought and organization which George directed from Moscow," then it can at least be affirmed that from his London-based extension of that school Padmore brought his radical political influence to bear upon many of the individuals responsible for Black Africa's emancipation in the 1950's. (1974: 284, citations omitted)

Kenyatta worked with Padmore in founding successive African student organizations in London and joined with African-American intellectual activist W. E. B. Du Bois, West African nationalist Kwame Nkrumah (later president of the first African country to gain independence from British colonialism), South African writer Peter Abrahams, and others to organize the momentous Fifth Pan-Africanist Conference in Manchester, England, in 1945. Building on various meanings of Pan-Africanism—Africa as the homeland for diasporic blacks, rehabilitation of the African past, solidarity across nation-states, and political and economic interdependence as the goal of African liberation movements—the 1945 Pan-Africanist conference focused attention more directly on struggles on the African continent and promoted resolutions demanding constitutional, economic, and social reforms in British and French Africa leading to immediate independence (Esedebe 1982).

A Wreath for Udomo, published in 1956, the first novel by Kenyatta's London colleague Peter Abrahams, a "colored" journalist exiled from South Africa, may be the best recollection of what life was like for future African leaders living in Europe and plotting the independence of their countries. In the novel, at the center of the group of African, West Indian, and British activists is the dedication, rhetorical power, and revolutionary commitment of Thomas Lanwood, a thinly disguised George Padmore. Kenyatta biographer Murray-Brown suggests that the title character, Michael Udomo, is really Kenyatta:

> Kenyatta was Abrahams's model for his hero, Udomo, and it is an interesting portrait of him from the point of view of a fellow African at this crisis in his career. In the thirties his IASB [International African Service Bureau] colleagues had not been over-impressed with Kenyatta's style; but they all recognized in him someone who was *authentically African.* Where Europeans were struck by his earthy approach to drink and sex, these negro intellectuals were impressed by his detachment from the European scene. (1972: 222, emphasis added)

Others suggest Kwame Nkrumah, the first president of Ghana, also a member of Padmore's study group, as the model for Udomo (see Stanlake J. T. Samkange's introduction to the novel, 1971). More than likely, Abrahams created the character of Udomo from features of both these now historic figures. What most brings Kenyatta to mind is the intensity of Udomo's eyes, his weakness for and dependence on women, and, in the midst of Pan-Africanism, his steadfast concentration on his own country.

The fictional Udomo is quite comparable to anthropologist Robert Edgerton's unflattering description of Kenyatta in London:

> During Kenyatta's early days in England he was known as a frivolous dandy who affected flamboyant costumes, brandished a walking stick, waved his large redstone ring like Merlin the magician, and seduced British women whenever he could. He also took advantage of several people who befriended him. (1989: 43)

In Kenya, Kenyatta had been seen as a detribalized native living and working in Nairobi; in London he learned to use his Africanness, his exoticism, for his own benefit. For instance, he changed his name to Jomo from Johnstone Kenyatta at the time of the publication of *Facing Mt. Kenya* and devised the hyrax- and monkey-fur cloak for the cover instead of the tweeds he wore in Kenya. He used his sexuality, his political connections, and his friendships to keep body and soul together. He even played a toadying minor chief in the racist imperialist film *Sanders of the River* (1935) starring Paul Robeson. Robeson had thought that the film was to be "the first comprehensive film record of African culture" (Duberman 1988: 179), but it is hard to suppose that Kenyatta could have believed that, given his own experience of British colonialism and the bowing and scraping to the colonial officer he was asked to perform in the movie. Both men repudiated the film when they saw the final product.

Peter Abrahams's novel was quite a different matter. Abrahams captures the feel of Africans living in Europe, maintaining a commitment to their countries' liberation while losing touch with the people in those countries, caught up in day-to-day survival and finding comfort in the arms of white women, dedicated comrades. In the novel, Udomo loses the esteem of his colleagues because of a sexual misadventure with his lover's roommate, just before he goes back to Africa to lead his country to independence. Once he is in his country, Pan-africa, the scourge of colonialism is defeated, but only by unleashing tribal passions and magic. In the end Udomo is brought down by the very forces that helped to bring about the revolution. Abrahams gives Udomo this long final speech:

> "As I say, our country has three enemies. First there is the white man. Then there is poverty. And then there is the past. Those are the three enemies.
> "When I first came back I recognized only one of the three: the white man. But the moment I defeated him I saw the others, and they were greater and more dangerous than the white man. . . . I've paid lip-service to the ritual of juju and blood ceremonies and worshipping at the shrines of our ancestors. Now I don't have to any more. There are enough liberated young people now for me to defy all that is ugly and evil in our past."(1971: 340)

Udomo is hacked to death as talking drums urge his murderers *"Udomo die Udomo die Udomo die"* and then *"Kill! Kill! Kill! Kill!"* (1971: 344–45). The defeat represented here is more Nkrumah's than Kenyatta's. From one who knew them both, St. Clair Drake (1978), anthropologist and spellbinding storyteller, I learned of Kenyatta's desire to modernize African tradition, to synthesize the best of African and European cultures, and of Nkrumah's determination to stand above tradition and tribalism. The irony is that Nkrumah's victories were based on his alliance with traditional chiefs and market women, and their displeasure destroyed his Pan-Africanist government. Kenyatta fared better, but the Mau Mau war against colonialism, with its violence and blood oaths, never had his central control. Writing during the Mau Mau period in Kenya while Kenyatta was in prison, Abrahams calls up the fears of many African nationalists.

I have presented the contradictions of Kenyatta as authentic native and cosmopolitan dandy, as Pan-Africanist and nationalist, and as traditionalist and modernist in order to reveal the conditions of the production of the ethnography *Facing Mt. Kenya*. The ethnography was published in 1938 at the midway point of Kenyatta's sojourn in Europe. In *Suffering without Bitterness*, he authorizes this summary of the place and time of production:

> It was during this long episode in Europe—strictly, between 1930 and 1937—that Mzee Kenyatta wrote *Facing Mount Kenya*. Whenever he could, he was collecting material, or attending to preparation and production. He typed the manuscript himself, and did much of the work on the book at a house in Bois de Boulogne, Paris. (1968: 34)

No doubt Kenyatta configured some of the material for *Facing Mt. Kenya* while he served as a native expert in linguistics at London University, but most sources agree that *Facing Mt. Kenya* is based on papers Kenyatta wrote for Malinowski's seminar at the London School of Economics, which he took in 1936 (Murray-Brown 1972: 190; Berman and Lonsdale 1991: 160-61). Unable to earn enough money to live on in England in the 1930s, Kenyatta had to make do with gifts from friends as well as what money he could make on the fringes of the academic world. He was able to make some good friends among aristocrats, such as another student of Malinowski's, Prince Peter of Greece, who traveled to Scandinavia with him and probably opened to Kenyatta the house in Paris where, in all likelihood, he put the final touches on his ethnography.

The ethnography was written in the 1930s as Kenyatta struggled to maintain his dignity while living as a poor student, a political activist, and a charming retainer while confronting the politics of the day, the fascist threat to Western democracies. By this time, Kenyatta had made an extended visit to the Soviet Union and had been to Nazi Germany. He heard Hitler give a speech in Berlin; he had organized rallies in support of Haile Selassie and against the Italian fascist invasion of Ethiopia. Holding democracy as an ideal, he plumbed the contradictions of Western colonialism in Africa: at the local level, democracy versus official hereditary chiefship; more generally, meritocracy versus racism; and underneath it all, rational bureaucracy versus dogmatic religious precepts (cf. Lonsdale 1989: 131). Asking Britain to be true to its own ideals, Kenyatta showed that the Kikuyu met and surpassed the European standard.

Imperialists at home and in the colonies were afraid that the colonized people would turn against them as the war heated up. Czarist Russian and Soviet policy toward Africa had always been motivated by two concerns: to undermine the imperial power of their European enemies and to prevent the use of colonial troops against their armies (Wilson 1974: 128-29). Soviet pursuit of national security led to their encouraging indigenous nationalisms and violent proletarian and peasant revolt. As World War II approached, Pan-Africanists asked whether Africans should fight on the side of the colonial powers, a question more than anything else condemning the hollowness of Western democracy and demanding self-determination as an "inalienable right of every people regardless of the stage of their social and cultural development" (Esedebe 1982: 135). The possibility of African resistance to the war effort, and of Africans' being won over to the ever-active communist effort, was an ominous part of the climate in which Kenyatta wrote his angry denunciation of the West, his ode to the harmony and democracy of the Kikuyu.

Facing Mount Kenya

I find it remarkable that an ethnography so overtly situated in anticolonial and antifascist discourses could survive as simply a "description of Kikuyu culture" (Edgerton 1989: 44), but it has. A review of the *Social Science Citation Index* (1966–1993) from the time of the index's first publication to the present turned up more than 150 citations of the ethnography, from law to history to anthropology to psychology journals. I followed up on about one-third of these references to see just what others were looking for and finding in Kenyatta. Scholars do not seek out this work to hear the particular voice of Kenyatta or to assess the situated knowledge of the African ethnographer in the 1930s, but to find out about Kikuyu culture. Most references were to Kikuyu gender relations, sexuality, and initiation, especially the operation and lessons associated with circumcision and clitoridectomy; the next most frequent citations were about political and legal institutions, land tenure, age grade, religion, and ethnic relations. Some people writing on Kenya cite the book without specific reference; it is an obligatory reference for anyone studying the Kikuyu. When I asked one psychologist how it was that she came to cite Kenyatta's *Facing Mt. Kenya* and whether or not she considered any problems with the text from which she took her citation, I learned of her confidence in the book's specificity and her reliance on passages already cited by others. Few comment on the context in which the book appeared, but those who do mention insider anthropology and Kenyatta's pervasive and determinant comparisons with the West. Kennell Jackson (1976) wrote about the conditions of the production of this ethnography, and Maxwell Owusu (1978) raised the problem of the acceptance of Africans' writing about Africa and also proposed criteria and standards for the evaluation of ethnographies.

My name appears in the *Social Science Citation Index*; I am one of the people who uncritically used Kenyatta's *Facing Mt. Kenya*, just as I, in order to say anything meaningful about virginity in Africa, must use a range of sources whose conditions of production cannot be examined. Do Kenyatta's (and Leakey's) politics jeopardize the work so that nothing is retrievable, or should every reference be accompanied by interminable contextualization? What's an anthropologist to do? Should we give up on ethnography? Abandon cross-cultural comparison? My solution, which may have as much to do with my being a black American woman as with anything else, is to take all knowledge as con-structed and partible, contextualized and capable of recontextualization. That is how I learned to watch television, to process advertisements, and to read an-thropology; to apply most of what I read to myself or my situation, I have to see similarities despite differences, understand the origin and maintenance of difference, reconfigure relationships, and make color adjustments.

At the time that Kenyatta wrote *Facing Mt. Kenya*, the world had never be-fore heard a voice such as his: an educated, angry African representing his own culture to the world. Kenyatta was aware of this, though he felt that he re-strained his anger. And he was aware that he was stepping on the toes of "pro-fessional friends of the African" in writing his own ethnography. Some say that with this phrase he referred to Louis Leakey. Here is the full quotation from Kenyatta's introduction to *Facing Mt. Kenya*:

> In the present work I have tried my best to record facts as I know them, mainly through a lifetime of personal experience, and have kept under very consider-able restraint the sense of political grievances which no progressive African can fail to experience. My chief object is not to enter into controversial discussion with those who have attempted, or are attempting, to describe the same things from outside observation, but to let the truth speak for itself. I know that there are many scientists and general readers who will be disinterestedly glad of the opportunity of hearing the Africans' point of view, and to all such I am glad to be of service. At the same time, I am well aware that I could not do justice to the subject without offending those *"professional friends of the African" who are prepared to maintain their friendship for eternity as a sacred duty, provided only that the African will continue to play the part of an ignorant savage so that they can monopolise the office of interpreting his mind and speaking for him. To such people, an African who writes a study of this kind is encroaching on their preserves. He is a rabbit turned poacher.* (1938: xvii–xviii, emphasis added)

When Kenyatta was put on trial as a Mau Mau leader, Louis Leakey was brought in by the colonial government as a court interpreter. The literalness of this irony was too much for Kenyatta, and his lawyers were successful in re-moving Leakey from the court case.

Kenyatta succeeds in making his ethnography credible by establishing the rationality of Kikuyu beliefs in the most matter-of-fact way—for instance, in the almost tedious description of the male and female initiation ceremonies—by the piling on of detail. Of the female initiation ceremony, after telling us that no men are allowed, he writes this seemingly firsthand report:

> Each of the girls sits down with her legs wide open on the hide. Her sponsor sits behind her with her legs interwoven with those of the girl, so as to keep the girl's legs in a steady open position. The girl reclines gently against her sponsor or *motiiri*, who holds her slightly on the shoulders to prevent any bodily move-

ment, the girl meanwhile staring skywards. After this an elderly woman, attached to the ceremonial council, comes in with very cold water, which has been preserved through the night with a steel axe in it. This water is called *mae maithanwa* (axe water). The water is thrown on the girl's sexual organ to make it numb and to arrest profuse bleeding as well as to shock the girl's nerves at the time, for she is not supposed to show any fear or make any audible sign of emotion or even to blink. To do so would be considered cowardice (*kerogi*) and make her the butt of ridicule among her companions. For this reason she is expected to keep her eyes fixed upwards until the operation is complete. (1938: 145–46)

How different this report might be if it did not tell us "shoulds," "supposes," and intentions, but rather the actual experience of a young woman going through this operation. Still, by use of phrases like "reclines gently" and "holds her slightly," and by painting a seemingly complete picture, Kenyatta creates a sense of verisimilitude.

He writes as the omniscient participant, understanding the meanings of every action, the lives of all individuals. He is the author and authentic native, the insider who learned the language of the outsider, and he shares enough of the understandings of the outsider to know that they will condemn the same things, and have the same goals. Where he feels that he must argue with the outsider, to whom his ethnography is directed, Kenyatta argues that the outsider cannot really know the psychology of the native and must allow Africans to change in their own way, in their own time.

Kenyatta's ethnography is almost completely reliant on his memory. As he explains in the preface to *Facing Mt. Kenya*:

The cultural and historical traditions of the Gikuyu people have been verbally handed down from generation to generation. As a Gikuyu myself, I have carried them in my head for many years, since people who have no written records to rely on learn to make a retentive memory do the work of libraries. (1938: xvi)

He bases the ethnography on stories told to him and events witnessed in his homeland between 1894, the estimated year of his birth, and 1929, when he first went to London. Throughout the ethnography Kenyatta makes references to the way that the Kikuyu keep records in the absence of writing; in court cases, for example, the plaintiff entered the circle of elders "holding a bunch of twigs as a record of his statement, or in other words as notes of reference" (215). The male and female initiation ceremony, *irua*, for Kenyatta is bodily inscription, marking more than the transition to adulthood, but he maintains that "without this custom a tribe which had no written records would not have been able to keep a record of important events and happenings in the life of the Gikuyu nation" (135). Writing for Kenyatta was a mark of civilization, and this Kikuyu author was determined to claim the benefits of writing for his people, or to show that vilified customs served the same high purpose.

Following Malinowski in the structure and organization of the ethnography—from mythological charter to economics, kinship, education, politics, religion, and change—Kenyatta represents the Kikuyu as a society integrated by consensual agreement, religious belief, and morally binding practices.

Facing Mt. Kenya, primarily a collection of essays on Kikuyu life and customs based on the papers Kenyatta wrote for Malinowski's seminars at the London School of Economics in 1936 (Murray-Brown 1972: 190; Berman and Lonsdale 1991: 160–61), was praised by Malinowski, but its value, and the value of the discipline that produced it, are called into question by the historian and Kenyatta biographer Jeremy Murray-Brown:

> The value of Kenyatta's contribution to anthropology must be left to experts to judge. It is a science which claims an objectivity outsiders cannot always recognize. The historian especially must remain sceptical of a discipline which places such emphasis on description and offers no criteria for critical appraisal. But the accolade Kenyatta earned from Malinowski showed that he had mastered the technique. (1972: 190)

Malinowski's appraisal of *Facing Mt. Kenya*, however, is not unequivocal. As an anthropologist most noted for his pioneering long-term fieldwork of an exotic other, Malinowski starts his introduction to *Facing Mt. Kenya* on an entirely different note, legitimating Kenyatta's study of his own people: "'Anthropology begins at home' has become the watchword of modern social science" (Malinowski 1968: vii). Pointedly saying that he does not have to justify the claims of an African writing an ethnography about his own people, Malinowski does just that as he iterates Kenyatta's credentials, commends Kenyatta's work in his class, and declares that the monograph "bears full witness of [Kenyatta's] ability to construct, and his clarity of thought and expression" (1968: viii). Kenyatta's peculiar position as "an African who looks at things from the tribal point of view and at the same time from that of Western civilisation" (1968: ix) is key in both Malinowski's praise and his criticism of the ethnography. Any African bias contained in the monograph, Malinowski states, is all to the good, but, Malinowski argues, Kenyatta showed too much European bias in his work:

> There is perhaps a little too much in some passages of European bias. I might have been tempted to advise the writer to be more careful in using such antitheses as "collective" v. "individual," in opposing the native outlook as "essentially social" to the European as "essentially personal." At many points unnecessary comparisons are introduced and European expressions such as Church, State,

"legal system," "economics," etc., are used with somewhat superfluous implications. (1968: xi)

The Kenyatta dichotomies with which Malinowski quarrels were also influenced by Marxist theories of evolutionary history, learned in London and Moscow.

Malinowski further criticizes Kenyatta for lack of skepticism in his account of Kikuyu beliefs and practices of magic. And it is in this critique that the Polish anthropologist reveals his greatest concern: Western democracies' fraud, corruption, and mismanagement, which led to their weakness in stopping the spread of fascism and communism in this period just before World War II. How can the West criticize Africa when it is in the grips of politico-religious occultism?:

> Do the religious convictions of those who accept Hitler as God, who have faith in the omnipotence of Mussolini or in the omniscience of Stalin, belong to savagery or to civilisation, to superstition or to faith? We are thus led to the reflection that Europe is as deeply immersed in occultism; that superstition, blind faith and complete disorientation are as dangerous a canker in the heart of our Western civilisation as in Africa. Indeed, since we know better, and have all the means to combat superstition among us, Mr. Kenyatta's somewhat ingenuous remarks should lead us to search our own hearts and not to indulge in another supercilious attack on the African's liability to superstition. There is more superstition among us; it is more dangerous as well as more despicable than anywhere among the most primitive tribe. (1968: xiii)

In almost a textbook example of the anthropological use of allegory as James Clifford (1986) describes it, Malinowski asks the reader to evaluate his or her own culture in light of cultural events reported in Kenyatta's ethnography. Moreover, in language that presages cold war discourse, Malinowski challenges readers to heed the recitation of political grievances in the monograph for fear that discontented Africans will be driven into the "open arms of world-wide Bolshevism" (1968: x).

Facing Mt. Kenya is unabashedly political, which has not prevented it from becoming a popular and widely read ethnography. But it did not start off that way. The ethnography was first published in 1938 and sold only 517 copies in its first printing (Edgerton 1989: 44). Although it was little noted in Europe during its first printing, Kenyan colonialists did take notice. John Arthur, the head of the Kenyan mission when Kenyatta was in school there, denounced it:

> What I remember is the Kikuyu filth, physical and moral, which produced smallpox, and terribly yaws-sore bodies, periods of famine, a people bound by fear of evil spirits, degraded with polygamy and all that that means in village

life. All that is hidden in J. K.'s book under a veneer of an ideal African home life. It is untrue. (Murray-Brown 1972: n. 1, 362)

Anthropologist Robert B. Edgerton in his impressive recent study of Mau Mau concludes that "the book was rejected by white Kenyans as Kikuyu propaganda, but it was not that at all. It was a description of Kikuyu culture, and it gave Kenyatta an intellectual and social status that he had hitherto lacked" (1989: 44).

A description of Kikuyu culture aimed at justifying traditional beliefs and derailing colonialism, *Facing Mt. Kenya* went into its second printing fifteen years later, in 1953, during the Mau Mau movement; the politics of independence, neocolonialism, and African and African-American cultural nationalism helped fuel its subsequent printings. I have for years called Kenyatta's ethnography a cultural nationalist tract, but it never really served the purpose of organizing people. *Facing Mt. Kenya* was written after the first wave of Kikuyu cultural nationalism in the late 1920s; the ethnography captured that moment in the language of the functional integration of the tribe. Through *Facing Mt. Kenya*, Kenyatta spoke to the growing number of African specialists who stood in opposition to colonialism, who wanted to see the little community survive, or who had faith in Africans' ability to change their lives.

The major theme in Kenyatta's ethnography is the destruction of a functionally integrated society by British colonialism and cultural imperialism. *Facing Mt. Kenya* is not, however, a eulogy for a society destroyed, but a cultural call to arms to create a modern Kikuyu culture, maintaining aspects of precolonial culture, incorporating features from the West, and implementing them without white domination. Who was Kenyatta's audience? Not the Kikuyu, but liberal and radical men and women, primarily in Britain, whose thoughts he had sought to influence through his reporting and pamphleteering.

In the chapter entitled "The Gikuyu System of Government," Kenyatta uses Kikuyu myth to show how the government changed: "From Oligarchies they passed in the first instance to Tyrannies and from Tyrannies again to Democracy" (187). The footnote for this passage, "*The Politics of Aristotle*, Book 3, Chapter 15, p. 151," one of a handful of footnotes to outside sources in the volume, legitimates Kenyatta's claim that "the Gikuyu system of government prior to the advent of the Europeans was based on true democratic principles" (186). All men were eligible to participate in decision-making councils or *kiama* at village, district, and territorial levels, depending only upon their age and kinship status. In this decentralized society, leaders among the younger men, the warriors, and the elders were chosen based on courage, "impartiality in justice, self-sacrifice, and above all, discipline in the group" (200). Revolution was institutionalized in Kikuyu society in that every twenty or thirty years a ritual celebration passed rulership of the country from one generation to the next.

While Kenyatta describes almost complete grassroots participation and representative democracy among men, his view of the "economic man" is not quite so rosy. Every man strove to become the head of a large family group or lineage, but not all men succeeded. Those in the right kinship and age grade position who had more land, cattle, wives, and children became managers of lineage property. Many of them attracted tenants or *ahoi*, who, Kenyatta explains, were given cultivation rights on the land of another man or family unit, on "a friendly basis without any payment for the use of the land" (22). It is on the role and obligations of *ahoi* that much of the differences between historians and ethnographers turn. Kenyatta and Leakey both minimize the differences between landholders and the landless, and neither suggests that this economic difference has political ramifications.

A later study of the Kikuyu political and social system by Middleton and Kershaw (1965), part of the ambitious ethnographic survey of East Africa, does give an indication of the integration of politics and economy in early-twentieth-century Kikuyu society. Middleton and Kershaw state that an elder who could put unused land at the disposal of *ahoi* would very likely become a wealthy and influential person in the elders' council (1965: 3).

Kenyatta's interpretation of *ahoi* relations among the Kikuyu is projected into an explanation of early relations between Kikuyu and European colonialists. His ethnography uses the openness of Kikuyu land tenure practices to charge the British with deception and trickery. The Kikuyu had welcomed the white strangers as wanderers, Kenyatta explains, giving them temporary rights of occupation, cultivation, and construction. The colonialists' abuse of these rights and their violence against the Kikuyu led to increasing enmity between the groups and, Kenyatta concludes, to demands for a return of appropriated land and security of land tenure for Africans. Kenyatta would have us believe that prior to the coming of the Europeans, access to land, while controlled by those who managed the property or first cleared the land, was, on the whole, quite easy and hardly the basis for major social differentiations.

Social and political conditions in Africa and in Europe influenced the production of this ethnography. Kenyatta lived in England for almost twenty years. There he was supported, in part, by the Kikuyu political party that saw him as its representative at the colonial office, by his friends and colleagues, and by his services as an assistant in phonetics at the London School of Oriental and Asian Studies. In the preface to Kenyatta's *Facing Mt. Kenya*, Malinowski provides a portrait of Kenyatta as a displaced native criticizing metropolitan culture while using it to try to bring about needed changes at home.

According to Malinowski, colonized people were justifiably angry at the denial of their rights and freedom and at the failure of Western democracies as the war against fascism approached in 1938. Because Western-educated Africans were tragically caught between two worlds, Jomo Kenyatta's anger at British imperialism was righteous, and his belief in the spiritualism and magic of his culture understandable. Nonetheless, his translation of Kikuyu practices into British idioms was overdone. The ethnography itself is imbued with a nostalgia coming not only from time past, but also from Kenyatta's spatial dislocation. The strength of Kenyatta's denunciation of the British colonial system was based on the internal critique of Western European societies and from his forays into socialist countries.

Even though Kenyatta's confrontation with colonialism was bolstered by his engagement in British and continental discourse, politics in Africa determined the topics highlighted in *Facing Mt. Kenya*. Land and women were major issues. The last of a series of commissions to study the land question in the Central Highlands had in 1933 made its determination of land boundaries, allocating far too little land as a part of the Kikuyu reserve. In acquiring land, the British said that they had negotiated and compensated according to Kikuyu custom as described in earlier reports by colonial administrators and missionaries. With great attention to land ownership and usufruct rights, and to the rituals associated with land and kinship, Kenyatta challenged these understandings.

In regard to women, Kenyatta held that doing away with female initiation (which included clitoridectomy), as many missionary churches were trying to do, would result in the loss of the functional unity of Kikuyu culture. In the final pages of the ethnography, Kenyatta praises the independent Kikuyu churches and schools that allowed for the practice of Christianity and of clitoridectomy and polygamy (see chapter 3 for more on Kenyatta's political use of clitoridectomy).

In sum, Kenyatta's ethnography was influenced by his position as native in the metropole, by his involvement in European politics, and by his anticolonialism. His representation of the Kikuyu as a functionally integrated, harmonious community being destroyed by colonialism and imperialism denied the significance of the structured inequalities later historians saw, and it presented the cerebral savage in contrast to Leakey's tradition-bound primitive.

Speaking for the African: The Professional Friend

Leakey often called himself a member of the Kikuyu tribe, having been, as he put it, "born and bred" among the Kikuyu, having been initiated into the tribe, and having paid the fees necessary to establish himself as an elder. This rendition of Leakey's life leaves out the quality of the missionary influences on him and on the Kikuyu among whom he was "born and bred" (Leakey 1977: xi). It proclaims him as a white man integrated into an African lifestyle, ignoring the mutually exploitative relationship that he developed with the Kikuyu over the years (these issues are taken up more fully in chapter 4). When Leakey undertook his study of the Kikuyu in 1937, he was primarily interested in funds to return to East Africa, where he and his wife could continue their research into African prehistory. Never securing a permanent academic position, Leakey often supported himself on royalties from his books, especially popular ones such as *White African*, an autobiography published in 1937. The opportunity to do an ethnography of the Kikuyu came at a "nasty moment" in his career when his research fellowship at Cambridge was not renewed and the expected funds for an expedition to East Africa were not forthcoming. The Rhodes Trust supported the research for two years, and Leakey fully expected that the ethnography would be published immediately. He completed the three-volume work in the two-year period. When the ethnography was turned down for publication by the foundation, ostensibly because of its length, Leakey circulated it unsuccessfully over many years to publishers in the United States, Canada, and Britain. In a later book, *Mau Mau and the Kikuyu* (1952), Leakey declares that "Mau Mau" might have been prevented or the disaster lessened if his ethnography had been published and attended to.

Once he was in Kenya to do research for the ethnography, Leakey used his relationship to an important chief to mobilize groups of senior elders for interviews about Kikuyu society and culture before 1903. Both Leakey's missionary background and the fact that senior elders were his prime informants determine the overall feel of the ethnography. On the whole, the elders presented a view of Kikuyu society that held them and the laws they intoned at the center of the society. But by the time Leakey did his research, elder councils had been replaced by the power and authority of chiefs appointed by the colonial government. The elders used the occasion of Leakey's interviews to assert their moral authority and to make a bid for power.

The political conditions surrounding the production of the ethnography also accommodated Leakey's view of the Kikuyu as a people governed by a rule of law, by the "Book," much as the ancient Hebrews were. While much of the assimilation of the Kikuyu to the sacred-law-governed Hebrew is implicit in the ethnography, Leakey makes it explicit elsewhere:

They worshipped a Supreme God—not wooden idols or graven images—a God who required blood sacrifices, but who also answered sincere prayer and liked to be thanked for his mercies.

Many of the customs which went hand in hand with religion were also very similar to those of Old Testament times: polygamy was approved of, a widow lived with her deceased husband's brother and by him continued to have children; circumcision was practised. Many of the forbidden things of the Pentateuch were among the taboos of the tribes, as, for example, the ban on eating the meat of any animal that did not have a cloven hoof. (1954: 128)

The Southern Kikuyu before 1903 (1977), in its constant references to the laws of the Kikuyu, penalties for transgression, and the religious rituals and sacrifices that accompany all aspects of social life, makes a broad assimilation of the Kikuyu to the "people of the Book." Like the ancient Hebrews of the Bible, the Kikuyu were governed by the laws of God. Some chapters of the ethnography, like some books in the Old Testament, are lists of the rules and laws of the Kikuyu. Before Leakey wrote them down, these laws were in the minds of the elders. In writing them down Leakey wrote the Kikuyu Bible (his father had translated the Christian Bible into Kikuyu, a different but not unrelated enterprise). Louis Leakey's book even includes the myth of the creation of the first man and woman, Gikuyu and Mumbi, in the Kikuyu "Garden of Eden." Leakey's massive indignation against the oaths carried out in the early stages of Mau Mau is in part explained by his perceptions of their corruption of the laws and rules for oathing. In books for Western consumption and in newspapers and radio broadcasts aimed at the Kikuyu, he argued that Mau Mau oaths were false and had no power because they did not follow the laws of the Kikuyu (see chapter 6 for a further discussion of Leakey and Mau Mau).

In representing the harmonious little community of the Kikuyu, Leakey constructed himself as the transcriber of the holy book as spoken to him by the male elders. Both Leakey and Kenyatta saw the continuity of women's roles as essential in upholding age-old tradition, a retraditionalizing move not unfamiliar in critical times of change.

Leakey was adamant in his defense of polygamy, which, as he saw it, allowed all women to be taken care of. He argued, as did independent Kikuyu Christian churches of the time, that polygamy and other Kikuyu customs were similar to those of the Old Testament, and therefore worthy of respect. Leakey later elaborated on the sexual freedom allowed women in precolonial Kikuyuland in an ironical defense of Kikuyu male prerogative and in an attack on European sensibilities (see chapter 3 of this volume). This representation of Kikuyu women was predicated on Leakey's defense of masculinist prerogative, shaped by his criticism of Western sexual morality, and made respectable by his assimilation of Kikuyu culture to the Old Testament.

The major themes of Leakey's ethnography of the Kikuyu differ very little from Kenyatta's. In this, the third of his books on Kenya, Leakey completes the precolonial half of the transition that describes movement from economic plenty to poverty, from egalitarianism to exploitation, and from moral society to immoral conduct. On the whole Leakey identified with the local-level colonial administrator who moved among "his" people and tried to cushion the effects of colonialism through education, better housing, and increased wages. The ethos Leakey shared emphasized the value of communalism over individualism and upheld the belief that the "untouched native system" preserved a stable equilibrium between the interests in the community and the rights of individuals (Throup 1988: 72). Differing interpretations of these rights and interests were weapons in battles among the Kikuyu and between the Kikuyu and the colonialists.

Leakey's discussion of Kikuyu land tenure, economics, and politics in his encyclopedic three-volume ethnography is much more detailed than Kenyatta's. According to Leakey, Kikuyu men granted usufruct rights only, and those with usufruct and tenancy rights were said to have given the landowners livestock for ritual occasions and a portion of each harvest in exchange for those rights. Tenants could be evicted if they were inhospitable or stingy, if they did not cooperate in building and maintaining the village, or if they were unwilling to obey the orders of the landowning family (1977: 119). Leakey, however, makes little of the conversion of the landlord's economic power into political power in the councils of elders. He emphasizes instead the moral authority of the elders and the democratic, egalitarian nature of the Kikuyu political system.

A life history included in Leakey's ethnography contradicts the overall vision of Kikuyu society he tries to create. The story (1977: 18-33) of the elder, Kabetũ, stands in contrast to the overall effort that Leakey made to represent the Kikuyu as leading an especially democratic, rule-governed life. The life history partially escapes Leakey's imprint because the job of conducting the interview was assigned to one of the elder's sons. Leakey claims that the account was taken down verbatim and only translated by him. Traces of Leakey are, of course, evident. Besides putting the words in English, he did choose this elder; he mentioned that he wanted to do a second work that would record the differences between Kabetũ and his first son, who, as Leakey put it, had been to England, "owned his own car" (1977: 18), and served as an interpreter for the High Court in Nairobi. Also, in one or two key places in the telling of his life story, Kabetũ seems to answer questions from the interviewer, but these questions do not appear in the uninterrupted narrative. Notably, one of the missing questions in this life history intimates the importance of the ethnography as a political instrument through which the elders mobilized the past for their own benefit and by which Leakey's search for the complete details of the no-longer-practiced itũĩka ritual was thwarted (see chapter 4 of this volume).

Social differentiation stemming from variations in property ownership and control of rights giving access to livestock, land, and relations with women figure prominently in Kabetũ's story. The pains and joys of his warrior days are central in the old man's reminiscences. He was teased and taunted by the warriors as a boy, but after showing his courage was given special honor by them. When the time came for his initiation into adulthood, into the warrior age grade, he joined the other boys in the most "evil" dance, going from compound to compound raiding women's kitchens and stealing from the elders' meat feast. This dance served its purpose, and soon the initiation ceremony was held; the initiates' conduct during circumcision would later be praised or ridiculed in dance and song. After what Leakey calls "ceremonial rape" and describes as rape and sexual assault of a married woman (1977: 24, 690-92, 1364), the young men were considered adults ready to engage in the limited form of sex play allowed junior warriors. When Kabetũ chose partners from among the young women whose rightful partners should have been senior warriors, the young women were beaten and he was sent away from the village. Later, as a senior warrior, he killed a Maasai and brought back his sword. Performing the dance of the hero, which this privileged him to do, Kabetũ went from village to village collecting the traditional gifts of livestock. With the herd so acquired he married and began his ascent into the elders' age grade, about which he says comparatively little. In relating his life history Kabetũ recalls the personal challenges of youth and warriorhood and the importance of individual achievement in attaining prestige and status. The most cooperative acts recounted in his life history had to do with the raids on the Maasai and the joint action of the warriors against Kabetũ and young women.

That the ownership of property was a major determiner of relative power and status Kabetũ underscores with a story of himself as a boy. Kabetũ had angered his father by eating some of his yams without permission. To protect himself from his father's punishment, he asked his mother:

"Mother, if a person, even if young, has property of his own, would his father take his life?" and she answered, "No, my son, he would not." So I said to my mother, "Please find me a bush-clearing knife," and when she had given it to me I went off to find a piece of ground and got permission to make a garden then and there." (Leakey 1977: 21)

Having land of his own, of course, did not effectively establish the boy's authority. He had many other tests before him. But this does point up the power and ambivalence associated with land and wealth.

Through a warning and a deathbed curse about land and wealth Kabetũ presents the dual mandate of the nineteenth-century Kikuyu: explore and domesticate new territory and accumulate just enough wealth. This theme begins Kabetũ's story and, I believe, contains the beginnings of a rival interpretation to the colonial pastoral of a stable, harmonious society free from economic individualism and the similar interpretation given collectively by the elders (see chapter 4). His grandfather's deathbed curse, "To turn back is to return to sorrow and poverty," and the warning from a *mundu mugo* (Kikuyu spiritual healer) was that Kabetū's father would die if the father ate meat from the bridewealth given for a daughter (a major form of redistribution of wealth). Kabetū's father left his grandfather's prosperous compound to avoid the envy and witchcraft of neighbors; he became a tenant elsewhere, and ultimately a wealthy landholder with tenants of his own. He died when he ate from a ram roasted to celebrate jointly the marriage of a daughter and the acquisition of a large tract of land. The death of his father and the impoverishment and death of an uncle who returned to where he had previously lived are explained as the fulfillment of the curse and warning. In discussing the movement to new territories and the deaths that resulted from wealth and from poverty, Kabetū is experimenting with the implicit social knowledge of the Kikuyu—recognizing the ambivalence of the dual mandate, the power inherent in the control of economic resources, and the danger to all those who distinguish themselves through abject poverty and through wealth and power over others.

The major chord in Leakey's rendition of the Kikuyu ethnographic past was of orderly, rule-governed life in a harmonious, egalitarian community. The counterpoint of "An Elder's Story," with its individual achievement, property differences, and inequalities of power, effectively changed the tune, but Louis Leakey did not hear the subtle shift.

The Future in the Past

In this chapter I have contemplated the ways the present captures anthropology's imagination of the past, but many anthropologists have particular images of the future for which they construct their ethnographies. Kenyatta's and Leakey's works were both attempts at influencing the future. The perfect constructions of the past by both Kenyatta and Leakey—the Kikuyu as egalitarian, harmonious little community—were shaped not only by contemporary politics, but also by their hopes for the future. Leakey and Kenyatta discerned discontinuities between the past and the present and hoped for further disjuncture between the colonialism they knew and future society in Kenya. Leakey advocated more humane colonial rule with civil rights accorded Africans. Kenyatta urged self-determination for Kenya's black majority through reference to the histories and challenges of Western democracies. Both engaged in redemptive ethnography, using the past to redeem the present for the future. Their ethnographies of times past are thoroughly grounded in the present and accomplish very particular presentations (productions [cf. Dening 1993]) of the past as a present (gift) to the future.

The view of the historians whose work I considered in this chapter is backward in contrast to the forward vision of the ethnographers. Historians benefit from hindsight. Instead of making a production that occasions a disjuncture in history, as Leakey and Kenyatta attempted, the historians draw lines through peaks and rifts to illustrate a clear pattern. In the case of the historians mentioned in this chapter, they suppose continuity between the past and the present—a past fraught with difference and inequality that leads into the intratribal hostilities of the Mau Mau movement, prompts anticolonial agitation, and explains the predominance of Kikuyu among the petite bourgeoisie in postindependence Kenya.

While I hold that the historical perspective has definite advantages over the model of homogeneous functional society presented by Leakey and Kenyatta, it errs in the rigidity with which class or protoclass distinctions are drawn, and it overlooks mobility of elders in and out of the landed "classes." Just as the life history of the elder Kabetũ undercut the homogeneity of Leakey's and Kenyatta's Kikuyu pastoral, so too does it point up the controls in traditional society that checked the powers of the wealthy. Kikuyu elders found wealth and power dangerous and attractive; they moved in and out of high position; and, before the coming of the colonialists, their common interests as landowners were not solidified.

The structured inequality historians say is typical of Kikuyu society and the rule-governed egalitarianism of the ethnographers both fall short of the mark. In an effort to more adequately describe late-nineteenth-century Kikuyu political economy, in chapter 2 I examined women's contribution to the political economy, where principles and resources from family, trade, war, and age grade produce an open political field. Chapter 3 continues this discussion with a study of the way virginity becomes one of the principles and resources in a fluid political field in which prestige and relative status are always open to competition. An ideology of achievement, within an economy where only low levels of accumulation were possible, combined uneasily with ambivalent attitudes toward wealth and power, resulting in modulated competition within an open political field.

Leakey's interpretations and images of the Kikuyu were shared by colonial administrators, as I will take up in the next two chapters. Here I would like to note briefly how Leakey's discourse on the Kikuyu shaped and accommodated future colonial reactions to and interpretations of Mau Mau. Colonial administrators, as opposed to farmers and businessmen, represented the Kikuyu as an integrated, organic community (Lonsdale 1982). Like missionaries (such as the Leakey family), colonial administrators typically were not drawn from the ruling landed elite of Britain, but from the bourgeoisie, who both aspired to and rebelled against the values of the ruling classes (cf. Hobsbawm and Ranger

1988). Many went to the colonies seeking riches, a better way of life, higher status, or escape from the near-poverty of the middle classes. In Kenya they got caught up in the paradoxes of colonialism: the African was seen as inferior yet noble, and Western industrial development confronted wealth and abundance in precolonial society (see especially Leakey 1977: 41-47). Many colonial administrators envisioned African society as an instantiation of democratic ideals that had been lost to the West with increasing proletarianization of industrial society. For them Africa represented social redemption, but colonialists' views are never singular. At the same time that colonialists rejoiced in the recovery of the little community, they also carried the white man's burden—the supposed need to bring higher moral, political, and economic development to the darker races.

Colonial officials and others who saw in Africa the possibility of a return to a simpler society and a new road to prosperity denied long-standing inequalities internal to African society. And, most importantly, they did not recognize the psychological and social violence inflicted on Africans by colonial domination. The social knowledge of these early-twentieth-century colonizers inarticulately and implicitly constructed a colonizable Africa from contradictory images of the African as noble savage and cheap labor, as self-sufficient tribes and incompetent subjects, and as democratic communities composed of immoral and childlike natives. When Africans revolted in the Mau Mau war, these officials adopted an explanation of the social situation, developed and promoted by Louis Leakey, that emphasized the confusion and trauma caused by the transition from tribal culture to the modern colonial state (cf. Lonsdale 1990; Berman and Lonsdale 1991).

Leakey's analysis of Mau Mau combined what has been called the "liberal paternalist" position (D. Kennedy 1992) and the "liberal" and "revivalist" positions (Lonsdale 1990). In essence, Leakey held that the psychological effect of rapid change from tribal culture brought about a pathological reaction to colonialism. According to Leakey, criminals and thugs took advantage of this confused state of transition and tried to institute a cultural revival through the inversion of traditional beliefs and rituals (see Leakey 1952, 1954). In a study of the different colonial imagings of Mau Mau, Lonsdale summarizes Leakey's position as follows:

> What disturbed Leakey was the mixing of moral and social categories which Kikuyu culture had previously separated in creating order. This was to take the liberal view, that Mau Mau was a product of cultural decay. . . . Leakey may also have come close to portraying the horror with which Kikuyu faced the problem of violence far more intense and internal than could be controlled by conventional ritual means. Mau Mau's offence lay in its confusion between persons of hitherto distinct legal status, gender and generation; its subversion of

morally responsible legal tests, which resolved disputes, into coerced submission to unknown wills; and its inversion of actions proper to the day, social time, into the deeds of anti-social time, of darkness visible and spiritual. (1990: 400-401)

The rule-governed Kikuyu, "people of the Book," as Leakey saw it, were destroyed by the inequalities of colonialism, and from the resulting confusion grew the psychic violence and ritual abuse of Mau Mau.

The distinctiveness of Leakey's representation of Mau Mau can best be seen in contrast to other contemporary images of Mau Mau. For instance, the "conservative" position held that Africans were savages: "Conservatives stressed the unchanging danger of the primitive. Race was the most obvious boundary under threat and was simplest defended by hardening the polemical frontier between white civilisation and black savagery" (Lonsdale 1990: 404). In contrast to Leakey's little community caught up in change, conservatives stressed the essential savagery of Africans and advised increased force and discipline to quell the uprising.

Kenyatta's representation of Mau Mau gives another contrast to the view of Mau Mau as pathological reaction to the trauma of transition. Before his arrest as a Mau Mau leader, Kenyatta spoke both for and against the movement (Edgerton 1989: 55–56, 63; Lonsdale 1990: 417–19). Calling up the suppressed anger of *Facing Mt. Kenya*, Kenyatta clearly promoted radical change in Kenya and self-rule for Kenya's black majority; but as a leader of the moderate Kenya African Union, he spoke both publicly and privately in favor of peaceful constitutional reforms. *Facing Mt. Kenya* was written with an eye to the future liberation of Kenya. The forward vision of the ethnography contained the revival of Kikuyu traditions in the future, especially the revolutions by which democracy replaces tyranny and one generation another. Kikuyu rituals were pushed into revolutionary service as Kenyatta helped spread the oath of unity after his return to Kenya in 1946. But the oaths and the movement they inspired got out of hand, as Lonsdale explains:

> The right to force political change was contested between the men of authority like Kenyatta, who was the son-in-law of not one but two official chiefs, and the dispossessed, legal minors. The reputable, it began to appear, could not win power except at the appalling price of owing its achievement to men they despised. These latter, the hard men of Nairobi, took over the oath of respectable unity which Kenyatta knew and pressed it, by force, deception, and persuasion on those who hoped that desperate deeds, *ngero*, would earn them what they needed, the adulthood which would entitle them to share the fruits of victory. (1990: 418)

In *Facing Mt. Kenya*, Kenyatta produced a version of Kikuyu history that could contribute to the imagination of African independence. But Kenyatta was no mere scribe in this cultural presentation: he actively used the past to shape the future and, like the fictional Udomo, became trapped by forces he helped unleash.

The ethnographic past as constructed by ethnographers and historians is a production of the past based on the authors' understandings of present conditions and, in some cases, the authors' attempts to influence the future. Kenyatta's and Leakey's ethnographies of precolonial Kikuyu were written around 1938, and they responded to events and discourses in metropolitan Europe and colonial Africa. Both ethnographies presented patterns of coherence and continuity and suggested that inequalities were introduced by forces outside the Kikuyu. Historians writing in the 1970s about precolonial Kenya had the advantage of knowledge of events Jomo Kenyatta and Louis Leakey could not foresee but were later caught up in: Mau Mau and postindependence political and social changes.

Louis Leakey envisioned the Kikuyu as an egalitarian, harmonious, and healthy little community transformed by colonialism into a detribalized urban population and impoverished rural traditionalists. Precolonial differences among Kikuyu people, inequalities based on status, property, and gender, showed up in Leakey's ethnography, in Kabetū's "An Elder's Story," but did not contaminate the representation of the southern Kikuyu before 1903 as a rule-governed, egalitarian community. Leakey's interpretation of Mau Mau was based on his sorrow at the destruction of the little community from within by criminals who would subvert traditional customs and from without by colonialists who made it impossible for the Kikuyu to continue to live their traditional lives but did not make room for them in white society. In actively working against Mau Mau, colonialists employed Leakey's knowledge in the construction of institutions, especially detention camps and confessionals, in which colonialists could wield power according to their definition of their African enemy.

Jomo Kenyatta's ethnography, *Facing Mt. Kenya*, produced on the eve of World War II for a European audience, foreshadowed his interpretation of Mau Mau in its condemnation of British colonialism and its insistence on sociopolitical changes that recognize Kikuyu cultural integrity as well as their syncretic innovations. Kenyatta believed that Africans should take the best of both worlds. He worked actively to bring about needed changes, and he was not above using traditional means to reach modern goals.

Peter Abrahams in his novel *A Wreath for Udomo* conjured the destruction of an African leader who would enlist the past, traditional forces, in the cause of African liberation. The prophecy did not come true for Kenyatta, who, as first president of Kenya, adroitly prevented a bloodbath after independence. Before independence, Kenyatta ironically was removed from the "bloody terror" of Mau Mau by his arrest and imprisonment for being a Mau Mau leader. Ignoring inequalities among the Kikuyu, differences later taken up in the works of historians and others, Jomo Kenyatta emphasized in his ethnography the conflict of the Africans versus the colonialists. Internal differences among the Kikuyu contributed to the particular development of the Mau Mau movement, as did the local and international discourse through which images of Mau Mau developed. The following chapter explores the history and the rhetoric of Mau Mau.

6

Mau Mau Discourses

Mau Mau existed at an imagined border between white civilization and black savagery, a cultural intersection. This borderland is a space of interculturality where local traditions and innovations, metropolitan laws and practices, and international economics and politics converged. In Kenya, the Mau Mau movement emerged among Africans most substantially subject to colonial domination, those most intricately affected by the colonial enterprise. The person the colonial government convicted of masterminding Mau Mau, Jomo Kenyatta, was mission- and metropolitan-educated and was believed by many to have used Kikuyu tradition and European occult knowledge as well as communist connections to move his people back to savagery. Kenyatta and Mau Mau represented the colonialists' fear that the white man's burden was for naught—that Africans were capable of only a thin veneer of civilization, which, with just a little pressure, would give way to violence and depravity. Colonialists feared the revenge of the subjugated.

In this chapter, I consider the discourse on Mau Mau in U. S. print news media during the period 1952–60. Mau Mau synecdochically stood for all black people, and especially for American blacks as we began to make moves to change the status quo—from integration of the armed forces to school desegregation to the civil rights movement. In the 1950s, in the midst of national hysteria over the communist menace, the border between black and white was differently configured in the United States than in Kenya. The most popular Mau Mau discourses brought together three great fears of white Americans in the fifties: blacks, communism, and unbridled sexuality. Discourses on Mau Mau resonated with competing American tropes on the naturalness of racial hatred, the communist threat to racial harmony, the inferiority of the Negro, and the limits of education. As Americans took up the colonialists' cause in the fight against Mau Mau in the 1950s, racial and cold war politics merged to construct Mau Mau as a threat to the civilized world of Western democracies coming from the dissatisfied lower classes and races who were stirred up by communist agitators.

The ordeal of Mau Mau has been written about in firsthand accounts by Mau Mau adherents and Mau Mau hunters, in reports from journalists and scholars, in novels and short stories, and in government papers and academic treatises. Mau Mau has been dramatized in plays and on film. Still there is a great mystery about the actuality of Mau Mau, in part because the movement was caught up in local specificity of rituals and loyalties while at the same time making universalistic demands for self-determination and independence. There is no doubt that Mau Mau contained elements of civil war, that oathtaking was sometimes coerced and could consist in loathsome acts, and that the overwhelming motive for Mau Mau was liberation from colonial domination. This mix of motives and acts and the preponderance of reporting on degeneracy, violence, and sexuality in Mau Mau oaths instead of political and economic analysis point to the power of the image of "the Negro" as essentially primitive, despite the best intentions of Western civilization.

Mau Mau

Mau Mau was a movement to overthrow the colonial government largely waged through guerrilla warfare by Kikuyu and closely related groups, the Meru and Embu, in central Kenya—the Highlands and the Rift Valley—in the 1950s. Of the many works on this period I prefer the classics by Rosberg and Nottingham (1966) and Barnett and Njama (1966), the recent review of historiography of the Mau Mau by Buijtenhuijs (1982), Edgerton's very readable 1989 work, and work I wish I could have written: Lonsdale (1990) and Berman and Lonsdale (1991, 1992).[1] The movement was ignited in 1952 with the colonial government's declaration of a state of emergency in Kenya. Before that time, probably starting toward the end of World War II, the Kikuyu Central Association (KCA) was banned as potentially subversive. During World War II, while it was still underground, the KCA began to administer oaths of loyalty in and around Nairobi to male elders and young men, who were asked to swear their loyalty to the Kikuyu people with "a Bible held in one hand and earth pressed to the navel with the other" (Murray-Brown 1972: 240). While oath taking is a long-established part of Kikuyu practices, I think that the loyalty oaths administered by the British to Kikuyu government officials—chiefs and headmen—during World War II were the inspiration for this particular organizational strategy.

By 1946 a more inclusive oath of unity was administered to men, women, and children in the Rift Valley, and by 1948 squatters, tenants on white farms in the Rift Valley, traders, and artisans carried this oath to the Kikuyu reserves and back to the capital city, Nairobi. The *batuni,* the warrior's or killing oath, also known as the "advanced oath," began with the emergency and demanded that Mau Mau adherents and active supporters vow to kill or destroy the white settlers. In the 1940s, the rural wage earners were more active in spreading the anticolonial movement than the Kikuyu in the land-poor reserves. In the cities, Mau Mau appealed to the unemployed, criminals, and prostitutes and, to a much lesser extent, to government employees, white-collar workers, and skilled laborers.

Government district chiefs and village headmen were among the first victims of Mau Mau. Violence against the colonial establishment increased from late 1951 on:

> It started with a large-scale riot against anti-rinderpest inoculations in Fort Hall District [Murang'a], late in 1951, followed by the burning of Government headmen's huts in Aguthi Location (Nyeri) and the murder of headmen in Tetu and, again, Aguthi in 1952. Soon afterwards, grassfires broke out at several European farms in Nanyuki District. . . . Later in the year in September, stables were set on fire and cattle were maimed on European farms in Timau area, while the Kenya Government was badly shaken, in the beginning of October by the murder of Senior Chief Waruhiu, a leading Kiambu loyalist, assassinated in broad daylight by alleged "'Mau Mau' gunmen." (Buijtenhuijs 1982: 39)

Direct attacks on private property on the islands of white in this black sea must have been particularly unnerving, but it was the murder of a government-appointed senior chief that spurred on the declaration of emergency. Within days of the assassination of Senior Chief Waruhiu, the colonial government declared a state of emergency, which escalated the violence and warfare. The emergency decreed the arrest of around 185 prominent African nationalists, banned publications, and restricted travel and associations among the Kikuyu, Embu, and Meru. Some of the Africans arrested at the start of the emergency were moderate leaders such as Jomo Kenyatta, who had returned to Kenya in 1946 and become active in the Kenya African Union, which had replaced the banned KCA, his benefactors during his stay in England.

The greatest immediate effect of the declaration of emergency in Kenya in October 1952 was to increase solidarity among the Kikuyu and in part to legitimize Mau Mau. The reasoning went thus: Kenyatta is a good man; he was arrested for Mau Mau; therefore Mau Mau must be good. Buijtenhuijs concludes that the all-out attack on the Kikuyu through collective punishment and repression "drove many ordinary peasants to fighting in the forest, a line of action they were not prepared for and had certainly never planned" (1982: 45).

The colonial government's declaration of a state of emergency prevented centralized organization of the anticolonial movement, but the arrest of most of the moderate leaders left more militant younger leaders in disparate centers of organization. Members of the Action Group who had begun collecting firearms and ammunition in 1948 were probably pulled into the leadership, as was the Forty Group, men circumcised in 1940, who felt it was their time to rule the country, not the time for whites nor for older African men (Rosberg and Nottingham 1966). The Forty Group's members included

> "hooligans" and the longterm unemployed, especially at the early stage of the movement, but they were joined quite soon by more respectable people such as traders and businessmen. Many members of the Forty Group were ex-servicemen from World War II, although all sources agree that it was not exclusively an old soldiers' association. (Buijtenhuijs 1982: 15)

Unlike their brothers, uncles, and fathers who in World War I were primarily porters, African soldiers during World War II fired guns and engaged in battle. They returned to Kenya with military experience and heightened political consciousness based on their interactions with whites, with black Americans, and with colonized peoples in south Asia and the Pacific. The Forty Group, which had been responsible for mass oathing in Nairobi and all parts of the Central Highlands and the Rift Valley, remained the main link between the pre- and postemergency organization. Urban women were a part of the Forty Group almost from the beginning, and rural women, most of whom were the backbone of the passive support, supplying food and information, also joined in the active fight. Some women enlisted with the fighters in the forests, building the camps and cooking; some carried and fired guns (cf. Presley 1988: 507-8).

Estimates of the number of people who actively participated in Mau Mau as forest fighters vary widely, with British estimates as low as 8,000 for the year 1953 and estimates from Kikuyu sources as high as 51,000 for the same year. Buijtenhuijs, using a wide range of sources, writes:

> Taking into account the rather high turn-over in the forest armies, due to battles, defections and surrender, we may very tentatively suggest that during the 1952-56 Emergency years some 25,000 to 30,000 people in all must have engaged in forest fighting for at least a period of time. (1982: 49)

The peak years of Mau Mau war were 1953-56; much of the Mau Mau activity during that time involved procuring guns and food. Women and children living in the villages near the forests were most important in getting food and supplies to the forest fighters. Forest fighters who came out of their hiding places to liberate guns and ammunition from jails, prisons, ammunition depots, and white settler farms were often helped by women, children, and men who formed a broad base of "passive" support for Mau Mau. Mau Mau also moved against loyalist Kikuyu, and there is little doubt that grievances not directly related to freedom from colonial rule played a part in Mau Mau hostilities toward other Africans, Kikuyu included.

Casualty reports from the emergency, like the reports of the numbers of Mau Mau in the forests, are also varied and unreliable. Edgerton (1989), in assessing the degree of lethal force directed at African anticolonial forces, came up with the following figures:

> The official government figure for the number of rebels killed by the security forces was 11,503, and there can be little doubt that this figure is a substantial, and intentional, underestimate. . . . But even accepting the government's figure, and allowing for a good many wounded who were unknown to security forces, the ratio of Mau Mau killed to those wounded was at least seven to one. . . .
>
> The Mau Mau rebels killed 590 men of the security forces, 63 of whom were whites. About 200 white soldiers or policemen were wounded. They also killed 1,819 loyalists and wounded another thousand. In addition, 26 Indian civilians were killed. Mau Mau's original target had been the white farmers, and many people in Britain had been led to believe by sensational press reports that rebels had killed thousands of white Kenyans. But during the entire Emergency, the total number of white civilians who died at the hands of Mau Mau rebels was 32. (106)

Mau Mau did not come anywhere near the destructive brutality of the colonial forces.

The British used bombs and heavy artillery against the fighters in the forest, but their most successful strategies were (1) the pseudogangs in which black-faced white soldiers joined rehabilitated former Mau Mau in forays into the forests; (2) "population sweeps" in which, "under Home Guard supervision, the entire African population of a district was turned out with their pangas to hack into the forest, clearing the underbrush and killing any Mau Mau incautious enough to be found in the area" (Edgerton 1989: 101-2); and (3) the villagization program. Through the villagization program, Kikuyu who had lived in scattered settlements in central Kenya were thrust together in compact villages, around which they were forced to dig large ditches that were patrolled by the African Home Guard, loyalist Kikuyu and other Africans. The concentration of people, the barrier of the ditch, and the police patrol prevented personnel, supplies, and messages from leaving the village and reaching the forest fighters. In addition to cutting off the contact between the forest and the village, the colonial government enacted a policy of land consolidation and registration as a part of the villagization program. Through this compulsory program, a man would receive title deed to a parcel of land equal to the acreage of scattered plots he had rights to on *mbari* or family land. Family members active in Mau Mau got nothing.

The origin of the term *Mau Mau* is a mystery. Some suggest that the phrase is a mispronunciation of *muhimu*, a Swahili term meaning "important," which was used to refer to a secret group of militant young men organized as the Central Committee within the Kenya African Union (KAU). Even though they called themselves the Central Committee, they saw the committee as an alternative to KAU's more moderate constitutionalist strategies (cf. Kaggia 1975: 108–9; Buijtenhuijs 1982: 18).

During my fieldwork I asked a few people about the origins of the term *Mau Mau* and got several answers, but no real engagement with the question. When I asked a prosperous older businessman in 1972, I was told that it was a play on the phrase *uma uma*, which is said to greedy children, but here referred to the desires of rebels for more land. Men who said that they had been forest fighters, a positive phrase for Mau Mau in 1971-72 in Murang'a District, where I lived, saw the term *Mau Mau* as a colonialist creation, but accepted it because of the terrible, powerful image it provoked. The most common referent for Mau Mau that I heard during this time was in English and definitely anti-Mau Mau, the term *terrorists*. Other referents with a more positive cast were the general term *kiama*, meaning "council" as in elders' council or warriors' council. Few people used the populist *Land and Freedom Army*. These referents show the divided loyalties in central Kenya less than ten years after independence. Many people said that more people came out of the forest than ever went in, meaning that people who believed that forest fighters would be rewarded for their part in bringing about independence from the colonial regime hastily formed an alliance with Mau Mau.

Even people opposed to Mau Mau felt that the Kikuyu deserved rewards for bringing about independence. I conducted a survey in a Murang'a location less than ten years after independence. Almost all women and men I interviewed believed that the "fruits of *uhuru*," the benefits of independence, had been won by the Kikuyu, Meru, and Embu and that the lion's share of the rewards of independence should go to members of those groups. Kenyatta, as first president of Kenya, did not reward Mau Mau or the Kikuyu, Embu, and Meru. In concession to the British government, he made land available on a willing seller, willing buyer basis. Kenyatta did declare an amnesty for Mau Mau forest fighters and tried to establish them in resettlement schemes, but when the former forest fighters found out how little land they would get, how poor it was, or that they might be expected to pay for it, they rebelled. Kenyatta had no sympathies with the continued lawlessness of Mau Mau and mobilized his armed forces against them. Furthermore, because of the colonialist strategy of land consolidation and registration, landless Kikuyu, such as the squatters in the Rift Valley who had fought for more land, found themselves even worse off after independence.

Kikuyu who profited from their position in the colonial government, for instance in the Home Guard of loyalist soliders and police, were able to maintain their wealth, power, and position after independence. Where I lived, one of the richest Kikuyu men had been a particularly cruel police officer during the emergency. He lived in a European-style house with his family, sent his sons and daughters away to boarding school, and owned rental property and a small store. In 1971-72, he was still feared because of his "character" and his economic power. He and his sons were considered at worst evil, and at best rude. His success, especially his European-style house, was held against him; the bedroom doors opened into the interior of the house, not onto a courtyard, encouraging rumors of incest. Stories of his cruelty were commonplace, but no one could afford to disrespect him openly.

Leakey and Kenyatta faced off against each other over Mau Mau, though they already had a long-standing animosity, some of it related to the desire of each to represent the Kikuyu authoritatively. Leakey did not want any study of the Kikuyu to come out before his, and he charged Jomo Kenyatta with plagiarism (Berman and Lonsdale 1991: 160–62). Kenyatta was suspicious of the "professional friend of the African" and decried Leakey's counterinsurgency work among the Kikuyu during World War II. Even though Leakey championed an end to the color bar, and better education and housing and more land for Africans, his representation of Mau Mau concentrated on its methods rather than its goals. He shaped one of the major interpretations of Mau Mau as an inversion of Kikuyu tradition consciously used to intimidate the population, a syncretistic religious movement promoted by thugs (Leakey 1952, 1953, 1954). Leakey was prominent in the anti-Mau Mau campaign; in fact, he encouraged the hiring of government medicine men, "Her Majesty's witch doctors," to cleanse Kikuyu of the moral pollution brought on by their taking oaths. Mau Mau oaths, according to Leakey (1952), were a calculated inversion of Kikuyu custom. Many colonialists believed that Jomo Kenyatta, based on his knowledge of Kikuyu customary beliefs and European witchcraft—gained from his years of study in London—introduced and spread Mau Mau oaths in a deliberate attempt to subvert Kikuyu custom and create a murderous force of Kikuyu loyal only to him and Mau Mau (Corfield 1960).

Kenyatta always denied that he was a member of Mau Mau. Before his arrest, during his trial, after his conviction, and after he became president of Kenya, Kenyatta maintained that he stood for African independence, an end to racial discrimination, improved education, industry, and peasant agricultural development. These were changes to be brought about using peaceful constitutional means. From his point of view, the declaration of the state of emergency was an attempt to eliminate the Kenya African Union as a political party. The following analysis is taken from Kenyatta's opening statement as he mounted his defense at his trial, which took twenty months:

> And instead of joining with us to fight Mau Mau, the Government arrested all the leading members of the Kenya African Union, accusing them of being Mau Mau. . . . They wanted—I think—not to eliminate Mau Mau, but to eliminate the only political organization, the KAU, which fights constitutionally for the rights of African people. . . . Most of the people behind bars today are people who would be helping to adjust things and eliminate Mau Mau from the country. (Kenyatta, 1968: 57)

Kenyatta was not playing word games; he meant that he was not a member of a militant organization that vowed to bring about the end of colonialism through violent overthrow. Colonialists had refused to see any profound differences between the banned KCA, the new KAU, of which Kenyatta was president, and the emergent militant movement they called Mau Mau. While it is hard to judge the veracity of a speech in which one defends oneself during a trial, a number of scholars of this period of Kenyan history suggest that Kenyatta was on the outs with the young men who became associated with Mau Mau. Edgerton reports that just a few months before Kenyatta was arrested as a leader of Mau Mau, he was threatened by members of the Central Committee (*muhimu*), the secret organization of young men who while using the KAU as a cover would have no KAU officials as a part of their groups: "They warned him to temper his criticism and they were not gentle about it; the young leaders of Mau Mau were ready to kill Kenyatta if he continued to criticize the movement" (1989: 56). Kenyatta supported the administration of the loyalty and the unity oaths, but he opposed the "killing oath" and the criminal element that surfaced in Mau Mau (Edgerton 1989: 49, 60–61). In many respects, he was not very far from Leakey's position, but instead of elaborating their similarities, Leakey actively worked to bring about Kenyatta's conviction and to effect what he thought would be a swift end to Mau Mau. Leakey served as official interpreter at Kenyatta's trial, but his translations of witnesses' statements were repeatedly challenged by Kenyatta's aggressive defense attorney, Indian socialist D. N. Pritt.

Leakey was demoralized as well as energized by Mau Mau. He saw friends and relatives killed; his Kikuyu blood brothers turned against him. But his knowledge of the Kikuyu, finally recognized as valuable by the colonial government, was significant in the definition of power: who and what are to be controlled and how. The colonial government sought Leakey's help for cultural and religious solutions to a problem they were unwilling to see as political.

Not only had Leakey believed, with wonderful anthropological arrogance, that the publication of his ethnography might have changed the course of history, he must also have felt, despite his public statements to the contrary, a lessening of his personal identification with the Kikuyu. The publisher's epilogue to his memoirs, *By the Evidence*, summarizes his feelings as follows:

> The Mau Mau revolt affected him deeply; it was a nightmare come true, a bloody desperate attempt to revenge wrongs he himself had warned of in vain. . . .
> A price was also put on Louis Leakey's head by Mau Mau leaders. (Ironically, many of them were his "blood brothers," members of the *Mukanda* age group with whom he had been initiated.) His crimes were his anti-Mau Mau radio broadcasts to the Kikuyu [in Kikuyu] and his participation in counter-oathing campaigns. There was also his role as official interpreter at the trial of Jomo Kenyatta on conspiracy charges. (1974: 258–59)

Louis Leakey used all his resources to fight beside the colonialists against Mau Mau, continuing to authorize himself as the voice of the African.

Through his radio broadcasts, two books on Mau Mau, meetings with government officials, and work as a colonial counterinsurgency agent, Leakey promoted the view of Mau Mau as a syncretic religious movement whose oaths had to be confessed, and adherents purified from its effects. Though the categories blur into one another, historiography on Mau Mau shows three primary interpretations of Mau Mau: cultural renewal as a syncretic religious movement; an anticolonial bid for land and freedom; and a civil war between the haves and have-nots or the older and younger generations of Kikuyu men. Leakey's view of Mau Mau as syncretic religion was held by many white settlers who thought that Mau Mau as cultural subversion, rather than strictly cultural renewal, outweighed the political dimension of the movement. Leakey led the way in suggesting that individuals confess their Mau Mau beliefs and be purified of the effects of the vile oaths they had taken. Colonialists were horrified at the nature of the oaths Mau Mau were said to take; they were believed to involve abhorrent sexual acts, ingestion of human blood, mutilation of European pets, and desecration of the bodies of killed Africans and Europeans.

Hundreds of thousands of Kikuyu from throughout the country were rounded up and brought to detention camps and screening centers in central Kenya where they were asked to confess to having taken a Mau Mau oath, questioned about their adherence to Mau Mau beliefs, and encouraged to inform on others who took or gave them oaths or were identified with Mau Mau. Torture and abuse were a part of the interrogations in the detention camps. Karari Njama in collaboration with Donald Barnett (1966) describes the torture in camps in Nyeri District as follows:

> [There was also an] increase of inhuman torture in the local camps, e.g. men castrated, beatings aiming at fracturing a limb, putting *thabai* or *hatha—*

poisonous stinging plant leaves of the nettle family which causes great pain and swelling for half a day—in women's vaginas, pressing hard breasts or testicles with pliers. (209)

Confession, torture, and the grisly spectacle of dead bodies were a part of the colonial repertoire for fighting fire with fire.

During my stay in Murang'a District I came across a record book of interrogations at the Fort Hall Screening Center in the township that is now the capital of the district. In 1972 the screening center served as a juvenile hall, a home for runaway boys, brought upcountry from Nairobi and held at the center until they could be repatriated to their homes. As I was given a tour of the center by a child development officer, I found the record book, apparently discarded in one of the rooms. He was embarrassed by the obvious irony that the center to which thousands of Kikuyu had been repatriated during the emergency still served as a repatriation center. He welcomed me to take the book, a reminder of the past.

The record book, a triplicate book of one hundred leaves, held the record of one hundred men and women from the local area interrogated by three different Kikuyu screeners between August 27 and October 24, 1956. About thirty-five of those interrogated at Fort Hall Screening Center were women; fourteen of them were referred to as "girls." Of the women and girls, about half confessed to having taken two Mau Mau oaths, two said that they had been with Mau Mau in the forest, and three said that they had supplied food to forest fighters. Four out of five of the men confessed to having taken at least one Mau Mau oath, but only one admitted to having been in the forest with Mau Mau. In almost all the cases, whether the person confessed or not, the outcome was a recommendation for further screening, either closer to the person's home where he or she was "well known" or in the district reception center where people who "know too much" (and often were not cooperative) were sent. The writing in the record book is formulaic, with a preponderance of words like *seems to* and *apparent.* Some "confessed the truth before screening," while others did not give "proper confessions."

There is no evidence in this recovered record of the construction of Mau Mau beliefs specifically as a part of the organization of power and knowledge associated with the act of confessing, as Foucault (1980: 61–62) would suggest. But it is clear that in confessing to having taken an oath or confessing to *not* having taken an oath, the construction of Mau Mau as religion was officialized and reinforced. Detainees at the screening center were asked to repent of their beliefs, and some were remanded to other centers to "ensure whether he has got any m/m [Mau Mau] beliefs." The few who did not confess one way or the other, fewer than ten individuals, were highly suspect. For example, the following passage was entered by the head screener on August 29, 1956, after the standard listing of the place of interrogation, name, and home location of the detainee:

> We have interrogated this man and he confesses nothing to the Screening team therefore we are suspecting him to be deeply implicated with m/m [Mau Mau]. [T]herefore we have to screen him at Fort Hall R/camp [Reception Camp].

A person who confesses to having taken an oath is remanded to his local, divisional screening center. This statement was written by the same screener on August 30, 1956:

> We have interrogated the above named person and he has confessed to have taken one m/m oath, and as he has been in the prison for so many occasions we are suggesting him to know too much having to do with m/m activities in the camps where he has been kept, therefore we recommend him to go to his Divisional centre for further screening to ensure whether he can give any information having to do with m/m movement.

Kikuyu working for the colonial government were sometimes caught in the net, rounded up and asked to confess, as evidenced by this statement on a loyalist working as a Home Guard policeman:

> We have interrogated the above named person and he *confessed that he did not take m/m oath*, and as we have received information from reliable sources that he did not take m/m oath and again he was a member of Homeguard, we therefore recommend him to go to his Divisional Centre for release and if taken to D.C's [district commissioner's] office for release we have no objection about this. (emphasis added)

The reestablishment of colonial discipline through repentance of sin seems to be the main goal of the confessional movement in which Leakey had such a prominent place. Christian missionaries and loyalist Kikuyu spiritual healers were present in some camps to redeem and purify the repentant. Entries in the record book such as "he seems to have repented" and "he seems to be a very dangerous person because when questioned by the team he again asked questions in return" underscore the relation between repudiation of Mau Mau as "bad religion" and the acceptance of the colonial order.

Mau Mau: Fiction and Fact

The term *Mau Mau* entered Western popular culture even before Tom Wolfe canonized it in *Radical Chic and Mau-Mauing the Flak Catchers*. Playing on earlier definitions of *Mau Mau* as bandits ravaging the rich, Wolfe's use of the term in the 1970 book was a send-up of pseudoradical blacks' manipulation of white guilt. In the 1962 international edition of *Roget's Thesaurus, Mau Mau* is listed as a synonym for *thief*, but is not listed under the items associated with terrorism, revolution, rebellion, or sedition (Clough and Jackson 1975: 2). Directly derivative from this is the colloquial expression "mau-maued," which Clough and Jackson in their comprehensive *Mau Mau Syllabus: Part I* provocatively describe as follows:

> More current several years ago than now, this verb form was a synonym for mugging, robbery, and small assaults on individuals in the cities. Mau Mau in this usage is a label for a variety of petty crime, prevalent in urban areas, unmotivated by ideological or political concerns, a condition produced by certain anomic factors of dense social living. To be "mau mau-ed" was an act that was produced in the context of the almost Dickensian reality of the declining American inner cities. (1975: 2)

Outside of Kenya, where Mau Mau as evil and as liberation are still contested, the most tenacious association with the term is of unwarranted assault, nonpolitical aggression carried out by society's lumpenproletariat. For some, however, the term still conjures up images of sex and violence associated with the totally depraved.

In American popular culture, the novels of Robert Ruark, especially *Something of Value* and the film of the same title made from it in 1957, along with newsmagazines and newspapers, secured the definition of *Mau Mau* as depraved, unmotivated criminal behavior. But I want to point out the fear that savagery lurks in all blacks that the American treatment of Mau Mau lets loose. In this section, I consider the representation of Mau Mau produced by Ruark in *Something of Value* and the coverage of Mau Mau and Jomo Kenyatta during the emergency in major American newsmagazines and newspapers.

Although Louis Leakey repudiated the novel, I consider *Something of Value* to be a narrativization of Leakey's theories, one of the many stories that could be created of Leakey's representation of Mau Mau. Ruark credits Leakey's works as well as those of Elspeth Huxley and Jomo Kenyatta as sources from which he drew heavily. (He regards Kenyatta's ethnography, *Facing Mt. Kenya*, as a "blueprint for terror.") In the first sentence of the foreword, Ruark proclaims that, "this is not a true story," but he complicates that statement with the following characterization of the book:

> This might be possibly a true story of Kenya and of the events over the last fifty years which led to the present tragedy of the Mau Mau uprising, with all its sadistic murder and counter-murder. The book is completely true in reporting that its early skeletal structure rests on stony fact, which may be found in reference as fact. Some of these facts have been altered and condensed to comply

with novel form, as is always customary. But they remain facts. The characters in this book are entirely fictitious. (1955: foreword)

Whether the work is true or fictional, it is tied closely to Leakey because of its elaboration of Leakey's essential representation of Mau Mau as a heinous religious cult. In this view Mau Mau was inflamed by racial injustice, but at its core it was not a political movement.

Writing in the *Nation* in 1953, Leakey foreshadows Ruark's theme. After describing the Kikuyu fall from abundance to poverty and their political protests for more land, Leakey discusses the other causes of Mau Mau:

The influx of whites and the accompanying religion, educational, and economic changes have broken down the well-tried social structure of the tribe and replaced it with very little of solid value. The medical services introduced by the Europeans have improved the health of the people and the schools have opened the door to economic progress, but unfortunately the new education has not adequately prepared the younger generation for the more complex way of life. (1953: 346)

Almost these exact words are put in the mouth of the chief protagonist in Ruark's novel.

What Ruark brings to this enterprise are American cold war sensibilities, the context of American race relations, and the gift of blood. He writes:

There is much blood in the book. There is much killing. But the life of Africa was washed earlier by blood, and its ground was, and still is, fertilized by the blood of its people and its animals. This is not a pretty book, nor was it written for the pre-bedtime amusement of small children. And it certainly is not a political book. (1955: foreword)

Claiming that the book is not political was probably the most disingenuous statement in the mystifying hyperbole of the foreword. Supporting the bloody violence of the Africans in the novel are the socialist Asian and the Russian agent. Ruark's creation of these characters, especially the Russian agent who is in cahoots with a treacherous, pipe-smoking, European-educated Kikuyu man, points to the communist threat that was believed to be present in any uprising against colonial authority in the 1950s and 1960s. In the foreword, Ruark alerts the reader that the events in Kenya are "but a symptomatic ulcer of the evil and unrest which currently afflict the world." It is not the demise of Christianity to which Ruark refers, but he echoes the fear of the rise of communism that afflicted the American political imagination in the mid-1950s, when this book was written.

Indeed, the first representations of Mau Mau in American popular media depicted Kenyatta as a communist agitator. Fascinatingly, those images changed very quickly to that of the educated man reverted to savagery—the savage in the heart of every black man. I suggest that Ruark, the southern American writer turned big game hunter in East Africa, spoke to white Americans' fears of blackness, communism, and homosexuality, the three threats to American security that so occupied J. Edgar Hoover, director of the Federal Bureau of Investigation and a prime force behind the investigations of the House Un-American Activities Committee and Senator Joseph McCarthy's witch-hunts in the Senate Permanent Subcommittee on Investigations.

Something of Value was an immense popular, but not critical, success in the United States. Ruark's novel was chosen as a Book-of-the-Month Club selection, and, according to *Publishers Weekly*, was the sixth top-selling novel in the United States in 1955, with sales of 93,757 copies.

A "morass of clumsy exposition and preposterous dialogue" is how literary critic Bruce Bliven Jr. characterized *Something of Value* in *Saturday Review* (April 23, 1955: 14), but it got a better reception as the lead story on the front page of the *New York Times Book Review*, where John Barkham called it a "pile driver of a book" (April 24, 1955, section 7: 1). Africanist Basil Davidson, writing for the *Nation,* dismissed the novel as "cliché-ridden affirmations of white supremacy" based on "speculations, errors, or mere absurdities" (May 21, 1955). When this controversial novel was chosen as a Book-of-the-Month selection, an unheard of dissenting letter in which one of the judges warned that the work was "shocking" went out with the selection (*Time,* May 2, 1955: 108). The popular appeal of this shocking rendition of contemporary events was attested to in the book reviews' mentioning that the movie rights to the novel had been sold before the book even appeared in bookstores.

The movie made from the novel, released in 1957, starred Rock Hudson and Sidney Poitier and featured a prologue by Winston Churchill pleading for a return to calm in the country where he had once had a glorious safari.

The novel tells the story of two Kenyans, one white, of British descent, and one black, Kikuyu. The white man, Peter, played by Rock Hudson in the film, is the son of a hard-working farmer who has sacrificed his wife and two of his four children to the tribulations and diseases of Africa. Peter, the farmer's only surviving son, was reared by a Kikuyu servant, learned Kikuyu as his first language, and was best friends with Kimani, the Sidney Poitier character. When as a teenager the white boy is pushed to assert his dominance over his black friend, he balks, but in the ensuing incidents an admired adult slaps Kimani and Kimani tries to kill the white man. Believing himself to be a marked man, Kimani runs away and joins up with a hardened gang of criminals who introduce him to Mau Mau. Kimani takes and administers Mau Mau oaths devised to make social pariahs of its adherents.

A highly educated Kikuyu who has lived abroad is the mastermind of Mau

Mau, and a Russian instructs Kimani to get arrested so that he might recruit Mau Mau in prison. What oath was to be used to bind men to one another in prison? Sodomy. Kimani is on the way to rack and ruin. It turns out that Kimani had not killed the white man—Peter's sister's husband—earlier, but during a Mau Mau raid at Peter's family's farm Kimani does indeed kill him as well as his young children.

While Kimani is away learning the evils of Mau Mau, Peter becomes a big game hunter, taking rich tourists on safari. Among his clients are a charming American couple to whom Peter explains how and why Africans are not like black Americans: Africans are only a couple of generations removed from savagery and can revert at any moment. Peter falls in love with and marries the girl next door, but the marriage sours as the emergency is declared and Peter turns his attention to hunting Mau Mau. The novelist suggests that white men became savages in their attempt to conquer the savage African, but in the end Peter kills Kimani and takes Kimani's young son to the farm to be reared by Peter's sister, whose husband and children had been killed by Kimani.

Secondary stories show the friendship between Peter's and Kimani's fathers. Peter's father respects and uses African magic to his own benefit, while Kimani's father is imprisoned for following an African tradition that requires killing a child born breech. Another contrast is between Peter's sister, a woman of pioneering spirit, who is disfigured in but survives a Mau Mau raid, and Peter's wife. The wife, educated in London, "should be made of sterner stuff," cannot abide the deprivations of the emergency, escapes to Nairobi, and eventually abandons Kenya to live in England.

A most unlikely proverb from a distant people in southern Africa begins this novel. Ruark's epigram is unlikely in that it speaks of the trauma of transition, the sloughing off of custom in ways seldom conceived of by "traditional" societies:

> If a man does away with his traditional way of living and throws away his good customs, he had better first make certain that he has something of value to replace them.
>
> —*Basuto proverb*

Ruark returns to this theme throughout the novel, but it is most elaborated in the comparison between Kikuyu and Maasai and the implicit comparison between American blacks and Africans. During their first conversation with Peter, an American couple criticizes the treatment of Africans in Kenya as being similar to the way that black Americans were once treated in the southern United States: "Treat 'em as not too bright children. . . . Don't associate with 'em. . . . Have them in your homes and you depend on them entirely for the success of your work, but you treat them as if they were some special sort of cattle" (198). Peter, explaining that all Americans ask the same thing, responds that just fifty years ago Africans were cannibals and murderers, living short, brutish, and nasty lives in nature. Europeans gave them a new religion and "threw 'em a pair of pants" (198). The Maasai, nomads who refused the pants, still wear their goatskins and do fine:

> But we take the Kikuyu, say, or the Wakamba, and teach them how to increase their herds and how to increase themselves, but we don't find any way to absorb them. We change their old crop rotation to money crops and ruin the land. They live bang on the fringe of white civilization, swelling and crowding their properties—and mark you, they've got more land than they ever used before—but it isn't enough. *They learn all our bad habits. We destroy every bit of their old logical living because it conflicts with our law, and replace it with bleeding nothing.* So now you have, excuse me, please, whores when once there was no such thing as prostitution, and robbers and spivs and sly loafers, because they've become detribalized without becoming decently citified. (201, emphasis added)

Ruark juxtaposes the noble savage of the Maasai—"carrying on with the old ways"—with the detribalized Kikuyu whose relationship with the white man is both mimetic and "other." The technology of colonialism constructed Kikuyu as dependent subjects, a position from which they imitated Europeans in dress and drink, in progress and prostitution. The failure of colonialism, from this point of view, is that it introduces a veneer of civilization to those who are unalterably other: "[They] don't think like us, and they don't react like us" (200) and "in the African make-up there is really no such thing as love, kindness, or gratitude" (202). Africans in the cities are the grotesque imitation of whites, their lives carnivalesque.

Ruark configures three major failings of colonialism in Kenya prominently in this novel: colonialists tried to civilize Africans too fast; European values could not replace destroyed African ones because Africans are intellectually and morally other; and partially civilized Africans will revert back to savagery under stress.

Even though black Americans are supposedly exempted from savagery because of the length of our sojourn in white America, Ruark's work signifies white Americans' fear of the repressed, of sexuality and violence represented by black Americans. The 1950s in the United States, often portrayed as a peaceful return to domesticity, was for blacks a period of change and political consolidation spearheaded by the successes of blacks in World War II, culminating in the integration of the American armed forces in 1948 and the start of the civil rights movement by 1959. I hazard that the popularity of Ruark's images of blacks reverting to savagery captured the imaginations of large segments of the book-buying public because of their concerns with an increasingly visible black population, and not just because of their sympathies with the white minority in Kenya. The association of Africans in Kenya and blacks in the United States was further underscored when Thurgood Marshall, not long after his school desegregation triumph, served as an adviser to the African delegation during the meetings to hammer out a constitution for independent Kenya.

In pulling in images of the communist agitator, Ruark went right to the heart of the 1950s mania. Percy Wood, reviewing *Something of Value* as the lead story for the *Chicago Sunday Tribune Magazine of Books*, attended to the alarm Ruark sounded:

> Ruark brings a Russian communist conspirator into one of his scenes, as a sup-
> porter and co-director of the Mau Maus, and this makes sense, whether or not
> it can be documented. The situation in Kenya today is made for the Reds; it's
> just the sort of confusion on which they have battened in other primitive coun-
> tries. They made great headway in Indo-China and Malaya because of the stub-
> bornness of the French and the British colonizers; they could do the same in
> Africa, if they are not already doing so.
>
> Sixteen years ago, as Ruark notes, Jomo Kenyatta, the now imprisoned top
> leader of the Mau Mau, wrote a book drawing an exact blueprint of what was
> to happen. Lenin did the same thing; so did Hitler. (April 24, 1955, part 4: 1)

As cold warriors of the Western bloc and the Soviet bloc squared off, each side tried to ensure the incorporation of Third World and newly independent countries into its sphere, or at least to prevent the other from gaining allies. Many socialists and communists in Kenya, like Indian trade union organizer Makhan Singh, did support the Mau Mau movement, though the strength of their influence has not been fully detailed. White settlers in Kenya consistently complained that leftists in government in England and a left-leaning press misrepresented their case and pandered to Mau Mau.

Mau Mau historiography in Russia and Eastern European countries, based primarily on their readings of English sources, show two competing representations of Mau Mau as: (1) a British invention of a mythical organization designed to delegitimate and destroy the Kenya African Union, portrayed as an organization of peasants, workers, and intellectuals, and (2) a true nationalist movement employing terrorism against colonialist oppression. Clough and Jackson (1975 vol. 2: 63–69) provide an annotated bibliography of about twenty-five sources published in Russian and a handful of others in Czech, Polish, and Hungarian. Communist historians and ethnographers disagreed over whether lack of arms and military organization caused the failure of the movement or whether the religious and spiritual component isolated the Kikuyu and stifled the movement—or some combination of both. The communist world was not disinterested in Mau Mau and probably had some effect in the organization of trade unions and strikes, but the implied centrality of communists in the institution of Mau Mau oaths of sodomy is purely a product of cold war, homophobic America.

America's Achilles' heel was its oppressed minorities—could they be enlisted to destabilize the West? In the United States, poor and disenfranchised blacks rivaled organized labor as the presumed opening to the communist menace. Ruark, like many Americans, wondered if blacks might not have been happy with the status quo if it were not for outside agitators. As Ruark paints the picture, racial inequality as well as inherent black weakness of character allow for possible manipulation by communists.

Ruark's explicit blending of blackness, communism, and homosexuality brought it all home: the United States' fears about its national security in the 1950s were exacerbated by the newness of its position as leader of the free world, the internal contradictions of its own racism, and the fragility of its reinvented domesticity. Homosexuality was a threat to domestic and national security; it represented weakness of character to an American public obsessed with building families and fighting the communist threat. D'Emilio and Freedman in *Intimate Matters: A History of Sexuality in America* (1988) summarize this position:

> At one level, Cold War politics seem sufficient to explain the irrational preoccupation with an alleged homosexual menace. A nation at the height of its power searched for answers about why the world was exploding with danger. Just as hidden traitors were undermining the nation's physical security, so too did sexual deviates deplete its moral resources. But the growth of a gay subculture also called into question the strength of another prop of Cold War society, the family. Having been buffeted by the Depression-era and wartime shocks to family life, Americans after World War II were returning to domesticity with renewed fervor as the foundation for social stability. In the baby-boom years of the 1950s, with their paeans to domestic togetherness, visible gay men and lesbians suggested the potential fragility of heterosexual familial norms. (294)

Gay men working for the federal government (few women held sensitive positions) were labeled security risks because potential blackmailers could prey upon them and because of their presumed emotional instability and weakened moral fiber from sexual indulgence (D'Emilio and Freedman 1988: 292). In the construction of postwar family and masculinity, homosexuality was the ultimate taint:

> The homosexual, rather than the man who patronized prostitutes in the red-light district, became the marker that divided good men from bad. As Barbara Ehrenreich phrased it in her study of postwar masculinity, "fear of homosexuality kept heterosexual men in line as husbands and breadwinners. . . . The ultimate reason why a man would not just "walk out the door" was the taint of ho-

mosexuality which was likely to follow him. (Ehrenreich 1983 quoted in D'Emilio and Freedman 1988: 295)

For Ruark, writing in the 1950s, homosexuality was a trope that readily conveyed degeneracy and the loss of order. As the novel continues, the stigma of homosexuality is displaced by what Ruark represents as even more loathsome and evil: oaths.

Ruark claims that his novel, based on fact, is not a true story. During my stay in Murang'a District in central Kenya, only ten years after independence, I argued late into the night with young men in their early to mid-twenties about the veracity of Ruark's vision. My interest in the novel to a great extent stems from their serious entertainment of what to me was blatant sensationalism. Notes I wrote in my journal one morning following such a discussion give a whiff of the argument:

> We also had arguments over Mau Mau oaths. M's first position was that oaths were given as a part of a trial to test the truth of adversaries' statements and not as a method of ensuring unity. He agreed with others that it could be used in the latter sense, but said that we have no record of what actually happened, since we cannot trust anything the white man says. K, whose position is somewhat similar to M's, said that some of the things are perhaps substantiated. At this point we were discussing a book called *The Shadow of Mau Mau* by Ruark, which K says is mostly true. W agrees with him except for its treatment [characterization] of the Africans, and M says it is all lies. (field journal, December 11, 1971)

Two different books were merged in this discussion: *In the Shadow of the Mau Mau* by Ione Leigh, published in London in 1954, and Ruark's *Something of Value*, published in New York in 1955. Leigh's work figures Mau Mau similarly to the Ruark representation, as an evil reversion to savagery by lazy, lustful, half-civilized natives with no real grievances against the colonial government but spurred on by Russians and other communist agitators. She holds that the Mau Mau oaths included excessive consumption of alcohol, sexual orgies, ingesting menstrual blood, murder and cannibalism, and nailing live cats and dogs as well as human body parts to Mau Mau altars (1954: 44–49). Ruark's oaths included some of the same practices as Leigh's, with the most fearful *batuni* or warriors' oath demanding that the male initiates eat the brains of a man and a boy and that female initiates place the severed, slightly roasted penis of a decapitated man in their vaginas (1955: 324–28). I was not horrified that young Kikuyu men argued about whether these oaths actually took place, but the power of colonial literature to shape their discourse did, to me, appear awesome.

The evil of Mau Mau lives on long after the death of the movement. Much has been written about Mau Mau oaths over the past forty years. While we can never know the content of all of the oaths of this decentralized movement, I want to explore one way of thinking about them that is not developed in the literature, that is, as a particularly gruesome example of interculturality: the political use of oaths was inspired by the colonialists, who with confessions induced by torture not only got what they wanted to hear but also encouraged some of the excesses of Mau Mau.

Descriptions of oaths were often confessed after torture, by people who learned what to confess (Edgerton 1989: 135). The process of confession abetted the establishment of practices that defined what is normal or abnormal, and what is innocuous or powerful. Catholic confession of sexual behavior, Foucault (1980: 62–64) suggests, facilitates the delineation of center and periphery, creates the normative and the perverse. African authors, both Mau Mau participants and others, deny the existence of the advanced oaths as described by Leigh and Ruark (see Buijtenhuijs 1982: 97). But some Kikuyu have written that they were disgusted by oaths they participated in or witnessed, such as the evisceration of an African guard whose heart and liver were used in an oath (Mathu 1974 cited in Edgerton 1989: 135). There is little evidence, however, of bodies mutilated in the manner necessary for the number and distribution of rituals supposed by colonialists (Edgerton 1989: 94–95; Buijtenhuijs 1982: 94–95, 105).

While none of the men I interviewed who claimed to have been forest fighters admitted to oaths involving more than goat's blood and soil from Kikuyuland, the literature on Mau Mau strongly suggests that later oaths were calculated to create *thahu* or pollution in the initiates, making outlaws of the adherents and intensifying their commitment to the cause. Edgerton summarizes as follows: "Although most oathing ceremonies never even approximated the grisly bacchanalia that the Europeans found so plausible, some units did conduct ceremonies involving ritual cannibalism and sexual behavior that many Mau Mau themselves found appalling" (1989: 135).

Excessive Mau Mau oaths were not merely the invention of Europeans. A peculiar cultural intersection or instance of interculturality occurred in the representation and probably in the actuality of Mau Mau oaths. In many ways, Mau Mau grotesquely upended European values—especially the cult of domesticity, with its protection of women, monogamous family, sexual fidelity, inviolate home and garden, and tenderness toward children and animals. The outrage over the slaughter of white family pets for Mau Mau altars that Leigh represents in *In the Shadow of the Mau Mau* is evidence of the fear some colonialists had that Mau Mau was deliberately copied from European witchcraft models (cf. Carothers 1954)—terror at the intersection of mimesis and alterity. In reality, and here I trust the insightful analysis of Buijtenhuijs (1982), Mau

Mau used little European imagery or paraphernalia. The power of the Mau Mau oaths was based on its use of images and materials psychologically and socially potent within Kikuyu culture.

The use of oaths as a test of political commitment may have been set in motion by colonialists; torture and confession shaped expectations of content of the oaths, but, as the war wore on, oaths that had taken their power from the particular transgression of Kikuyu boundaries of gender, seniority, place, and time began to tap other dimensions of Kikuyu belief. Louis Leakey disapprovingly pointed out that the Mau Mau oaths were performed at night instead of day, were done in secret instead of consolidating the community in public, were given by juniors to seniors, and were taken by women and children. These inversions and transgressions of orderly society did not invalidate the oaths, but imbued them with potency to transform the oath taker and the society.

The widespread references to blood, especially menstrual blood, and to the manipulation of corpses point to two dangerous areas of taboo further appropriated by Mau Mau. Contrary to Ruark's assertion that precolonial Africa was drenched in blood, Kikuyu found blood dangerous; no woman could handle materials stained with the menstrual blood of another woman without incurring some form of pollution. Late-nineteenth-century and early-twentieth-century Kikuyu also found the manipulation of dead bodies anathema. Even at the Christian funerals I attended in 1971–72, mourners would mention that in the old days the bodies of ordinary people would be thrown in a special place where hyenas, the "walking graveyard," would eat them. When an old person was about to die, a village could move away and leave him or her to die alone or build a special hut outside the village to which the ailing person could go to die. If a few isolated Mau Mau oaths did involve ritual cannibalism and menstrual blood, the power of transgression was at work. Buijtenhuijs, after showing how Europeans projected their fears and fantasies on the Kikuyu in their imagination of Mau Mau oaths, turns to assess the ways in which the advanced, *batuni* oaths fit Kikuyu psychology:

> The taboos infringed upon during Mau Mau ceremonies correspond fairly well to Kikuyu notions of *thahu* [ritual pollution]. This is the case, for example, with menstrual blood, allegedly an indispensable ingredient of oathing ceremonies, and a highly impure matter in traditional Kikuyu culture. The same holds for manipulating a corpse, which was loathed by the Kikuyu to the extent that they often preferred to abandon a dying relative in the bush rather than have him die in their hut, exposing them to *thahu*. For the average European, touching a corpse may be frightful, but it certainly is not a taboo engendering guilt when infringed upon. This is even more the case with some ways of sexual intercourse that are less common in European practice than the "normal" missionary position, but that do not engender guilt as in traditional Kikuyu culture

169

where they are *thahu*. Again, deviant methods of sexual intercourse are mentioned by some sources as elements of the "advanced" oathing ceremonies. (1982: 104)

European representations of Mau Mau oaths were exaggerated, but they contained enough elements of Kikuyu beliefs that young Kikuyu men a decade after Kenyan independence earnestly puzzled over their accuracy. Mau Mau was not a reversion to savagery, but a revolutionary appropriation of the past in the service of the future. It got out of hand.

Mau Mau News

Coverage of Mau Mau in popular American newspapers and magazines featured the tragic manipulation of African tribesmen by communist agitators, the romantic return of the primitive—this time with the ignoble savage—and the farcical potential of African nationalism. I studied Mau Mau news in the *New York Times*, and *Time* and *Newsweek* magazines for the period from 1952 to 1960. The two newsmagazines consistently used the themes of communism and primitivism, and occasionally nationalism, in their reports on Mau Mau. The *New York Times* was the only one of the three to give space to an African to present his views during Mau Mau, and, as should be the case with the premier American newspaper, the overall presentation of Mau Mau news was more nuanced and considerably less sensational. Jomo Kenyatta, who appeared in pages of the newsmagazines as "Burning Spear," "bearded," "London- and Moscow-educated," "married to an English woman," united the three themes of communism, primitivism, and nationalism: all the best hopes of Kenya in this British-educated African fell prey to communism. Moreover, despite the civilizing influence of a white woman, his animal instincts took over as he led his people in bloody, savage oaths to restore or establish African nationalism. In the final section of this chapter, I reflect on print news media reporting on Mau Mau and Jomo Kenyatta and consider the ways in which the internal politics of race relations and the ascendancy of the United States as a political and economic power after World War II influenced Mau Mau news.

By definition, news is information that is fresh or current and is thus short-lived, ephemeral. The production of the news is constrained by conditions different from the production of ethnography and history—news cannot afford to be boring. The journalism industry demands a readable story, eye-catching headlines, and noteworthy events or interpretations. Some journalists try to present balanced stories, searching out the counterpositions to the main story, but Mau Mau news saw little of this, especially in the newsmagazines. American reporting on Mau Mau was strongly influenced by the same ideological positions that shaped Ruark's *Something of Value*. These were the national se-

curity issues related to the communist threat, demands of blacks for school desegregation and civil rights, and the fear of extramarital sexuality as destructive
of the moral fiber and domestic tranquility.

Even though news, unlike history or ethnography, is current and fleeting—
not reflective and ponderous—it also is a presentation of the past with an eye
to the future. Between 1952 and 1960, as the cold war heated up, Americans
worried about the future: would the world be destroyed by nuclear war? Mau
Mau news provided a glimpse of the past, a primitive, bloodthirsty past from
which they had been delivered by Yankee ingenuity, the very ingenuity that
had led them to win World War II and to emerge as the dominant world
power. Would this know-how lead to a return to primitivism through a nuclear holocaust?

Think for a moment on another holocaust, the mass extermination of Jews
by Hitler's Germany. I speculate that this past was a specter of European
atavism that shaped the discourse of Mau Mau. True, the rhetoric of Mau
Mau, with its "barbaric savagery," "inhuman monsters," and "primitive instincts," is not unheard of in Orientalist/Africanist literature, but the news
media's indecent delight in using these terms brings to mind their use just a
decade before to describe the excesses of the German Third Reich. This specu-
lation leads me to contemplate the union of opposites in the representations of
Nazi Germany and Mau Mau in Kenya: in Nazi Germany, modern technologies (gas chambers and biological experimentation) were used to meet the hor-
rific ends of European tribalism (extermination of an "alien" population),
while in Kenya, tribal means (rituals and oaths) were employed to reach modern ends (majority rule in independent Kenya). White prestige was redeemed
with the rise of Mau Mau as a black monster.

Still, the news media was not above criticism of whites in Kenya. Colonel
Blimp (a David Low cartoon character of an elderly, pompous British reactionary) metonymically stood for the British military and the colonialists in
Kenya in *Time* magazine's coverage of Mau Mau (December 8, 1952: 32-35;
March 30, 1953: 31). But pompous and ineffectual or not, the British were
white, and American arrogance did not blind the news reporters to the racial
prestige at stake. Whites in Africa were besieged by marauding savages, while
blacks at home wanted to sit next to white children—girls—in classrooms. In
1954 the United States Supreme Court decided in favor of desegregation in the
public schools, and many state and local governments in the southern states
decided not to comply. Open confrontation between blacks and whites followed. The interpretation of Mau Mau as reversion to savagery, of Kenyatta as
an educated African leading his people back to barbarism, of cannibalism and
debauchery by African tribesmen, accommodated the implicit knowledge of

many Americans that all black people are savages, only tenuously connected to civilization.

The images of Mau Mau as blacks for whom civilization did not "take" peppered the American populace. Like a vaccination gone bad, civilization did not bring progress for Kikuyu tribesmen in Kenya, but brought instead social and psychological pathology by way of the "trauma of transition." Educated Africans, with Jomo Kenyatta as the prime example, could revert to primitivism. American media sometimes recognized possible political or economic issues at stake in Mau Mau, but more often referred to "primitive instincts" and occasionally employed the trope of "racial hatred." Take, for example, the opening paragraph of one of the earliest reports on Mau Mau in an American newsmagazine:

> On lonely upland estates, in back-country settlements, even in crowded cities, the white man in Africa could imagine he was hearing something like the throb of drums in the jungle—an insistent, ominous warning of trouble and more trouble from the black man. In the heart of the Dark Continent, from South Africa to Kenya Colony, the Negroes were turning on their European masters. The Communists doubtless would try to exploit the conflict. But it had a simpler and far more dangerous basis in an outburst of racial hatred. (*Newsweek*, November 3, 1952: 44)

In this passage and, I venture, for much of the American population, racial hatred is axiomatic. Racial hatred need not be explained by politics, history, economics, or social relations; it is part of a state of nature. The term *Negroes* used in this passage, rather than African "natives" or the more frequently used "tribesmen," makes a clear association with American blacks, who at that time preferred the term *Negro*. The message for whites in the United States: do not ask for whom the drum beats, it beats for thee.

Newsweek had the least coverage of Mau Mau of the three American news sources I studied. In the second week of coverage of Mau Mau, *Newsweek* uncritically reported the colonial secretary's speech to Parliament after a visit to Kenya:

> A "horrible poison . . . of nostalgia for barbarism" runs deep in the Kikuyu tribe, British Colonial Secretary Oliver Lyttelton told Parliament on his return from an emergency visit to Kenya. That, rather than genuine economic problems, he concluded, was the cause of the terrorist movement that has infested the 1,000,000 tribesmen (4,600,000 natives belonging to other tribes in Kenya have not been affected so far). (November 24, 1952: 33)

Throughout the period from 1952 to 1960 *Newsweek* maintained the rhetoric of pathology as well as a discourse of fear of reversion to primitivism and of communist agitation. If Mau Mau is nationalism, *Newsweek* reporters concluded, then its nationalist impulses are antiprogressivist, rolling back to a time when "change is impossible" and "thinking unnecessary." Even this desire for a return of the past was suspect as communist agitation:

> The vital question is what will take its [colonialism's] place—a carefully tended reservoir of cooperative understanding or a deadly well of hatred, Communist-inspired wherever possible, poisoning black-white relations for generations. Red agents already are at work in detribalized areas telling witch doctors that their ancient power will return after the white man leaves. (*Newsweek*, October 31, 1955: 46)

Positive race relations are possible in Africa, this later article suggests: racial hatred is not natural, nor is it a product of colonialist oppression; it is stirred up by communists—another popular trope in cold war America. The American assistant secretary of state for Africa, according to the same news item, recognized African mineral resources as vital to the United States, and he expressed hope for gradual, "orderly development of self-determination" for colonial Africa. In the same article, *Newsweek* reports that "responsible Africans" say that the white man is not through in Africa: "They need white brains and white capital if Africa is to be saved from Communism and from itself" (46).

Some Mau Mau oaths were described in *Newsweek* in the early years—"Thus he feared to violate the Mau Mau oath, which was administered with rites involving banana blossoms filled with blood, goats' eyeballs stuck on thorns, and the magic number 7" (November 3, 1952: 44)—but later they were "too obscene for public distribution" (March 15, 1954: 40). The reporting on oaths served to undermine the political content of the nationalist anticolonial movement and bolster the interpretation of Mau Mau as primitive mind control, horrible rituals that sap the individuality and humanity of participants, turning them into unthinking killers. (At this time Americans were also coming to grips with communist brainwashing and using similar kinds of arguments in anticommunist propaganda.)

In the final days of the colonial period, the Corfield Report (1960), commissioned by the British government, was published. *Newsweek*'s parting shots at the end of this era were taken from this report, which emphasized Mau Mau as transgression, breaking taboos that put its adherents beyond psychological and cultural redemption.

In *Newsweek* Jomo Kenyatta was labeled a founder of the "savage Mau Mau" who led his people in "blood-drinking oaths to exterminate the whites" (October 31, 1955: 44). *Newsweek* did not keep the question of Kenyatta's communist associations in the forefront in the way that *Time* did, but there was intermittent mention of Moscow's and *Pravda*'s interest in African unrest and of Kenyatta's having studied in Moscow during the 1930s. Kenyatta's image as a "human monster," a description quoted from a colonial official and often repeated, was not repudiated in *Newsweek* even in 1960 as Kenyan independence approached. On the eve of black rule in Kenya, *Newsweek* cast Kenyatta as a "white-bearded Othello" and warned that his influence was "a great dark shadow [that] still looms over the land" (March 7, 1960: 44). As Kenyatta, still in detention for conspiracy charges related to Mau Mau, received visitors with ministerial portfolios for the new government, *Newsweek* revived the colonialist epithet: "[White settlers] were particularly outraged by the British Government's talk of releasing Kenyatta, a man whom most of them regard as a *'human monster'*" (August 22, 1960: 44, emphasis added).

The *New York Times* downplayed the communist threat (early on they implied USSR support and agitation and later reported that pro-Soviet Egypt supported Mau Mau) and played up the civil war among Kikuyus. Mau Mau were often reported attacking Kikuyu loyalists, and loyalists were reported as giving aid to the government efforts. The *Times* also brought out different interpretations and political positions taken by whites in Kenya, the uneasy relations between the colonial government and colonial office in London, and the battles between labor and conservatives in England. The paper carried the debate in Kenya over whether a South African-style apartheid system was best or whether a multiracial goal should be sought (June 1, 1954, 8: 5). Articles and statements by Louis Leakey (May 3, 1953, 6: 14) and Elspeth Huxley (June 6, 1954, 6: 12) were published, and the *Times* offered one of the only commentaries by a Kenyan African that appeared in the press: J. Gecau held that Mau Mau was a revolt against white minority rule (December 28, 1955, 7: 4). Intermittent tallies of body counts on both sides and the number arrested and detained were reported, as were charges of brutality by whites as well as Mau Mau.

This daily paper gave more in-depth coverage than did other sources of the arrest, trial, and conviction of Jomo Kenyatta; the hunt for and trial of the leader of the forest fighters, Dedan Kimathi; the rise of labor leader Tom Mboya; and Kenyan constitutional reform. There was little coverage of the oaths, though early on the paper reported that Christians who took the oath would be excommunicated, that the colonial government hired witch doctors, and that the advanced oath ostracized its initiates from tribal life.

Time was the most rabid in stirring up anticommunist sentiments. One of the magazine's first articles on Mau Mau appeared under the headline "Black and Red Magic" and raised fears that communist inroads like those made in Malaysia could happen again (September 1, 1952: 25). Repeated references were made to Malaya and to Jomo Kenyatta's being "Moscow trained" and once having been the "student-guest of the Kremlin." Rhetoric of this sort kept up through 1953; it went hand in hand with the portrayal of Mau Mau as a terrorist secret society out to "destroy all authority." Land hunger was ventured as one of the causes of Mau Mau, but again and again the brief stories on Kenya insinuated race war and the "something of value" theme—the destruction of tribal culture and African maladaptation to Western civilization leading to social and psychological pathology. This is the description of Mau Mau in one of the almost weekly articles that appeared just after the state of emergency was declared:

> Part land hunger, part savage revolution against domineering white men and the bewildering 20th century, the Mau Mau's blind fury, could, if left unchecked, turn the Crown Colony of Kenya into another Malaya. (*Time*, November 1952: 36)

Even though Mau Mau was represented as a war of black savagery against white civilization, whites were in for some criticism from *Time*. Taking the white settlers' perspective, and implying the superiority of American bureaucracy, *Time* called on the image of Colonel Blimp to criticize the colonial power structure:

> [Since] Nairobi is by & large run by the sons of old Colonel Blimp, the ex-Indian army colonels, the not-so-young younger sons of aristocratic families with hyphenated names, it is not surprising that the embattled farmers explode with numerous complaints about Nairobi's incompetence and muddle-mindedness. (March 30, 1953: 31)

Time's International News section on April 6, 1953, placed an article on Mau Mau next to one on the issue of assessing the guilt for Nazi Germany: to what extent were the German people to be blamed for Hitler's government's "bad and amoral management" (40)? Mau Mau news for the day included the escalation of the war in Kenya and the mass arrest of Kikuyus: "Dragged from their mud huts, 20,000 Kukes [a derogatory term used by whites in Kenya] were herded into compounds; 2,500 suspected Mau Mau terrorists were culled from among them and clapped into jail. Next day there were more arrests: another 3,500 'suspects' were seized near Thika" (40). Colonial policies of mass arrests and reprisals against the entire population of Kikuyu, Meru, and Embu left little doubt about the guilt of Kenyan people, whose leaders were not just "bad and amoral," but also "barbaric."

Of the three American news sources I studied, *Time* devoted the most attention to the oaths, depicting them as cannibalistic and bestial, with Mau Mau drinking blood and eating sheep eyes in 1953, taking the eyeballs from living people in 1954, and drinking menstrual blood and semen cocktails in 1960. Vivid, graphic descriptions of Mau Mau killings with large machetes or *pangas* were the core of many articles on Kenya. The maiming and killing of domestic animals, especially European pets, said to stand for Kikuyu loyal to the colonial regime, was represented in a November 3, 1952, *Time* article with reference to "the Mau Mau habit of nailing headless cats to their victims' doors" (36) and an article the following week that showed a picture of a dead cat hanging from an arch of saplings. The caption under the photograph reads:

SYMBOL OF DOOM: A dead cat, left hanging from a bent sapling in a forest clearing, bears a threat written in blood that any person who works for whites "will be destroyed by the power of this oath." Some 5,000 suspected Mau Mau members are in police compounds. (November 10, 1952: 31)

Time had fun with Mau Mau. Even as it produced dozens of column inches on bloody violence, *Time* played Mau Mau for laughs with headlines like "The Meow-Meows" (November 3, 1952: 36), "Land of Murder and Muddle" (March 30, 1953: 30), "Burning Spears" (a persistent translation of Jomo Kenyatta's name, April 20, 1953: 42), "Challenge, Then Shoot" (May 13, 1953: 38), "Mow Them Down" (May 25, 1953: 36), "No. 2" (January 25, 1954: 26), "General China and His Friends" (March 15, 1954: 28), "Mau Mau in the Cathedral" (March 21, 1955: 32), and "Bwana Tom Goes to Court" (June 23, 1958: 23). The pronunciation of the term *Mau Mau* was said to rhyme with "yo-yo" on September 1, 1952 (25), with "mo mo" on October 20, 1952 (40), and with "bow-wow" on October 27, 1952 (40). *Time*'s flippant style saturated its reporting with bemusement: If the story was about whites besieged by blacks, the underlying tone smirked that only the "blimpish" British could let themselves in for this. In reports on the oaths concocted by Mau Mau, the reader was led to wonder at the magical thinking of those benighted natives.

An article published after the height of hostilities is strictly for laughs; here is the final paragraph of the news item entitled "The Munitions Makers":

The Mau Mau rebellion was now at an end, but a British district officer, passing through Nandi [who had fought with the British against the Kikuyu] territory recently, noted that the tribesmen were still making arrows. The witch doctor was arrested. As he was hauled to jail, mooning all the while over a withered setiot blossom (the symbol of virility among the Nandi), the remaining Nandi meekly and with some relief surrendered their stock of nearly 15,000 newly made bows and arrows. "We had to do as the witch doctor said," one explained apologetically, "otherwise he would have bewitched our children." (May 27, 1957: 39)

Time profiled Jomo ("Burning Spear") Kenyatta several times between 1952 and 1960. In almost every mention of Kenyatta, his name is first printed just as I used it in the previous sentence; he is then referred to as Kenyatta or Burning Spear. Not until the fifth article on Kenyatta is the appellation Burning Spear explained: "His first name had been of his own choosing, the Kikuyu word for an unsheathed dagger or a poised, burning spear: Jomo" (April 20, 1953: 42). In fact, all of his name was of his own choosing; Kenyatta remade himself at different points in his career. His earliest name was probably Kamau wa Mugai, Kamau of [son of] Mugai, his father. When he went to missionary school, after his father's death, he was Kamau wa Ngeni, Kamau son of Ngeni, his father's brother. He was baptized Johnstone, having decided to take the names John and Peter; being told he could have only one baptismal name, he combined John and Peter, the rock, or stone. Sometime around 1918, he changed from Johnstone Kamau to Johnstone Kenyatta, taking his last name from a *kinyatta*, a Maasai beaded ornament that he wore as a belt. As I noted in chapter 5, it was not until he wrote *Facing Mt. Kenya* that Kenyatta adopted the name Jomo, probably as a part of his re-Africanization, as he donned borrowed furs and crafted a spear from a wooden plank he found in London (Edgerton 1989: 44 n. 44; Murray-Brown 1972: 194) to present an authentic image of the African native to the public (see fig. 4). *Time* kept the violent image before the public.

Standard fare for *Time*'s coverage of Kenyatta, unvarying over the years, was Kenyatta's connection to communists, his education as an anthropologist, his support of clitoridectomy, and his participation in Mau Mau oaths. *Time* reported on, but did not make much of, his marriage to an English schoolteacher. The following is the first description of Kenyatta in the magazine, taken from an article appearing before the declaration of the state of emergency:

> The Mau Mau's leader, Kenya officials are sure, is black-bearded Jomo ("Burning Spear") Kenyatta, 50, a thick-set Kikuyu dandy, who runs the outwardly respectable Kenya African Union (K.A.U.), whose stated purpose is Negro advancement. A London-trained anthropologist who wrote (1938) a first-rate study of his people, *Facing Mt. Kenya*, Kenyatta is a devotee of Red magic. He spent the '30s in Moscow as a student-guest of the Kremlin, returned to Kenya after World War II, now heads a chain of 135 bush schools which spread anti-British propaganda and uphold old barbaric rites (e.g., female circumcision). (September 1, 1952: 25)

This description is reiterated in other profiles, and to it were added terms of condemnation having to do with his participation in oaths. Kenyatta was said to have "used the skills civilization taught him to give savagery a new kind of power" (April 20, 1953: 42). While he was in prison, most references to him were to his being the mastermind of Mau Mau, to his "dreaded name" (March 6, 1959: 30), and to his being "father of the terror" (May 27, 1959: 26). Tom Mboya rose to prominence as the leader of Kenyan Africans during this time, and some news articles pitted him against Kenyatta. In a March 7, 1960, cover story on Mboya, Mboya acknowledged that Kenyatta was the true leader of

Kenyan Africans, but *Time* portrayed Kenyatta as an "alcoholic wreck" (March 7, 1960: 30). As the end of the colonial period approached, the Corfield Report on the causes of Mau Mau, commissioned by the British government—calculated to bring fear back to whites who might have buried the evil of Mau Mau—was published. Just when Kenya should have been turning toward reconciliation, the newspapers and newsmagazines were filled with stories of Mau Mau oaths and atrocities, and Kenyatta was blamed for the reign of terror:

> Personally responsible for the "general pattern" of this horror, charges the Corfield report, was Jomo ("Burning Spear") Kenyatta, sixtyish, longtime Kikuyu nationalist leader still under house arrest in a remote Kenya mountain village. A mission-educated nationalist fanatic who spent 17 years in England and Europe, where he made himself an expert in primitive anthropology and published a scholarly work on Kikuyu customs, Kenyatta diabolically parodied the traditional religion of his people in Mau Mau ritual—much as occultists did in the legendary Black Mass. (*Time*, June 13, 1960: 31)

By the end of the decade *Time*'s anticommunist fervor had cooled: Mau Mau was a colonial revolt, nationalism gone berserk, seven years of terror unmatched for sheer grisliness (June 13, 1960: 30).

The figure of Mau Mau constructed in Kenya reverberated in the United States, where it took on new inflections in relation to the civil rights movement, the cold war, and the return to domesticity. In Kenya, Mau Mau was fought on many fronts, the most effective of them not the cultural, but the military. The villagization program was basically a military operation, but the associated land consolidation and registration strategies shut out Mau Mau once and for all. In the end, Kenya colonialists constructed an image of the ignoble savage to distance themselves from the Africans who were most like them. With excesses on both sides influenced by the representations of the other, Mau Mau images grew out of mimesis and alterity of part societies. In the next chapter, I return to the part societies of colonial Kenya and the intersections of race, class, gender, and sexuality in the production of colonial subjects and discourses.

7

Race, Class, Empire, and Sexuality

Popular discourse on Mau Mau as bloody savage was short-lived though deep-seated; it was succeeded in popular imagination in Kenya by representations of the Kikuyu as aggressive merchants and avaricious government bureaucrats, a present-day image many Kikuyu themselves accept. The father in the family I lived with in the early 1970s contrasted the Kikuyu with the Luo, who had become their enemies when they were employed by the colonialists against the Kikuyu during Mau Mau. "The Luo," he said, "are good at school; they go to university. The Kikuyu do business; we make money." In this chapter, I explore images of "the other" that preceded Mau Mau, images of Africans and of European colonialists. As I have tried to show in the discussions of Leakey, Kenyatta, and Mau Mau, European colonialists, according to their position or situation, variously imagined Africans as representative of a lost communal past, the brutality of uncivilized nature, the tragedy of transition, and the hope of personal autonomy. Africans, according to their degree of incorporation into the colonial system, saw themselves as advantaged or disadvantaged by colonialism and saw European settlers as arbitrary rulers, self-important bosses, and competitors for land and power.

Winston Churchill, as British colonial undersecretary on his first visit to Kenya in 1907, caught many of the dichotomies of colonial discourse in the following depiction of the conflicting and divergent interests in colonial Kenya:

> There are already in miniature all the elements of deep political and racial discord. . . . The white man versus the black; the Indian versus both, the settler as against the planter, the town contrasted with the country; the official class against the unofficial; the coast and the highlands, the railway administration and the protectorate generally; the King's African Rifles and the East African Protectorate Police; all these different points of view, naturally arising, honestly adopted, tenaciously held, and not yet reconciled into any harmonious general conception, confront the visitor in perplexing array. (Churchill quoted in Best 1979: 70)

My study further complicates black-white relations by concentrating on class and gender differences within the colonialist population and on the generative power of the images colonialists constructed of Africans.

Colonialists created stories to justify their rule, stories to rule by. But the hegemony of the colonial powers was not complete: Africans had competing narratives and images of themselves and others; they both accommodated and subverted colonialist narratives in their own construction of colonial society. These images and representations, the products of discourses on race, class, gender, and sexuality, shaped colonial policies, reactions against colonialism, and the particularities of interaction within and between communities. Colonial culture of necessity developed in the intercultural environment of the borderlands between European and African knowledge and experience, images and representations.

In popular novels and autobiographies, Kenyan whites tell the story of the hardships and sacrifices that have tied them to the land. They point to the graves of mothers who died in childbirth and children lost to tropical diseases, to the farms redeemed from grasslands, to their civilizing influence on the people who work for them, and to the proud pastoralists whose presence reminds them of what they gained and what they lost.

Despite their romantic, utilitarian, and melancholy ties to the land, whites in Kenya had to negotiate relations to one another in order to secure their dominance in colonial Kenya, a job never successfully completed. The relationships among white populations—aristocrat, middle class, and working class; British, Danish, and South African—were greatly influenced by each group's fantasy of life away from metropolitan conventions and by particular representations of the African other. Many aristocrats lived a life of sexual license in "Orientalist" splendor, while the upwardly mobile British middle and working classes struggled to maintain white prestige in the face of the "progress" of educated Africans and the degeneracy of white Africans. Some white women called upon to participate in the civilizing mission balked, while others took up the white man's burden with relish, but many also used their stay in this new land to reexamine metropolitan sexual and gender roles in an African landscape. Europeans brought with them ideologies of difference that shaped their perceptions of Africans and were the origins of change as they adapted to Africa.

Colonial Landscapes

In Kenya, Europeans were confronted with vast plains dotted with human settlements surrounded by abundant wildlife. Writing in Denmark years after she left Africa, Karen Blixen, who published *Out of Africa* under the name Isak Dinesen, recalls the view from her farm:

The views were immensely wide. Everything that you saw made for greatness and freedom, and unequalled nobility.

The chief feature of the landscape, and of your life in it, was the air. Looking back on a sojourn in the African highlands, you are struck by your feeling of having lived for a time up in the air. (1937: 4)

The political geography of this gaze from the heights figures importantly in colonialists' appropriation of Africa: the feeling of being in the air, on the top of the world, a small part of a great landscape, but the pinnacle of the human pyramid. Colonialists could own all that they could see, people and land, or could claim the wilds of Africa as their happy hunting ground, slaughtering many of the species Western environmentalists now try to protect.[1]

"Assuming that the landscape will play a key role in any colonial imagination," as does Gaile McGregor in *The Noble Savage in the New World Garden* (1988: 11), I follow her lead in investigating figures, images, and discourse by which colonialists structure their relation to nature. In following this path I am brought to contrasting notions of the noble and ignoble savage and of the garden and wilderness in Kenya. I come first to the flower garden, where European householders in Kenya lavished time and resources on the cultivation of ornamental flowers, in an effort I see as displaced eugenics. Colonialists wanted a European transplant to take root in Africa, and they wanted to improve African humanity as they improved African plant species. In the Kenyan colonial landscape the flower garden stood for European high culture, for the possibility of civilization in the wilderness.

Flowers as a thing unto themselves had little place in precolonial African cultures, Goody (1993: 12) speculates as he launches into his study of the culture of flowers. He came to this study of flowers in Europe and Asia after recognizing the relative absence of wildflowers in the tropical forests and savannahs of Africa and the unimportance of flowers in African public life. In Africa, flowers are a sign of the harvest to come, and as such may be incorporated into ritual and ceremony, but the features of plants most valued are "leaves, roots and bark, the attributes of trees rather than flowers" (Goody 1993: 23). Goody associates the development of a culture of flowers in Europe, like the development of cooking as an art, with the growth of literacy and "cultures of luxury":

Africa did not have the same prerequisites for a culture of luxury, let alone its rejection. For the growth and use of domesticated flowers, like their representations in art and literature, in graphic and in verbal media, are part of the growth of "cultures of luxury" and subsequently "cultures of mass consumption," consumer societies. (24)

The culture of flowers for Kenya colonialists represented the attainment of high culture. Elspeth Huxley recoils at the poverty and baseness of a South

African's home not graced by flowers, both in her novel and in the television series based on *The Flame Trees of Thika* (1959: 167). The absence of lawn and ornamental blooms was in itself testimony to the inferiority of the South African's life. Flowers and gardens are so taken for granted by middle-class English colonialists that the remark made by an American settler to Huxley's mother—"My, you have flowers . . ."—is noteworthy in underscoring the visitor's destitution.

I see gardens as a metaphor for the transplanting of whites into Africa—what would be necessary for them to survive? Karen Blixen helps me to develop this idea with her reflections on a single white peony, which I quote in full:

> Once, when I was at home, an old lady in Denmark gave me twelve fine peony-bulbs which I brought into the country with me at some trouble, as the import regulations about plants were strict. When I had them planted, they sent up, almost immediately, a great number of dark carmoisin curvilinear shoots, and later a lot of delicate leaves and rounded buds. The first flower which unfolded was called *Duchesse de Nemours*, it was a large single white peony, very noble and rich, it gave out a profusion of fresh sweet scent. When I cut it and put it in water in my sitting-room, every single white person entering the room stopped and remarked upon it. Why, it was a peony! But soon after this, all the other buds of my plants withered and fell off, and I never got more than that one flower.
>
> Some years later I talked with the English gardener of Lady McMillan, of Chiromo [Kenya], about peonies. "*We have not succeeded in growing peonies in Africa,*" he said, "*and shall not do so till we manage to make an imported bulb flower here, and can take the seed from that flower.* This is how we got Delphinium into the Colony." In that way I might have introduced peonies into the country and made my name immortal like the Duchesse de Nemours herself; and I had ruined the glory of the future by picking my unique flower and putting it in water. I have very often dreamed that I have seen the white peony growing, and I have rejoiced because after all I had not cut it off. (1937: 200, emphasis added)

Blixen's desire to be remembered, which I will revisit later, is a self-conscious theme here, but implicit in this passage is the importance placed on gardening and the hope of truly adapting something European to the African environment, that the next generation, if not the pioneer colonialists, would be sturdy and strong, would survive and thrive in Africa. The discourse on gardens brought together European aesthetic appreciation (see Leddy 1988 on gardens as fine art), ideology of cultural or class hierarchy, practical knowledge about improving the race or species, and the desire to make something European out of Africa.

How does the savage, noble or ignoble, fit into the garden? Well, neither is typically in a cultivated flower garden. But Gaile McGregor's work suggests that the discourse of landscape and nature produced by colonialists influences the conception of the savage and conversely that the image of savage is projected onto particular conceptions of landscape and nature. In her study of British and American primitivism and romanticism, McGregor (1988) traces three important dichotomies in the development of the figure of the noble savage in the New World: garden versus wilderness, cultivated garden versus natural garden, and city versus country. McGregor's thesis is that in the American colony, as long as the settlers (she concentrates on the Puritans of New England) saw themselves as symbolically in "the wilderness," they deemed native peoples demonic, satanic. The image of the savage changed with political and economic relations, but it was not until the Enlightenment presented nature as good and beneficent that the association of savage with nobility gained credence. With the notion of a beneficent nature, human labor in the creation of cultivated gardens took on greater positive associations. As cities increasingly became a place of oppressive discipline, the contrast between city and country also affirmed the beneficence of nature. Not until the institution of an American literary canon does McGregor perceive the full development of the American Indian as noble savage in the New World garden, and then it is "conventional rather than truly symbolic, a chauvinistic celebration of American unity rather than a viable image of the disturbing ambiguity implicit in the nation's inherent sense of self" (1988: 97). Never has the Native American as noble savage totally replaced the ignoble savage in American thought; both remain available for imaginative use.

In Kenya, the noble savage was projected onto the majestic, expansive landscape, while the ignoble savage, the ignominious servant, was close by in the cultivated garden. The outward gaze fell on the nobility of the colonial landscape, but at home, work on colonial farms, estates, and ranches did not ennoble African laborers. Moreover, Africans who lived in the recently developed Kenyan cities were especially reviled for their association with the corruption of European progress and their distance from the noble landscape. The cultivated flower garden in colonial Kenya represents fighting back the wilderness, the possibility of civilized life. The wilderness here is less figured in the biblical sense and more influenced by European romantic traditions. Karen Blixen, as I intend to show, invites nature in as a part of the process of domestication and cultivation. Those who are close at hand to the colonialists, domestic and agricultural workers, are themselves cultigens—capable of being cultivated, shaped, molded. Those who are far away are noble, taking on features of the landscape itself.

Errol Trzebinski, writing about the European men and women who colonized Kenya, captures the feelings of nobility, freedom, and possession that the juxtaposition of wilderness and cultivated landscape inspires in one "pioneer" woman who sometimes had doubts about her mission in the Kenya colony:

[Lady Francis Scott] writes of her doubts as to the wisdom of "living out here, being a drudge and meeting no-one except delightful farmers . . . then, I order a pony and gallop up the hill in the sunshine and stand at the top gazing over the limitless spaces of Africa with the glorious wind blowing the delicious mimosa scent against my face and wonder if I haven't got the best possible kind of life after all . . . "
There was a feeling of unequalled nobility in this freedom, a greatness which overpowered the white men who were new to Africa; once they had experienced it they would never settle for less. (Scott's 1922 diary quoted in Trzebinski 1986: 4)

The scent of the cultivated garden, mimosa, made the appropriation of nature all the more wondrous. In this limitless, free, and noble landscape, just beyond the hint of civilization, lived the pastoralist noble savages of Kenya, of which the prime example was the Maasai.

The noble savage and the spiteful servant were two different representations of African subjects in the colonial landscape. These representations of Africans supported and subverted colonial laws and policies and shaped and were shaped by European and African colonial discourses. The figures of the noble savage and the spiteful servant are both of a male generic; women are either absent or ambiguous. A discourse that saw Maasai men as beautiful and free in a way that heightened their nobility and regarded Kikuyu men as domesticated and lazy or contentious and deceitful dominated the colonial imagination and defined the areas of instantiation and contestation.

A racial aesthetic that gave nobility to lighter skin, sharper features, and a taller and leaner body contributed to particular patterns of subjugation and resistance in colonial Kenya. The Maasai were ruled as "wild" and relocated when European ranchers wanted their land, while the Kikuyu were ruled as servants, and ironically assimilated to the indispensable yet despised "lower orders" of European society. My research also suggests that sexual and other social relationships among colonialists were influenced by colonialists' perceptions of and identification with Africans, especially the Maasai. Discourses on class and sexuality shaped by racism in the space of interculturality were especially significant in Kenya, a colony with an important early influx of aristocratic settlers from Britain. In contrast to the colonialist differentiating discourse of beauty and body, class and race, both the Kikuyu and the Maasai, through folklore and other oral traditions, feature noncorporeal discourses on their interrelationship, achievement and property.

The Politics of Representation in Colonial Kenya

Notions of race and class developed in Europe traveled to Africa and were transformed there. Jan Nederveen Pieterse (1992), in a volume designed to accompany the "Negrophilia Collection" exhibited at the Tropical Museum in Amsterdam, The Netherlands, writes convincingly of the construction, redefinition, and reassertion of black stereotypes in European intellectual and popular culture. Especially adept at charting the twists and turns of the European concept of savage through the dichotomies of warrior-child and noble-ignoble embedded in European ethnic, class, and gender relations, Pieterse maps the contribution of the discourse on the internal other to European representations of racial difference. He also draws out the changing images of the "children of Ham" through historical epochs from Aristotelian natural hierarchies to medieval monsters and saints to Renaissance "people without history" to nineteenth-century colonialist conceptualizations of savage warriors and lost souls to contemporary representations of Africans in advertising and tourism.

According to Pieterse, the colonial encounter in Africa was a replay of earlier subjugation and control in Europe:

> Europe's nation-states came into being through a process of subjugation of regions, in which missions and Christianization, pacification and exploitation formed a colonial scenario similar to that of the later imperialism overseas. To put it differently, the nation-states were the first empires. It follows that for virtually all the complexes which arise in relation to non-Europeans we can find precedents in Europe itself. (31)

Pieterse's course brings together race, class, gender, and sexuality in establishing the various images and narratives of the African used in the domination and humiliation not only of Africans but also of white women, Jews, the Irish, and other "white Negroes." In conclusion, he asks, "What do the parallels between racism, sexism, classism and other forms of stereotyping tell us?" (222). Pieterse answers as follows:

> In the first place, that racism never comes alone. It forms part of a hierarchical mental set which also targets other groups. In the second place, the features attributed to groups defined by "race," such as blacks, are not peculiar to racism, but are also attributed to entirely different categories defined according to social status, gender, age, nationality, and so forth. The similarities to other forms of stereotyping in terms of structure, content, even down to details, are so far-reaching that we must conclude that it is not racial phenotype, colour, or ethnicity that is the decisive factor, but the *relationship* which exists between the labelling and the labelled group. Irish people may as readily be branded as "human chimpanzees" as Africans. This says nothing about Africans nor about Irish people; rather it says something about the British and the relationship that

existed, exists, or is being constructed, between the British and Africans and Irish people respectively. (222–23)

Like Pieterse, I want to show the interrelationship between forms of oppression, but my focus is different: in examining the racism of Europeans toward Africans, I seek to reveal the continuities of their earlier class relations, the persistence and mutability of anti-Semitism, the resilience of the tropes of the industrious north and the lazy, lustful south, and the longevity of the dichotomy of the noble-ignoble savage.

The Lower Classes

Late-nineteenth-century theories of degeneracy applied to working-class whites in Britain held that lower classes had a "tainted hereditary" that worsened with each succeeding generation, causing lewd and lascivious behavior in women and criminal behavior in men.[2] The physical differences between the upper classes and the lower classes were often matters of facial features, though stature and body build were also evaluated. On the whole, the lower classes, conceived of as a separate race, had fleshy noses (sexual capacity), small or misshapen eyes (the windows of the soul), large mouths (sexual appetite), and blemished skin (impurities of the body and soul) (see Chamberlin and Gilman 1985).

Class relations were also influenced by racial imagery. With the immigration of large numbers of Irish people to England after the famines of the 1840s, and with Irish resistance to British domination, a discourse that likened the Irish to blacks and apes increased in Great Britain. Pieterse observes:

> Irishmen were depicted with low foreheads, prognathous features and an apelike gait by cartoonists such as Sir John Tenniel of *Punch*. In 1862 a satire in *Punch* attacked Irish immigration under the title "The Missing Link": "A creature manifestly between the Gorilla and the Negro is to be met with in some of the lowest districts of London and Liverpool by adventurous explorers. It comes from Ireland, whence it has contrived to migrate; it belongs in fact to a tribe of Irish savages: the lowest species of Irish Yahoo." (1992: 214)

European class prejudices were overlaid on racist notions overdetermining the style and rhetoric of subordination of Africans by European colonialists.

The Jew

The Jew is the ultimate European internal other—a participant in the same political community, but with different goals and values, different food and body. Again a male generic seems to predominate in the stereotypes of Jews. The Jewish body is marked by the circumcision of men and the often parodied large nose. The nose and circumcision may be different versions of the same story. For centuries Europeans have expressed fear of Jewish hypersexuality and condemned circumcision as primitive and backward (see Lyons 1981).

In Shakespeare's *Merchant of Venice*, Shylock, the Jewish moneylender, professes his similarities to Christians in a famous passage: "Hath not a Jew eyes?, hath not a Jew hands, organs, dimensions, senses, affections, passions? fed with the same food, hurt with the same weapons, subject to the same diseases, healed by the same means, warmed and cooled by the same winter and summer as a Christian is?" (act 3, scene 1). In an earlier passage, Shylock also lays out his differences from the Christians as he declines an offer to dine with the Venetian merchants with whom he has just sealed a deal:

> Yes, to smell pork; to eat of the habitation which your prophet, the Nazarite, conjured the devil into; I will buy with you, sell with you, talk with you, walk with you, and so following; but I will not eat with you, drink with you, nor pray with you. (act 1, scene 3)

Shakespeare declares the humanity of Jews in marking their similarities to Christians, but he also marks differences in their everyday lives that set Jews apart from Christians: Jews do not eat with Christians or eat what Christians eat. Beyond the gaze of Christians, what do they eat? Pieterse suggests that the medieval European accusation of cannibalism against Jews is a precedent for colonial encounters of the other:

> Perhaps there is a parallel in the "blood libel" of the Jews in medieval Europe, as a group whose place in the hierarchy of the estates was based on a series of exclusions which served to fix its place in the overall scheme of things. When new lands were found and strange peoples encountered, whether in America, the Pacific or the African interior, the accusation of cannibalism served to affirm and secure the central place of Christian civilization. (1992: 115–16)

The attention given to black facial features also has a precedent in the depiction of Jewish physiognomy. In the politics of racial aesthetics, the nose is the marker of class and morality; note the reverence for a classical profile and the reviling of the Jew, portrayed with a large hooked nose as immoral and sexually rapacious.

I do not mean to insinuate that once anti-Semitism traveled to Kenya and was adapted to attitudes regarding blacks, anti-Semitism itself disappeared among the colonialists. Much the contrary. When in 1903 the British began negotiations for a Jewish homeland in East Africa, in the eastern province of Uganda, the Kenya colonialists rose up against it, fearing Jews were not good mixers, were not farmers, would "lead to trouble with half-tamed natives jealous of [Jewish] rights," and "would tend to form a poor white class" (Trzebinski 1986: 82). East Africa was not established as an antechamber to the Holy

Land. From the beginning, a small segment of the colonialists had been Jewish; the most well known was probably the farmer and hotelier Abraham Block, whose Norfolk Hotel was at the core of Nairobi high society. Anti-Semitism was one aspect of the discourses of inequality that European colonialists brought to Kenya, and it played a part in the development of a colonial racial aesthetics.

North and South

For the British and the northern Europeans, the southern Europeans—in particular the Greeks, and the Italians and Spanish with their Moorish influences—represented the tropical types found later in the colonies. Shakespeare once again confirms the longevity of these tropes. His Italian plays (for instance, *The Taming of the Shrew*, *Romeo and Juliet*, and *Much Ado about Nothing*) underscore a concern with domestic relations, the person, role reversal, and turbulence that the southern climes entail. Ann Stoler's (1989) study of tropical sexual fantasies that have inspired Europe goes back even further, to the displacement of repressed desires and doubts onto a tropical landscape developed with the popular studies of geography.

In explaining this attraction to the darker races, Kenya colonialist Karen Blixen, writing in *Out of Africa* under the name Isak Dinesen, calls on a familiar European trope of the dark, lazy southerner:

> As it is almost impossible for a woman to irritate a real man, and as to the woman, a man is never quite contemptible, never altogether rejectable, as long as he remains a man, so were the hasty red-haired Northern people infinitely long-suffering with the tropical countries and races. (1989 [1937]: 16)

Blixen celebrated the unity of opposites, especially as represented in the master-servant relationship in her later memoirs, *Shadows on the Grass*: "The servant may be the more fascinating of the two, still it holds true of him as of his master that his play of colours would fade and his timbre abate, were he to stand alone" (1960: 379). Her personal experience of difference in Africa expanded her world, deepened and enriched her song of life. Available to the colonialists as they began the colonizing enterprise was a range of tropes of the lazy and lascivious south that they found amenable to the construction of an African other.

The southern sun was seductive. Kenya's European colonialists carried on a dangerous flirtation with the sun, whose rays were believed not only to damage the spine but also to cause immorality. Medical manuals of the time advised that too long a stay in the tropics would cause fatigue, individual and racial degeneration, physical breakdown, "cultural contamination and neglect of the conventions of supremacy, and *agreement* about what they were" (Stoler 1989:

646). Men, women, and children were cautioned to wear pith helmets and spine pads—a thick strip of gauze that stretched from neck to buttocks. Women wore even more, being counseled to line their dresses and headgear with scarlet cloth. Popular writer James Fox, whose story of Kenyan socialite settlers *White Mischief: The Murder of Lord Erroll* was made into a major film released in 1988, concludes:

> [The Kenyan colonialists' fears of the sun] seem to revive the Victorian shibboleth that exposure to the sun was improperly sensual and immodest, and certainly not something that could easily be shared with Africans on an equal basis. Thus taboos were raised against it, the most peculiar reserved for women, who were advised to line their dresses and headgear not with flannel, but with bright scarlet cloth. (Fox 1988: 15)

In the latter part of the twentieth century, Europeans less ambivalently embrace the sun, and the north-south discourse most often describes hemispheric economic disparities. Yet the tropes of the industrious north and the lustful south abide. In the United States, these geographic determinisms have been reclaimed in Afrocentric discourses that praise the creativity and warmth of the "sun people" (people of African descent) and damn the rapacity and formality of the "ice people" (people of European descent). Karen Blixen might not have disagreed.

The Red Indian and the Black Slave:
Paradigm of the Noble Savage and the Spiteful Servant

The development of the figures of the noble savage and the spiteful servant is historically determined. This is absolutely the case in terms of the American images of Native Americans and African slaves, whose images changed with the frontiers, with industrialization, with nationalism, and with waves of ideology. Even before the first long-term British colonialists arrived in the New World, they had contradictory images of the West as the land of darkness, sunset, and death and as the land of rebirth, renewal, and higher reality. These contradictions were variously played out in colonial perceptions of Native Americans. When the American colonialists represented themselves as the righteous in the wilderness, Indians were imaged as bloodthirsty and devil worshippers. But the idea of the noble savage grew with the notion of nature as good and beneficent, with natural law, with the Enlightenment and the French Revolution; then the noble savage was represented as in harmony with a moral environment (see McGregor 1988: 71). McGregor finds that Americans warmed to the idea of the Indian as noble savage as a "safe" kind of romanticism, counterbalanced by rationalism, developed within the context of national self-consciousness and national literature (93).

Two different kinds of Puritan literary genres represent the differences between Indians as noble and ignoble savages. In the first, war tracts construct vile enemies to be killed and victories to be celebrated; the second, captivity narratives (see Rogers 1989), told stories of the gender equality and personal freedom of North American Indians.

Black folks were not originally incorporated into the American imaginary as the ignoble savage or the wild man (see Dudley and Novak 1972). Before the explosion of slavery in the United States, black indentured servants were assimilated to the lower classes—with attendant discourses of moral and physical difference. Only when African Americans became such an indispensable part of the American economy and took on power as representatives of American consciousness in the American literary canon and popular discourse did the black as spiteful servant gain prominence (cf. Toni Morrison 1989). Like the Jew in Europe, the black American is an ultimate internal other whose differences from the hegemonic self mark the fear of both self and other.

In a study of the people of early America, Gary Nash (1974) identified four incongruities that describe white ambivalence toward the Indian constructed as noble savage and the African American I have termed the spiteful servant. These paradoxes, as aspects of discourses on difference, contributed to the foundations of knowledge and power by which colonial discourses were constructed in Africa:

> *To assimilate or not:* "Europeans in America claimed that they wished to assimilate Indians and Africans but they found that the most effective way to exploit the land of one and the labor of the other was to follow a non-assimilationist policy" (Nash 1974: 310-11).

> *Defeated enemy versus despised servant:* "White American culture developed the most pervasively negative attitudes toward the cultural minority in its midst that was indispensably valuable to it—the Afro-Americans—and held the more positive attitudes toward the cultural minority which stood only as an obstacle to white society once their military assistance was no longer needed—the Indians" (312).

> *The price of freedom:* "The cultural group that was enslaved, degraded, and despised survived and flourished demographically in America, while the group that maintained its freedom, much of its power, and a considerable amount of European respect suffered depopulation and gradual decline" (313).

> *Dashed dreams:* "Many Indian societies embodied what Englishmen and other Europeans had come to find in the New World but were

destroyed or driven westward while daring to be what Europeans could not" (317).

The story of the Native American and the African American creates the trope of nobility free in nature versus the oppressive disciplines of labor. Native Americans, of course, were not free in nature, but marginalized in a capitalist economy. To the extent that the power of the contrastive pair, Indian and slave, is grounded in Europeans' dissatisfaction with their political economy, we can expect that the noble savage versus the spiteful servant forms a master narrative in the West, one to which the Maasai and the Kikuyu could be assimilated. In both colonial and contemporary discourse in Kenya, Maasai are like Native Americans, noble but doomed (or is it noble *because* doomed?), and Kikuyu are conceptually assimilated like the corrupt and corruptible black American.

The following formula may be the most succinct statement of the noble savage as marginalized other:

1. The X (the Maasai, American Indians, for example) are not like the Y (the Kikuyu, African Americans) because they resist modernization, do not deign to compete, are aloof; they are nature's aristocrats.

2. The X (Maasai, Native Americans) even have the features of aristocrats, at least compared with the Y (Kikuyu, black Americans): narrow faces and noses, fairer skin, proud bearing.

3. But the X (Maasai, Indians) are doomed because they are too proud and aloof. See how marginal they are, out on the boundaries, an anachronism, dying of disease.[3]

Historically, the European discourse on savages provides more commentary on attempts at hegemony and internal contradictions within Europe, and on the nature and quality of European imperialism, than on any actual condition of the native other. Pieterse captures class elements in this discourse as follows:

The theme of the "noble savage," with its classical-aristocratic overtones, implied that the humanists were striving for autonomy from clerical authority, and possibly the uneasiness of nobles over their loss of status in relation to absolutism; the "good savage" on the other hand was a theme with primarily bourgeois overtones which implied a criticism of both feudalism and absolutism. (1992: 33)

Discourses of inequality in the Kenya colony were overdetermined by what the colonialists brought with them from internal distinctions already with the capitalist nation-state and empire.

Living Off the Land

Karen Blixen's *Out of Africa* combines the trope of the noble and ignoble savage with European discourse on northern and southern peoples. Blixen's stories recreate the mood and mystery of Africa. Calling on an array of rhetorical and philosophical strategies—melancholy, the unity and interdependence of all things, the greatness and scope of the African landscape, irony and humor, union of opposites, the order of things, and the personification of nature—Blixen creates a pastoral that seeks to escape the progress and industrialism of the north through a move south and a return to the primitive, to the little community, to nature.

This novel was recommended to me by many white expatriates when I first went to Kenya in the early 1970s, but I actively resisted reading it until just a few years ago. I was not interested in reading a beautiful book about African colonialism. Today I am still trying to understand what makes this book beautiful, to understand the relationship between racism and romanticism, and to understand how a recent reviewer could make the following statement:

> This unashamed aristocrat despises the English for their besottedness with the monarchy. She seems to favour the idea of revolution, which fits uneasily with her hatred of all things bourgeois. She has a Romantic notion that there are true aristocrats of the spirit, among whom are many of the black Africans whose love and respect she never lost. She was, I suppose, essentially a feudalist—but of an unconventional kind. A feudalist and a feminist—it is a strikingly odd combination. (Bailey 1984)

Blixen's romanticism never removed Europeans from their pinnacle. She delights in nature, and her belief that Africans had not quite severed the umbilical cord with nature results in both admiration and disdain for them. This is paternalism (maternalism), and it is racist.

As one reviewer put it, *Out of Africa* is written against Europe:

> Isak Dinesen has been able to reinvigorate the romantic tradition because she rediscovered in Africa the validity of all the romantic myths, myths that locate spirit in the elemental—in nature, in the life of primitive people, in instinct and passion, in aristocratic, feudal, and tribal societies that have their roots in nature. She could not, however, have seen Africa as she did had not she brought to it eyes prepared by European romanticism, had she not discovered Europe in Africa. (Langbauam 1984)

Imbuing the African landscape and people with a consciousness that comes out of the contrast between Europe and Africa, Blixen created an orderly world of oddities and eccentricities, of masters and servants, of animals who think and of people who are like animals. *Out of Africa* is not divided into chapters. There are five major sections: the longest section, sixty-four pages, is divided into thirty-two subsections, little stories, and the shortest, fifty-four pages, into four subsections. The resulting fragmentation denies the reader anticipation, creates no internal tension; neither chronology nor character is consistently developed. Hard times come and go, people join the household and grow older, others pass through, even wars happen, but all in a sense of time out of time. Yet Blixen's Africa is caught up in change. She admits this, sees it, but writes with such a sense of irony that this reader was led to believe that all change is on the surface—Africa is essentially timeless. This timelessness inspired the critic who wrote the introduction to the 1952 Modern Library edition of *Out of Africa*. She exclaims:

> In no other book I know—even remembering Joseph Conrad—is there the glow that shines through *Out of Africa*. You are transported to a land as remote as the moon; huge pachyderms from another eon wander there freely; the dark narrow-headed tribesmen become your familiars. You are on a continent as it was ten million years ago, yet vibrant and exhilarating. (Kielty 1952: xii)

In her juxtaposition of the stories of the Kikuyu boy Kamante, whom she saved through medical treatments, and a gazelle, Lulu, that wanders into her house, Blixen constructs the romantic story of the dark southern man's incorporation into nature and her wise northern musing at it all. "Lulu," Blixen writes, "came to my house from the woods as Kamante had come to it from the plains" (1989 [1937]: 61). Blixen brings together the wild of nature and the uncivilized of humanity. Of Lulu's entrance into her household, she writes:

> It also seemed to me that the free union between my house and the antelope was a rare, honourable thing. Lulu came in from the wild world to show that we were on good terms with it, and she made my house one with the African landscape, so that nobody could tell where the one stopped and the other began. (73)

The situation is different for Kamante, but not for all the other herd boys on the farm:

> These little boys, who wandered about the farm in the company of their fathers' herds of goats and sheep, looking up grazing for them, did in a way form a link between the life of my civilized house and the life of the wild. (44)

Kamante, who had learned much of European ways while he was in a mission hospital, was humorously represented as believing that he shared beliefs and outlooks with the author. Africans taken into the house form an uneasy alliance with civilization.

An old Kikuyu man I interviewed in 1971, who estimated his age as ninety-five, said that the white man betrayed or became unfaithful to the Kikuyu. This is just what Karen Blixen tried not to do. In paying wages, tending wounds, educating children, throwing dances, provisioning feasts, adjudicating disputes, and making a way for her retainers to carry on after her departure, Blixen sought the love and respect of the native. She naively believed that she alone among the whites truly cared for the natives, and she delighted in the approval of her servants and retainers (Huxley 1980: 9-10).

Certainly Blixen could not have gotten the love and approval of Burugu, the old man I interviewed, for the white man's betrayal of the Kikuyu itself involved incorporation of Kikuyu men into the bottom rung of the colonial labor ladder. Burugu explains that the chiefs told the warriors not to attack the white man who came to found the district administrative headquarters, Mr. Hall of Fort Hall:

> *Burugu:* The chiefs gave stories to the warriors that Mr. Hall was one of those white men who exchanged cloth for ivory for the Africans at the coast so that he would not be fought.
>
> *Question:* When did you come to dislike the white man, before Mr. Hall's arrival or after his arrival?
>
> *Burugu:* We came to hate the white after Mr. Hall's arrival. When we built a house for him in Murang'a [then Fort Hall], he with some other men would come to collect our *anake* [young men] and send them to Nairobi to work there. The young men would be asked to carry heavy loads or iron sheets, boxes and other articles. These heavy loads made the young men grow weak and their backs pained. Even today my back pains because of these heavy loads. The white man always came in the evening to collect us to go to work for them. We were paid three shillings a day. When this went on we found or rather we realized that the white man wanted to tire us; then we began to dislike him gradually as time went on.
>
> Then we began to attack the white man. [We] *asked the white man why they had become so unfaithful to the Agikuyu.*

An important subplot of the film version of *Out of Africa,* released in 1985 and starring two top-ranked American movie stars, Meryl Streep as Karen Blixen and Robert Redford as Denys Finch Hatton, is Karen Blixen's alienation from Nairobi society and her faithfulness, her devotion, to "her Kikuyu." The love story between Finch Hatton and Blixen dominates the movie, and its success touched off a spate of romantic imperialist nostalgia films about relations among whites against the backdrop of the colonies. Nicholas Best, in a journalistic history of whites in Kenya, credits Blixen with getting the respect of both the Kikuyu and whites: Kikuyu "warmed to her anyway for the enthusiasm with which she invariably espoused the black man's cause against the white" (1979: 113); Blixen was "a woman of strong character who became a pillar of Nairobi society in the years following the Great War" (114).

Denis Boyles's recent exposé of the lives of Kenya's colonialists takes a different tack. Those he interviewed who knew Karen Blixen much preferred Meryl Streep's version. Blixen, they said, was affected and pretentious, her patronizing attitude toward Africans offensive to both the white and native communities, and whatever did she see in Finch Hatton (Boyles 1988: 24-25)? About this affair, Elspeth Huxley says subtly, "something in his nature held him back from any full commitment to a woman, a cause, or even to his own career" (1980: 11). Boyles comes closer in presenting gossip that intimates that Blixen's lover was gay or bisexual:

> I was sitting in a coffee bar in Nairobi one morning gossiping with a local writer, a lifelong Kenyan with an acute sensitivity to local history, when the current feature topic [the film version of *Out of Africa*] came up. "Blixen was quite intense, quite passionate," she said. "And I think she actually believed the things she said, even though we all often knew better. That affair with Finch Hatton, for example." She paused for effect, then ever so slightly lowered her voice. "We all knew he had other *tendencies*, wandering off all the time with those boys," she said, referring to Finch Hatton's frequent and lengthy excursions into the bush accompanied only by native youngsters. "But she was quite imaginative, and nobody wanted to say anything." (1988: 23-24)

Blixen's letters confirm that "her friendship with Denys Finch Hatton was a fully consummated love relationship" and that in 1922 she believed herself to be expecting his child and "was in the depths of despair when this proved to be a false alarm" (Lasson 1981: xviii-xix). Her willingness to bear a child out of wedlock, even her willingness to stay on in Kenya after the breakup of her marriage and her possible acceptance of Finch Hatton's *"tendencies"* must have set middle-class colonial tongues a-wagging. Karen Blixen's relationship with Finch Hatton, however, unlike the movie version, ended well before his death in a plane crash.

Denys Finch Hatton, like Baron Bror von Blixen, Karen Blixen's ex-husband, was a big game hunter, pioneering the use of the airplane to spot game. Sport hunting on long safaris became fashionable in Kenya colony almost from the beginning, often drawing in rich visitors from Europe and America. A whole hunting and safari industry grew up in Nairobi in the first decade of the twentieth century (cf. J. MacKenzie 1988: 161). In his retrospective of the socialite settlers of the colony, Best describes the place of these men who lived off the land in a very different way than did the farmers:

> Lording it over everyone else, however, were the white hunters, kings of the safari, legendary names some of them, who emerged only infrequently from the bush but by God were ready for a snort and a long talk when they did appear. The hunters were almost larger than life, festooned with slouch hats and bullets and gaiters of buffalo hide, invariably accompanied by a jungly looking native

tracker as part of the props. Every one of them possessed a fund of stories.
(1979: 65)

In *Out of Africa* Karen Blixen asks, "Will Africa remember my name?" It
has. There is an area of Nairobi called Karen, after her, and her house is a national museum, Karen House, and a minor tourist attraction. One Kenyan
brand of instant coffee recalls the Karen Blixen of the film *Out of Africa* on its
label: a white woman astride a horse in the coffee fields, with "Out of Africa"
emblazoned overhead (fig. 5).

Racial Aesthetics in Colonial Kenya

Red Strangers

Elspeth Huxley, the daughter of British settlers, spent most of her childhood in Kenya. Against this backdrop, she wrote political analyses of African
colonialism in her novels, memoirs, and biographies of Kenyan "pioneers." In
the 1930s Huxley experimented with a literary form that she called the "documentary novel" in her work on the Kikuyu of the pre- and early colonial period. Like Kenyatta, Huxley was a student of Malinowski; along with Kenyatta, Leakey, and innumerable colonial administrators and missionaries, she
sat in on his seminars at the London School of Economics (see Kuklick 1991:
210). Malinowski's influence is not readily apparent in the novel she published
in 1939, around the same time that Kenyatta's *Facing Mt. Kenya* was published—which, of course, was around the time that Leakey was finishing his
ethnography of the Kikuyu.

Red Strangers is not a precursor to the postmodern ethnography. Huxley
disclaims any anthropological interest: "I am not an anthropologist and have
not been able to adopt the methods of long study and thorough checking and
rechecking essential to that social science" (1939: vii). Her claims to verisimilitude in her documentary novel are based on her personal experience and rap-
port with others: "All the characters, without exception, are imaginary, but
many of their adventures occurred to real people who related them to me; and
such events as smallpox outbreaks, famine and so on, are matters of historical
record" (vii). Huxley creates a story following one Kikuyu family across generations to encounters with white colonialists, "red strangers"; the novel ends
with an African marveling at the miracle of the airplane. This in effect captures
the main trajectory of the novel, for Huxley sees colonialism as freeing the personal spirit, a spirit encumbered by the rule-bound superstitions of the
Kikuyu. Acknowledging the Routledges (1910) as her predecessors and Leakey
as a contemporary whose notes she checked, Huxley focuses on the impossibility of a Kikuyu man living an upstanding life without breaking some rules and

Fig. 5. "Out of Africa," Kencaffe instant coffee label (registered trademark of Bidco [Kenya] Ltd.)

paying fines. The rules and fines seem to have no rhyme or reason; Kikuyu notions of contamination and disgorgement are not developed. What is clear is that elders, parents, and fathers-in-law all demand and deserve payments of some kind. Differences in wealth and personal achievement are of utmost importance; the protagonist must leave his own tribal group and join hunters in the forest before he can attain the wherewithal to succeed at home. But instead of the rule of elders that Leakey presents, Huxley finds great power in the medicine man, the *mundu mugo.*

Huxley does not often describe women or much attend to the distinctive ways in which they were affected by colonialism. When she does describe women, she seems to emphasize their connection to nature, as in this introduction of the first protagonist's mother: "Dappled sunlight spotted his mother's brown goatskin cloak as though it had been a leopard's back. . . . The shaved shiny head of the baby on her back bobbed up and down as she laughed" (1939: 5). A few pages later, we find this:

> How pleasant it was, she thought, to be again among the goats in the warm thick atmosphere of which she seemed herself to be a part; how pleasant to sense the familiar tang of goat sharp in her nostrils, to hear their scuffles and soft stampings in the darkness. (17)

Kikuyu men are differently assimilated to nature. Their features often recall animals, as in this passage:

> Mahenia, Waseru's father, was small and brittle. His face was networked with wrinkles as if a horde of ants had been scurrying over his skin, each one leaving a little furrow in its track. He had shrewd black eyes that darted swift glances about him like a forest rat. He was known as a quick-witted man who drove hard bargains in goats, and if luck had been with him he might have become rich. (16)

Huxley does not write about white people like this. The descriptions of whites in *Red Strangers* are all written from the Kikuyu point of view, since the book is about the coming of the European to Kikuyuland. An example of her descriptions of whites from a later work is Lord Delamere, the "white man" of her work on Kenyan history, *White Man's Country* (1935): "a short, stocky figure in a big mushroom hat with long greyish hair (he was then in his fifties) and a beaky nose, clad in a mud- or grease-stained brown cardigan" (1987: 92). Here is the sister of a beleaguered colonial administrator:

> Like her brother, Dolly was lightly built, wiry and deceptively strong. She had a nut-brown complexion, dark hair that tumbled about at will, somewhat prominent teeth and large dark-blue eyes, and was impetuous in movement, often funny and quite ruthless in getting her own way. (1987: 172)

In her first mention of the Maasai people, in her most recent book on Kenya, a memoir, *Out in the Midday Sun,* about her return to Kenya in 1933 after an eight-year absence (published in 1985 after the success of the television series of her memoir *The Flame Trees of Thika*), Elspeth Huxley pictures the Maasai living in harmony with nature where "no animal oppressed or tortured another" (1987: 12). The Maasai are to her the best example of human integration into this environment:

Even man, the arch-killer, fitted into this harmonious-seeming state of affairs. To the left of the railway line, as far as the eye could see and farther, lay the Maasai reserve; the Maasai, by and large, left the animals alone. They killed lions to protect their livestock, and young boys might hunt birds with bows and arrows, but otherwise they did not molest the wild creatures. Being nomadic, they had no crops and gardens to protect. Wild animals could come and go as they wished on their seasonal migrations. (1987: 13)

Contrast this to the first mention of the Kikuyu, workers on her parents' farm in the Rift Valley whom she was seeing for the first time in eight years. With this contrast, major ways of conceptualizing the native in Kenya begin to take shape:

Small totos in their skimpy cloaks feverishly shooing herds of bleating goats out of the way; women in goatskin cloaks and aprons bowed under their loads— one never saw a loadless woman. . . .
    Then came Karanja in his red fez, scarcely changed at all, and then Mbugwa, who had changed a lot, having grown from a kitchen toto into a well-built young man, both of them grinning from ear to ear and pumping my arm up and down. (1987: 27)

The red fez was an affectation that most Europeans of means used for their household servants. This, along with a long white Muslim-style robe, vest, and sash, none indigenous to the Central Highlands of Kenya but representative of imperial power when India was the jewel in the crown of the British empire, distinguished the household servant (see Hansen 1989 for an excellent study of domestic service in another African colony). Huxley introduces the Kikuyu in a European household, all members of the family working, the men named and identified in specific relation to the European household. Kikuyu women were at the edge of the European sphere, called in as hands at crucial times in the agricultural cycle, much of their time given over to subsistence duties supporting their own families. (No mention of the forced labor of Kikuyu women on European estates occurs in these works.) Within Kikuyu society, women were praised for their industry and fertility, and men for wisdom, wealth, and managerial ability.

The Maasai, in nature, free and nomadic, were unabashedly praised, while the Kikuyu, in the realm of European civilization, were variously reviled and defended. Huxley set Kikuyu enterprise and humor against Kikuyu craftiness and deceitfulness. Explaining her mother's high regard for her Kikuyu workers, Huxley states:

Enterprise always appealed to her, and so did a sense of humour; it was their possession of these two qualities that underlay her liking for the Kikuyu people. . . . Some Europeans thought them deceitful, crafty, much given to

199

squabbling and to becoming barrack-room lawyers, and were reluctant to employ them, preferring men and women of more straightforward tribes. (1987: 182)

Leakey and Kenyatta, in different ways and from different charges, also defended the Kikuyu. In his ethnography, Leakey (1977) defends Kikuyu men against the accusation by whites that they are lazy and that women do all the work; he represents Kikuyu women as influential in their society and champions the women's sexual freedom. Kenyatta's (1938) functionalism normalizes Kikuyu society, declares Kikuyu superiority to the destructive colonialists, and exults the industry and achievement of both men and women.

Colonialists reveled in the sexual glories of the Maasai, but thought of Kikuyu male workers as neuter and women as workhorses. Kikuyu men were trebly neutered: by their female roles in European households, through attempts to negate the potential sexual threat from their living in such close proximity to white women, and through the overriding image of the strength and industry of Kikuyu women.

Maasai men were male-defined, male-identified sexual beings. In the following passage Huxley summarizes the attraction of the Maasai and the problem with the Kikuyu:

At heart, I think, [Europeans] envied these young men's apparent freedom, their status, their physique, the spice of danger in their lives and their sexual opportunities—the warriors could take their pick of lovers among unmarried girls. In fact they had just about everything a young man could want, so why try to turn them into disgruntled, trousered clerks? (1985: 75–76)

Trousers were always associated with the disgruntled and with the Kikuyu, or rather with certain groups of young Kikuyu men. Kikuyu elders who wore blankets had greater legitimacy in the eyes of the colonial administration and the white settlers. Colonial administrators were quite antiprogressivist, using "evolutionist arguments to resist whatever innovations they saw as threatening to their authority; primitive peoples would suffer cultural degeneration unless their progress was negotiated very gradually" (Kuklick 1991: 222). On the whole, Kikuyu rather than Maasai wore trousers, were educated clerks, and agitated for change. The Maasai, the authentic natives, were decked out in "traditional" garb:

The young warriors with mops of red pigtails were free-striding, graceful, arrogant and proud, but when they stood still, often with one arm draped around another's shoulders, there was a curiously soft, moulded, feminine look about their greased and well-proportioned limbs and torsos. Certainly there was nothing soft or feminine about their behavior. From infancy they were trained for war, in the shape of raids to capture their neighbours' cattle and sometimes women. You could say they were the fascists of East Africa, not to mention racists, but because of their physical beauty, their bravery and their uncompromising pride in themselves, a kind of Maasai-worship prevailed among many Europeans. (Huxley 1987: 75)

What does this beauty consist in? Socially, their very marginality and distance contributed to their beauty, but on the physical level they had the beauty of grace and elegance of body, a proud demeanor, and noble facial features—white features sculpted in black. The Maasai, like several other pastoralist peoples in the area from the Nile valley to the Great Lakes and Rift Valley of East Africa, have been called one of the lost tribes of Israel. Caucasian influences were believed to have resulted in the high-bridged, narrow nose, the thin lips, and the elongated bodies typical of many of these people. Physical anthropologists theorize that these traits are associated with adaptation to a hot, dry savannah climate, but such conjecture was neither available to nor amenable to colonialist interpretations.[4]

Reading Faces as Political

In the West, the nose is a supreme marker of class and morality, and of gender and sexuality. In the European imagination all Maasai noses are thin and narrow. Here is a passage from a 1961 novel by Richard Llewellyn, author of *How Green Was My Valley*, who also turned his hand to a Maasai colonialist pastoral. A Maasai man greets a young Maasai woman whom he has not seen for a long time:

> The girl laughed down at him, and the honeyed, coppery-black hair fell forward and the gold-gray eyes in the whitest white of health were wide in surprise, and the nose was thin and the mouth showed the perfect teeth, with the telltale gap in the middle of the bottom row. (34)

The skin is lightened by the honey, copper, and gold references, and the nose is thin. Large noses in Europe were associated with the lower orders, with Jews, and with the besotted. Large noses, large feet, large hands, large penises, and large sexual appetite go together in European folklore. Today "nose jobs" for women are the most popular forms of plastic surgery, as women try to create the appearance of beauty and refinement through their noses.

Turning to the question of skin color, the evidence of European association of immorality and degeneracy with dark skin is legion. Following work done by Harryette Mullen (1990) on American slave narratives, I would like to point to signs that are typically read from white skin, signs that black skin masks, that supposedly show virtue. Mullen believes that it is the inability of black skin to redden in a blush that, from the white perspective, denies modesty, virtue, and innocence to the darker races. A recent documentary film on the racist Aryan white power movement in the United States uses the phrase "blood in the face" as its title, connoting the importance placed on reddened skin as a sign of the honor of whiteness. This is particularly crucial to women whose honor is vested in control of the body, in maintaining the inviolate body: the skin of black women in the context of the white slave master showed no signs of modesty. The English middle class sometimes had an obsession with modesty and its display in young women, Yeazell concludes in her study of blushing in Dickens's *Our Mutual Friend*, where she finds "a narrative event in the coming of a blush" (1982: 343).

The face should show what is on the inside. Black American composer Fats Waller aptly captures the problematic for blacks of the relationship between the inside and the outside in his composition "Black and Blue," which asks, "What did I do to be so black and blue?" The answer is, "I'm white, white inside, but that don't help my case, cuz I can't hide what is on my face."

What is on my face? Political statements and moral precepts written in skin color and features. The blues come from the opposition between black and white, inside and outside, an opposition heightened by Christian ideology and racism. In Africa too the same opposition is noted by a Maasai man. After being baptized by a German priest, Tepilit Ole Saitoti, in his 1988 autobiography *The Worlds of a Maasai Warrior*, recounts the following feelings:

> We were congratulated by our teacher, and everybody else around told us that our souls were now white as snow, having been cleansed of all our sins. I felt so pure that I wanted to die before messing up again. I knew it would be hopeless to try to live a whole day without sinning. It was hard to remain pure when it was demanded that you not desire, swear in God's name, or even cheat a little. (1988: 39)

All of the demands Ole Saitoti fears would deny his purity, his white inside, relate directly to Maasai cultural expectations of the warrior. Warriors are permitted sexual relations with unmarried girls, and married women often take warriors as their lovers. Warriors swear by that which defines them—their own names, names of cattle, age grade names, clan names; in this case, what is denied is the use of the name of the Christian god who claims the baptized. Cattle raiding and stealing, while no longer a major part of warrior activities, remain as a symbol of what it meant to be a warrior. To be white inside requires denial of his external blackness. Christian Maasai are thereby denied the right to act morally according to Maasai beliefs.

The missionized African, the Christian convert, felt the dilemma of black and white symbology, but it was shades of black and nobility of profile that captured the colonialists' imagination. What is on my face? Eyes (bulging or squinting), nose (big, wide, open), teeth (gapped, bucked), jaw (protruding or square), forehead (sloping, wide)—all make statements about sensuality, poverty, intelligence, brutality, and honesty. Racial political aesthetics are part of a discourse on subordination and in colonial Kenya were used to define and differentiate groups for immediate and indirect domination by colonialists. Colonialists used body and facial features along with notions of bravery and arrogance to define the differences between the Kikuyu and the Maasai, reifying the concept of tribe and making absolute distinctions between the two tribes. This reification of tribe does not correspond to the experience or the internal discourses of these two populations, but it does highlight the constructed quality of the racial aesthetic and its use in a discourse of domination and subordination.

African Discourses on Tribe and the Other

The Maasai and the European

British settlement in Kenya followed the railroad, built to link neighboring Uganda to the sea at Mombasa on the Kenya coast. As settlers moved west, many Europeans moved into Maasai territory and began struggling to turn pasture into agricultural land or cattle and sheep ranches. This period saw warfare between the Maasai and the British until the establishment of the so-called Pax Britannica, when much of the overt warfare ceased. (Historian Mungeam was struck by the Maasai's "failure to provide the expected military opposition to British entry" and the tenacity of the Kikuyu's opposition [1970: 129].) The incorporation of former "respected" adversaries into the armed force of the colonizer is common in the noble savage trope; after defeat Maasai *moran* [warriors] accompanied colonialists on pacification raids on other Kenyan groups. The railway divided Maasailand in two, effectively creating two reserves by 1904 and alienating large tracts of fecund grazing land from the Maasai. The colonial government agreed to provide a half-mile-wide road linking the two reserves, and to preserve the territory for the Maasai "so long as the Maasai race shall exist" (Trzebinski 1986: 35). This agreement lasted less than ten years.

In the first decade of the twentieth century, European sheep and cattle ranches around the northern Maasai reserve, Laikipia, were notoriously unsuccessful as a result of a lack of minerals and water in the pastures, while the excellent pasturage on Laikipia had so swelled the Maasai herds that they had outgrown the area.[5] Trzebinski, in *The Kenya Pioneers,* summarizes the situation as follows:

> By now the European farmer openly recognised that in choosing land for stock formerly occupied by the Maasai, they could not go wrong. These age-old pastoralists instinctively understood the nature of the land. (1986: 161)

Trzebinski quotes a settler as saying that the Laikipia reserve "is a splendid tract of grazing country, the Maasai would not be there if it weren't" (161). The settlers pressed for removal of the northern Maasai from Laikipia, and so did the Maasai *laibon*. The *laibon*, sometimes spelled *loibon*, is a prophet, and among precolonial Maasai was a leading integrative, political figure. Lenana, a customary *laibon*, acted as government-appointed paramount chief for this divided tribe. In 1909, a second "treaty" removed the Maasai from Laikipia and consolidated the reservation in the south (see Rigby 1985: 114).

Maasai social organization changed once negotiations over territory began at the turn of the century. Before that time, the power of the elders who held sway by virtue of their monopoly of ownership of cattle and exercised power primarily through the age grade councils was held in check by the alliance of alternate generations as played out by the cooperation of the prophets and the warriors (Rigby 1989: 425-27). Male elders controlled marriage and access to adult status, but younger men, as cattle-raiding, lion-hunting warriors, were the heroes of the culture (Llewelyn-Davies 1978). At the highest, most integrative level were the prophets (*laibon*), a hub of districtwide integration. Negotiations over the Maasai reserve pushed the *laibon*, Lenana, to the fore and diminished the sharing of power among the Maasai. This increased centralization of power resulted in closer control of the *moran* [warrior] age grade and greater rule of the prophet in external relations with colonial powers (cf. Rigby 1989: 427). Rigby concludes:

> Internally, these transformations weakened the secular power of the local elders, the representatives of influence and authority over the *ilmurran* [warriors], making this relationship more ambiguous and contradictory than it already was . . . , especially in the elders' capacity to appropriate the labour of *ilmurran* [warriors] for the reproduction of the community as a whole. (427)

The removal of the Maasai sets in clear opposition colonialists' narratives about the noble savage and European progress. Some colonial officers wanted to preserve the integrity of the Maasai, and the issue, one way or another, caused the resignation of two governors. In 1912, after a disastrous first move, the Maasai went to court to fight the eviction of the northern Maasai, citing the treaty that gave the land to the Maasai forever. They lost. During the years of political and legal wrangling, the northern Maasai migrated south on their own.

During these moves many Maasai died, and they lost a large percentage of their herds. Eventually the Maasai did recover their herds and their own population increased, but the balance of cattle and humans that had been their strength was not replicated in the new territories. Neither was the famed freedom and autonomy of the warriors, nor was the power of the elders regained in the new territory. The moves marked the official end of the special status in government policy the Maasai had enjoyed since 1895 (Waller 1976: 52), but aspects of colonial discourse were resistant. The colonial government eventually did campaign against the *moran* [warriors], manipulating the *eunoto* ceremony in which junior warriors became senior warriors, after which warriors were bound to cattle raids and stock theft. This further weakened the tie between the prophets and the *moran* and strengthened the power of the elders. Elders increasingly collaborated with the colonial authorities to bring *moran* under control and to reduce the fines for cattle raids and stock theft for which elders had collective responsibility. *Moran* mounted primary resistance to change, fought schooling, rejected road work, and struggled to maintain their autonomy and esprit de corps (Tignor 1972). Rigby's excellent overview of Maasai resistance and accommodation to capitalist "penetration" contains the following passage from Tignor:

> The elders' support for government programs was not hard to understand. Collaborationist elders could benefit from government support, as was happening in Kikuyu society. More significantly, the military organization of the *moran* had become a serious liability to the elders. Not only were the defensive and military aspects of the system growing unnecessary in the new colonial era, but the illegal *moran* raids were (again) bringing onerous government fines. . . . Since the elders were obviously the wealthier element, they shouldered the heaviest burden of repayment. Their economic interest dictated cooperation with the government. (1976: 81–88)

Maasai resistance to capitalist "penetration" resulted not in the conservatism that colonialists praised and that is extolled by tourists today, but in a transformation of institutions and practices. To keep to themselves under colonialism, there had to be changes in Maasai social organization, just as there were changes in response to colonial initiatives. Two opposing accounts have been proposed as explanations for Maasai continued resistance and conservatism today. Rigby holds that the *moran* "constitute a threat to the ability of some current elders to profit (literally) from the government-mandated process of land commodification, and hence its accumulation" (1989: 437). On the other hand, David Campbell once again rings the doomsday bell for the Maasai, whose cattle-based pastoral subsistence has become increasingly undermined with individual ownership of land:

> While cattle may still represent the core of being Maasai, it is access to land upon which to graze them that now defines participation in cattle raising. Further, for many Maasai, control of land is seen as a means of acquiring wealth, not in cattle, but in the monetary economy. (1993: 269)

Within touristic Kenya, Maasai claim and refine the image of themselves as conservative, authentic natives in a rhetoric of cultural autonomy and integrity, despite the substantial changes taking place in their everyday lives.

The Kikuyu: Myth and History

A rhetoric of incorporation predominated among the Kikuyu in the early twentieth century. They demanded economic equality with Europeans—more land allocated to the Kikuyu reserves, for example, and the right to plant coffee and to sell their produce in European markets. Kikuyu demanded the respect that democratic Western principles taught them that they as God's children deserved. Many Kikuyu young men and fewer women took advantage of the colonial infrastructure of transportation and communication to expand their networks and resources. Women on tenant farms in the Central Highlands were often unpaid labor, the subsistence support system or forced labor on European estates, but women who migrated to the cities asserted their economic and social independence (see Bujra 1975; White 1990a). Working women were at the forefront of labor unrest in Nairobi (see Presley 1986; Wipper 1989).

Educated Kikuyu men, along with Luo and Indian men, were the backbone of British civil service and commerce. They saw themselves as potential equals of the white man, but they did not want to be white. Two complex sets of competing discourses moved the Kikuyu at this time: a discourse of democracy that pitted European liberty and mobility against the entrapment of tradition, and a discourse of economic equality in the face of discourses of social and political subordination. Using Laclau and Mouffe's (1985) analysis of hegemony and social structure, what is evinced here is the development of social movements spurred on by antagonisms that arise when subjects who are constructed as subordinate by a set of discourses are, at the same time, interpolated as equal by other discourses. Kikuyu were caught up in a colonial Christian discourse of equality, implying upward mobility, that was at odds with the antiprogressivist colonial discourse of subordination.

By the 1920s the Kikuyu, in the bosom of colonial habitation, were feeling the loss of land as well as the loss of culture that came with Christian mission education. This period saw the beginning of independent Kikuyu Christian churches and schools (mentioned in chapters 4 and 5). From these schools came leaders of political parties that challenged British rule by using British democratic traditions, and from these schools eventually came Mau Mau, which achieved a revolutionary amalgam of Kikuyu and British traditions. When the Kikuyu rose up against the settlers and colonial government in the Mau Mau movement after World War II, the colonialists, inspired by interpretations like Louis Leakey's, did not see their acts as politically motivated, but, as I explain in chapter 6, as an evil, nativistic religious movement run by thugs and extortionists, a throwback to primitive mentality—the result of try-ing to cram a thousand years of civilization into fifty years. To support their position, the colonialists pointed to the vile and disgusting oaths that Mau Mau used to bind adherents. But as I argued earlier, these oaths were in part in-novations based on Kikuyu practices and the British oath of loyalty that the local native council was compelled to take to show loyalty during World War II. The feature of Mau Mau that colonialists marked as most backward had clear influences from the colonialists themselves. As I tried to show in chapter 6, Mau Mau inverted a discourse that had constructed the Kikuyu as domesti-cated but deceitful, and Kikuyu were seen as wild and uncivilized.

African Discourses

The colonial discourse of subordination was based on a reification of tribe and race. From Maasai and Kikuyu perspectives, as well as others, however, there is a great deal of social, cultural, and physical overlap between the two groups. How do the Maasai and Kikuyu see their similarities and differences? While many Kikuyu and Maasai men, especially, acknowledge differences be-tween the two populations, they are not the same differences, with the same va-lences, that the colonialists used. Colonialists inscribed political identity and morality in the body, but the Kikuyu and Maasai were more likely to see it in dress, weapons, and body ornamentation. Women in each group wore distinc-tive jewelry on their necks, ears, arms, and ankles. Men used special styles of knives, spears, and shields, as well as war paint designs. The Kikuyu are some-times called Hamiticized in recognition of their many borrowings from the Maasai. Note that the old anthropological term *Hamitic* assimilates the Maasai to the children of Ham, and again places them within the Judeo-Christian tra-dition, the power of the profile.

Oral traditions of both the Kikuyu and Maasai speak of long-term links be-tween the two groups. Kikuyu and Maasai folklore suggest that a Kikuyu man rich in many cattle becomes a Maasai, and that a Maasai man poor in cattle might join forces with the Kikuyu until he rebuilds his herd. One Kikuyu cre-ation myth holds that Kikuyu farmers, Maasai herders, and Ndorobo hunters are brothers whose legacy from their father defined their different occupations and lifestyles.

Historically, the Kikuyu adopted much of Maasai military culture and or-ganization, as well as some of their religious beliefs. They valued Maasai age grade organization, and many Kikuyu groups had a "Maasai" moiety as a part of the age grade organization for men. In a study of relations between the Maa-sai and Kikuyu over the past two hundred years, Lawren (1968a, 1968b) found that cultural "transmission" from Maasai to Kikuyu was primarily limited to military and age grade organization. With first contact estimated at around

1759, the Kikuyu and Maasai met in warfare on the plains around Mount Kenya. Later in the eighteenth century the Kikuyu moved into the protective forests and, while there were occasional raids, Kikuyu-Maasai relations took on a more peaceful quality. With trade relations predominating, Kikuyu and Maasai lived in different ecological niches but in close proximity, and they intermarried over the years. At the beginning of the colonial period, around the turn of the twentieth century, "close economic and social ties between the two societies were symbolized by the Maasai concept of *osotua,* a term for 'bond friendship' that expressed the idea that preferential exchanges between two partners created a kind of kinship transcending social boundaries" (Waller 1993: 228). In a study of "acceptees and aliens" in the Maasai reserve, Waller concludes that a discourse of ethnic difference between the two groups heightened during the colonial period with the creation of separate Kikuyu and Maasai reserves:

> The state now defined what was criminal and in some circumstances ethnic identity could be a crime. Squatters [Kikuyu] in Maasailand were "out of place" both as Kikuyu in the Masai Reserve and as cultivators in a pastoral area when these categories of residence and occupation were elaborated as an integral part of the reconstruction of ethnicity by Maasai and colonial administrators alike. Their plight thus illustrates two lines of investigation—the moral economy of marginality and the criminality of "tribe"—which have yet to be fully explored in the historiography of colonial Africa. (1993: 247)

"Maasainess" was defined by pastoralism, being bound to "tradition," but could encompass moving back and forth across cultural and ecological borders. On this last point Galaty is eloquent in noting the specific and general meaning of ethnic border crossings and boundary maintenance:

> Ethnic shifting may, in fact, represent a coherent cultural process of managing long-term intergroup relationships and the negotiation of ethnic boundaries is a way of defending and reproducing, not obscuring or erasing, lines of demarcation between communities. The way Maasai identity is defined and transformed is not unique, although it appears startlingly complex given the naive simplicity of folklore concerning their pastoral identity. The interplay of linguistic, cultural and economic symbolism; the existence of boundaries marking distinctions of honour, status and class; and the negotiation of identity between distinct groups joined through affinity and co-residence may be quite general phenomena in the construction of identities and the creation of communities. Where Maasai experience may be noteworthy is in the emergence of a strongly pronounced sense of personhood and group character which has been historically strengthened rather than weakened as the group has served as an ethnic vortex, providing itself with recourse in times of stress by pulling neighbouring people into an orbit and, selectively, defining them as "Maasai." (1993: 192)

Maasai feel superior to their neighbors, but they are inclusive (see Spear 1993). In a study of aesthetics, expertise, and ethnicity in personal ornaments among the Maasai and their Okiek neighbors, who are sometimes mistaken for Maasai, Klumpp and Kratz (1993) found that with the introduction of colored beads into trade in the nineteenth century, ethnic distinctions among Kenyan tribes hardened as ethnic groups elaborated and developed color codes as diagnostic indices of ethnicity. Using strict rules for sequencing and combinations, Maasai are able to identify personal ornamentation that is Maasai, supposedly made and worn by Maasai. While other groups, like the Okiek, imitate Maasai-style beadwork, during the colonial period and today personal ornamentation was and is used by Kenyan groups as a marker of identity and membership. Klumpp and Kratz conclude:

> They [Maasai women] advertise their own identity through the beaded ornaments they create and wear. Even when they are absent, they also help state and negotiate that of their husbands, sons, brothers, and friends who wear their creations. Finally, they help create one of the principal marketed versions of Maasai-ness with the beaded ornaments sold to tourists and others, and with the displays of beadwork in popular images of Maasai. (1993: 218)

In sum, Kikuyu and Maasai recognize overlap between their two groups, and distinctions between the two groups actually heightened after the colonialist romance of the pastoralist began. Integrating some of the colonial discourse into their discourse of ethnicity, Maasai and Kikuyu do not elaborate a discourse of bodies and faces, but negotiate differences having to do with pastoralism, "tradition," language, and aesthetics. While many Maasai represent themselves as distinctive and conservative, their cultural process is one of interculturality, inclusion, and inequality.

The Air up There: The Visible Minority of Socialite Settlers

Representations of the Maasai as noble savage along with interpretations of the Kenyan landscape itself as noble contributed to different strains of colonial and national identities among Kenyan whites. Colonialists' perceptions of the sexual freedom of the Maasai encouraged the notorious "Happy Valley" lifestyle in which adultery, drugs, and alcohol were rife, inspiring the London musical theater line, "Are you married, or do you live in Kenya?" Middle-class white settlers were outraged by the shenanigans of the British aristocracy in Happy Valley, especially as they contradicted their interpretation of themselves as classless and morally superior to the sex-driven Africans. Elspeth Huxley in her 1987 memoirs goes to great pains, not one, but three times, to dissociate the majority of hardworking colonialists from the socialite settlers: there were "Never more than perhaps a dozen individuals . . . with a taste for gambling and for sexual promiscuity" (38–39), the women among them who were divorcées were not invited to Government House for official state functions (49), and some respectable women's reputations were ruined by their friendships with members of this group (56). In *The Flame Trees of Thika*, Huxley's mother was scandalized by the goings-on among the socialite settlers in Happy Valley. Trying to turn a blind eye to ladies waking up in the parlor on the afternoon after a late-night party, she upheld the middle-class values of thrift, industry, and moderation against the indulgences of the aristocracy and the indolence of the poor.

Denizens of Happy Valley (Wanjohi Valley in Maasai territory of the Rift Valley, see frontispiece) were young socialite settlers whose scandalous lifestyle echoed not only the colonialist interpretation of the sexually free Maasai, but also the European Roaring Twenties. Focusing primarily on the period between the two world wars, I contend that the internal distinctions within the white populations were created in the colony as well as in the metropole. Moving beyond unitary representations of black versus white, I indicate that particular constructions of what it meant to be white in Kenya were differently intermeshed with the African landscape and people.

Animosity between the European settlers and the British colonial government tore at social relations in this colony, which had one of the largest white settler populations in sub-Saharan Africa. Colonial officers changed as the government of the United Kingdom shifted back and forth from conservative to labor. But all in all there was something steady in the British civil service in Kenya, a longing for a golden past, a communal golden age, which they imagined was their lost heritage in Britain, now regained in the nonhierarchical organization of Kenyan tribes. For their part, settlers opposed the red tape the colonial bureaucracy imposed on their expansion and what they saw as the protection the government offered certain tribes. In various parts of the country, but especially in the White Highlands, settlers turned their country clubs into political organizations to counter the executive and the legislative branches of colonial government. This is a conventional rendering of Kenyan colonial history, which reveals an important tension between the government and the settlers but also disguises equally important differences among the settlers, implying homogeneity or at best leaving unexamined the differences among them. I would like to open up the category of white settler and discuss the construction of two different kinds of whiteness, both of which contribute to past and present tensions in Kenya.

Many of the earliest colonialists in Kenya came from a wide array of backgrounds and places, but not until the 1920s did the socialite settlers' community get started in earnest. Elspeth Huxley defends middle-class morality and the reputation of Kenya's European settlers against the disgraceful doings of the socialite settlers:

The apparent prevalence of Earls and old Etonians in Kenya's white society has created an impression that the settler population was drawn mainly from Britain's aristocracy. This was far from the case. Afrikaner transport riders, Scottish cattle traders, Italian mechanics, Irish garage owners, Jewish hoteliers, and farmers drawn from the despised and mediocre middle classes, were all there too, in much greater numbers. They did not make news, whereas errant Earls and dashing barons did. They were in a small minority. (1987: 132)

The socialite settlers were aristocrats, landed gentry, nobles and peers who as second sons might not succeed to the title. They tended to be Edwardian troublemakers, gamblers, and philanderers sent to the colony to avoid disgrace at home or wealthy adventurers following earlier European explorers. In his chatty history of whites in Kenya, popular writer Nicholas Best characterizes these settlers as "fugitives in disgrace from Edwardian society, exiled perhaps for losing too much at cards or for getting a debutante in foal, [bringing] with them the unmistakable stamp of the English upper class and printing it firmly on the new earth" (1979: 47). Socialite settlers were never in Kenya in great numbers, but had sufficient influence that their culture of sportsmanship and indulgence leaves traces in the safari tourism of Kenya today.

Only a few European women were in the colony during the early years before World War I. In *The Flame Trees of Thika*, Elspeth Huxley contrasts some of the women who made up white Kenyan society: a retired nurse who blushes at the sight of African male genitals and mends bashed skulls with aplomb; a wealthy middle-class woman bent on uplift but not willing to work hard at anything; and Huxley's own mother, optimistic, humane, and industrious. Most of these women, who came as wives or married shortly after their arrival, had the same sense of adventure as their husbands. Still, there was the job of making a home of Africa; on this Huxley is poetic and I quote at length:

They came in quest of adventure, stayed to make a colony and, in the process, destroyed what they had come to seek. They brought wives, and wives make homes. An inexorable process began. Patterned chintz replaced the sacking and amerikani spread over packing-cases to be used as tables; curtains went up over unglazed windows; china cups bought at local sales replaced tin mugs. Soon prints of the Midnight Steeplechase hung on mud-block walls, followed by the Laughing Cavalier and Van Gogh's sunflowers on roughly chiselled stone ones; creepers half-concealed corrugated-iron roofs; then came dressed stone bungalows with wide verandas, and tennis courts and stables, herbaceous borders, tea on the lawn. By stealth, civilisation had arrived. (1985: 132)

Most of the male socialite settlers married women in Britain and brought them to Kenya, though divorces and second marriages did take place in Kenya. The social and sexual relations among socialite settlers, much influenced by their perceptions of the African land and people, caused tension between them and other white settlers and with the colonial government. These men and women saw in the openness, freedom, and grandeur of Maasai territory of the eastern Rift Valley a playground for Orientalist splendor, pursuit of game, and sexual license. Alcohol, altitude, and adultery marked the lives of these socialite settlers:[6] they were "sybaritic white men and women luxuriating in a land of sunshine, parties and affairs, waited upon by servants with endless glasses of champagne" (Trzebinski 1986: 88-89).

One valley in the great Rift Valley metonymically stood for Kenya for this group of whites: Wanjohi Valley, also known as Happy Valley. At the center of the Happy Valley set was Lady Idinia Gordon, twice-divorced daughter of the eighth earl of De La Warr, who married and ran to Kenya with Josslyn Hay, earl of Erroll, whose family, as one of the "Hereditary Lord High Constables of Scotland since 1315, walked directly behind the Royals at coronations" (Fox 1988: 30). Hay had been asked to leave Eton, but had around him many Etonians. He is reported to have been very handsome, the object of many crushes among schoolboys and irresistible to women. I would think from the accounts of his womanizing and disdain for women, and his close friendship in Kenya with a man Fox calls homosexual (35), that the whole story of the sexual exploits of this Don Juan has not been revealed. We do know that he and his wife enjoyed and expected mate swapping at their parties, and that Lord Erroll took delight in cuckolding men in elaborate affairs with their wives. Lady Idinia and Lord Erroll set up housekeeping in 1924 in a large rambling house in the Wanjohi Valley called Clouds. At Clouds, there were expansive gardens, tennis courts, a horse stable, and a polo field. Clouds was also the staging place for luxurious safaris and the site of jackal hunts, which replaced the fox hunt of the English countryside. When Lord Erroll was killed in an unsolved murder in 1941, the Happy Valley scene ended.

While Happy Valley was in full swing, the socialite settlers, like other Kenyan colonialists, went into Nairobi for the horse races during the established race week and were members of the exclusive Muthaiga Club in the capital city. Visiting royals were also entertained at the Muthaiga Club. Edward, Prince of Wales, who years later, after his abdication from the British throne, became known as the duke of Windsor, visited Kenya in 1928 and was entertained by socialite settlers. Three anecdotes of events that took place at the Muthaiga Club during his trip give perspective to this period. In the first, the prince was said to have been so annoyed by the music being played at the Muthaiga Club that, assisted by the wife of one of the settlers, he threw both the records and the record player through the glass window. On another occasion a guest was roughly removed from Edward's presence by one of the erstwhile white hunters. The following explanation was offered: "Well, there is a limit, even in Kenya, and when someone offers cocaine to the heir to the

Throne, something has to be done about it, particularly when it is between courses at the dinner table" (Fox 1988: 37). Fox quotes several people who were a part of the socialite settler set or close observers who say that cocaine and morphine were in great abundance; one admired woman openly injected herself at the dinner table, between courses. The last anecdote involving the Prince of Wales is reported by Karen Blixen. It seems that his date, who later became quite an outrageous character in the socialite settler set, had at dinner at the Muthaiga Club bombarded the prince with big pieces of bread from across the table, then "finished up by rushing at him, overturning his chair and rolling him around on the floor" (quoted in Fox 1988: 54). While visiting royalty had given over to the spectacle of Africa, the colonial government, in opposition to the socialite settlers, was at the same time trying to set standards of decency and morality (Huxley 1987: 47).

A popular history of this period, published in 1979, describes the Happy Valley lifestyle:

[There were] days of opulent manor houses, flowing green lawns and syces to hold your horse's head while you picnicked on the grass overlooking a wide view that somehow always seemed to include Mount Longnot, volcanic setting for the Kingdom ruled by Ayesha, Rider Haggard's *She* [a popular image from the adventure story of the archetype of the great white hunter]. The altitude was high, the air clean and it was a life of laziness and laughter and long, lingering looks between fit men and their best friends' wives, leading invariably to strange beds and a reputation for casual promiscuity that ultimately gave the place and the people the enduring nickname of Happy Valley. (Best 1979: 103-4)

The opulence and indulgence of life in Happy Valley was founded on the openness and freedom felt by these privileged people outside of the metropole.

I argue that their appropriation of the sociality of sexuality of Kenya and of the much-praised noble Maasai is at work in this colonial discourse. Elspeth Huxley in *Out in the Midday Sun*, a memoir of her experiences in Kenya, states that a type of Maasai worship prevailed among many Europeans, sparked by their envy of the freedom and excitement in the young Maasai warriors' lives, especially the danger of the hunt and their sexual freedom (1987: 75). Huxley complained that the sound of African drums in the distance hinted at "human sacrifices" and the "walking dead" (38), but foremost in her mind (and body?) in the presence of African dancers was the erotic:

The male dancers jumped up and down with tremendous energy and thumping, the ground seemed to shake under their feet, and all the time they chanted a refrain. Drums beat—no other instruments were played—with a compulsive rhythm. The young women, with bunches of grass fore and aft and masses of beads, like the men painted with chalk and smeared with red ochre, also jumped and thumped, but went in even more for swaying and rolling their hips. After a while the dance became what was generally called suggestive; explicit would be a more accurate word. No bones were made about the dance being a thoroughly erotic affair. (37)

Despite the government and missionary attempts to curtail them, colonialists indulged in support of large-scale African dances or *ngomas*. Nicholas Best recalls that Karen Blixen was always coming into conflict with the government because of her *ngomas*, which usually consisted of "naked men and women waffling their private parts at each other before dashing off into the darkness" (1979: 119). For people like socialite settler Raymond Trafford, this was intoxicating. Evelyn Waugh writes in his diary of Trafford: "He got very drunk and brought a sluttish girl back to the house. He woke me up later to tell me he had just rogered her and her mama, too" (quoted in Fox 1988: 36). Is this an English perversion of the Maasai warrior's (and Kikuyu) taking two young women to bed with them?

One of the best chronicles of the sexuality that was a part of this particular construction of whiteness is the volume *White Mischief: The Murder of Lord Erroll*, first published in 1982. Like Huxley, James Fox, the author of *White Mischief*, presents the Happy Valley feather game, in which sexual partners for the evening were determined by blowing a feather and seeing where it landed. Only in the movie version was the possibility of same-sex partners broached. Fox goes on to describe parties given by Lord Erroll and Lady Idinia, which began in Lady Idinia's elaborate bathroom, where typically their guests watched her bathe and dress. After this, feasts, alcohol, drugs (cocaine and heroin), and sex—private and group—were on the party agenda.

I do not mean to say that these sexual practices occurred only in Kenya: the period of Happy Valley supremacy, from before World War I to just after the start of World War II, saw a loosening of sexual mores in many parts of Europe. But I do suggest that a particular group of whites, with the wherewithal to buy tracts of thousands and sometimes hundreds of thousands of acres of land and with a sense of mastery over African land and people, identified themselves with the majesty of the land and the open sexuality of the people they ruled. Their own story of how they came to identify as Kenyans emphasizes the money they poured into the country as one after another of their ranching and farming schemes failed, bringing bankruptcy and suffering. But I suggest that the identity of these white Kenyans was equally involved with their perception of the nobility of the spirit of the Maasai, with the freedom and sociality of Maasai sexuality.

Socialite settlers left their mark on Kenya in the horsey set, polo fields, sport hunting, and luxurious safaris, but a different population of whites who probably never had the audacity to ask to be remembered has probably had a more profound effect on the black people and the land of Kenya. They are the women and men of the British middle class who, granted land in Kenya as their military pensions, came to Kenya in large numbers after World War I. They found there not only the socialite settlers but also missionaries, civil servants, railway workers, and other farmers and ranchers. After the first decade of the twentieth century, more white women came into the colony, and divisions along color lines hardened. Even while women as farmers and farmers' wives set up first aid stations and clinics for Africans, interrelations between Africans and whites decreased. Middle-class women's civilizing mission put a stop to everyday practices of open sexual exploitation of African women, girls, and boys. Trzebinski and Best both underscore the sexual exploitation of the African population before the influx of domesticating white women. Citing a report of a railway chief of police at the turn of the century, Best comments that "wee Nandi girls and some Lumbwa and Wa-Kambasie and a whole lot of little boys and girls" were used for sex (1979: 26). Trzebinski is almost apologetic in her ode to the rugged men who pioneered Kenya who traveled freely, mocked authority, and took "an African girl for the night" (1986: 31). She praises these early settlers, even as she recognizes the excesses of some of the later generation of white hunters who did not live off the land, but on the fees clients paid or on illegal trade in elephant tusks (see also J. MacKenzie 1988):

> The early pioneers and administrators lived mostly alone. Few men had white female companionship or domestic ties. They were free to travel, at liberty to mock authority, to take an African girl for the night and remain as anonymous as they wished. . . . Their lives were their own to put at risk and sometimes they died as a result. (Trzebinski 1986: 31)

Middle-class men, it seems, were not above having sexual relations with Africans, but the openness of those relations, within the context of racial inequality, decreased with the civilizing influence of colonial women.

Ann Stoler (1989), in an examination of the politics of race and sexual morality in twentieth-century colonial cultures, reaches a conclusion relevant to the changes that occurred in Kenya once the settler population expanded and the colonial government began to enforce more rigid racial policies:

> The tropics provided a site of European pornographic fantasies long before conquest was underway, but with a sustained European presence in colonized territories, sexual prescriptions by class, race and gender became increasingly central to the politics of rule and subject to new forms of scrutiny by colonial states. (635)

Many of the middle class settled on generous plots in the eastern part of the White Highlands not far from the capital city of Nairobi in Kikuyu territory.

Like the socialite settlers, they had their differences with the colonial government: they wanted more financial help in building their farms, more land to be
made available from the African reservations and Crown land, and white settler
rule rather than rule from the metropole. Unlike the wealthy and privileged socialite settlers whose distinctiveness was vested in their sensibilities and sensu-
alities, the middle class was concerned with establishing control and with creating a laboring class of Africans. To this end the Kikuyu who were displaced
from their land were hired back by the white settlers as workers on their farms,
in their houses, and in their businesses.

The success of the farmer in the White Highlands was dependent upon the
Kikuyu. Perhaps because of this, the farmer most feared the Kikuyu, and
maybe feared becoming like the Kikuyu. Robert Ruark in *Something of Value*
(discussed in chapter 6) configures the white man's fear that the savagery of the
African is only masked by civilization, and that in learning to adapt to African
sensibilities his own mask might slip.

The representation of the Kikuyu created by white farmers is similar to the
colonial pastoral of the British civil servant. Both long for a golden past, and the
possibility of gaining even a glimpse of the great communal past is lost as the
once egalitarian natives become grotesque imitators of the British or, worse, the
savage destroyers of a civilization the British both love and despair of.

In making their claim to Kenyan national identity, the middle-class white
farmers also emphasize their suffering and sacrifice, the loss of children and
other loved ones to the ravages and diseases of Africa. In addition, they point to
their knowledge of the land, their transformative technical know-how, and the
social and economic institutions that they built. White expertise and knowledge were the ways middle-class colonialists appropriated Africa. As Ranger
puts it, "It emerged clearly that the claim to 'expertise' was an essential part of
the local white self-image in Africa from the beginnings of colonialism" (1979:
468). Middle-class whiteness was constructed in opposition to the socialite settlers who brought opulence and decadence to the colony; the middle class,
with all its discontents, brought civilization.

Noble Savage, Spiteful Servant, Socialite Settler: Sex and Power in Kenyan Colonial Discourses, A Summary

Colonialist narratives of the Maasai as beautiful and noble justified a colonial
policy of preservation of Maasai culture, even if the Maasai had to be moved
from one part of the country to another to do it. The colonialists' racial aesthetic not only enabled them to maintain the myth of the noble savage while
appropriating Maasai land, but also, by contrasting the untouched native to
the untrustworthy servant, reinforced restrictive colonial labor practices for the

Kikuyu. The Kikuyu, farmers in what became known as the White Highlands, were among the first to pressure the colonial government in Nairobi and the colonial office in London for more land, greater participation in government, and recognition of the viability of their cultural traditions and innovations. Mission-educated and landless young Kikuyu men argued for more land and for schools and churches independent of missionary influence, while many older men strove to keep the privileges and rewards of colonial-government-backed chiefs and councils and also argued for more land for the Kikuyu people. The Maasai, proud of their independence from Europeans and superiority to other African groups, ironically changed their society in their efforts to preserve it.

Kikuyu women, like Maasai women, were at first subject to colonialism through the men of their groups, but within the first two decades of the twentieth century Kikuyu women had risen up with men in opposition to colonial policies. In white colonial discourse, young Kikuyu women, unlike the alluring Maasai maidens, were seen as workhorses, laboring under heavy loads for their male relatives in the native reserves or mobilized for forced labor by those in the employ of whites. As the colonialists saw it, the Maasai following their herds of cattle were unmoved by the appeal of European culture: they were the authentic native in a familiar narrative in which nature's aristocrats resist modernization but, because they are proud and aloof, are doomed. The Kikuyu, on the other hand, were increasingly thought of as cunning young men in trousers trying to outwit both the colonialists and their own no longer revered elders.

Images of the Maasai as arrogant black racists helped justify European racism, and images of the Maasai as physically and sexually free fueled the European imagination. Europeans played out their pornographic fantasies within the racial divide in Happy Valley with "glorious entertainment in an exhilarating landscape, surrounded by titled guests and many, many servants" (Fox 1988: 2).

An imperative for the British middle class was to maintain the prestige and standing of the white race, to protect white privilege through control of morality and through control of the means of production. But such a neat moral order could not be maintained in the face of aristocratic dissoluteness, white African degeneracy, downward mobility of the middle class, and the demands of Africans for more land and cultural autonomy. White prestige was built on middle-class morality and discipline and on the maintenance of distinct boundaries between the colonizer and the colonized. This boundary was transgressed by poor and uneducated whites. The existence of second-generation British youth who could achieve little more than artisan status and the influx of minimally educated whites from South Africa threatened colonialist hegemony. The trouble with the English in Kenya, as Huxley puts in the thoughts of an Afrikaner colonialist, is that they value feudal loyalty to their retainers over solidarity of the white race against the blacks (1959: 51).

The Kenyan landscape attracted a wide range of colonialists. For some of them, their ability to live high up, to possess a vast, majestic landscape, made their heads light with power and possibility. While many whites wore pith helmets and covered their spines with strips of felt to ward off the debilitating and lascivious effects of the tropical sun on the central nervous system, the socialite settlers reveled in the effects of the land and people of Kenya. In reassessing colonialism in Kenya, I have highlighted the role of racism and sexuality in constructing political subjects and the multiplicity and overlapping subjectivities among white settlers and African natives. With this work I challenge conventional wisdom about what whites made out of Africa, and I indicate what Africa made out of them.

Notes

1. Introduction: Social Theory and Colonialism

1. The Imperial British East Africa Company (IBEA) was awarded a Royal Charter in 1888, after Germany and Britain signed accords defining their spheres of influence in East Africa. In 1895 the IBEA relinquished its interest and Kenya became part of the East African Protectorate. Kenya became a colony in 1905.

2. My original fieldwork, conducted in Murang'a, Kenya, in 1971–72, was supported by National Institute of Mental Health grant number 71-1238. I returned to Kenya in 1982 and 1984.

3. Cross-checking and contextualizing several sources (Routledge and Routledge 1910; Middleton and Kershaw 1965; Cagnolo 1933; Lambert 1956; Leakey 1977; Kenyatta 1938) on the late-nineteenth- and early-twentieth-century Kikuyu provides this brief sketch of the Kikuyu. Later I will more fully take up the production of colonial ethnographies of the Kikuyu.

4. Peter Rogers (1979), in a study of early relations between the Kikuyu and the British in the years 1890–1905, recounts many of the names of Kikuyu leaders. These include as major players Waiyaki, Karuri, and Kinanjui and as lesser players Mugi, Gatama, Katchundo, and Kirago.

5. From the Old Testament:

8 And the Lord said unto Moses, Make thee a fiery serpent, and set it upon a pole: and it shall come to pass, that every one that is bitten, when he looketh upon it, shall live.

9 And Moses made a serpent of brass, and put it upon a pole, and it came to pass, that if a serpent had bitten any man, when he beheld the serpent of brass, he lived. (Numbers 21:8–9)

6. Novels and interviews give some clues to this discourse. In Nigeria, Chinua Achebe writing *Things Fall Apart* against Joyce Cary's *Mister Johnson* created a world almost parallel to colonialists', but when the two do converge, it is disastrous for the African. Kenyan novelist Ngugi wa Thiong'o, previously known as James Ngugi, in his first novels, *Weep Not Child* and *The River Between,* similarly insists on representing Africans not in relation to particular colonialists but in relation to the hegemonic power and discourse of colonialism. What is called for is a deconstruction of the figure of the colonialists and the metaphors of power and subordination.

7. Orvar Lofgren's study of the development of Swedish national culture (1989b) has led him to some general insights in understanding how "traditional culture" is constructed through "itemization, fragmentation, reshuffling as elements are organized into new patterns" (1989a: 368).

2. The Production of Women: Kikuyu Gender and Politics at the Beginning of the Colonial Era

1. In using older colonial sources I look for consistency but scrutinize the exceptions for telling surprises. I measure the arguments and theories against standards for social analysis, always wary of the unparsimonious, and of biological or racial explanations. The language and rhetoric of the works themselves sometimes become serious elements in my use of colonial sources. I pay attention to who published the works and whom the authors cite. I ask if the authors have presented any information that can be used outside of their own frameworks. Chapters 4 and 5 are thorough examples of this reading strategy.

2. There is some controversy about where the Kikuyu Garden of Eden, Mukurue wa Gathanga, the chief area of dispersal within the Central Highlands, actually is. Muriuki (1974) offers a reasonable reconstruction of the introduction of the Kikuyu into the area generally known as Kikuyuland. By the middle of the nineteenth century, Kikuyu had expanded north and south from the central district and were moving westward toward the Nyandura (Aberdares) Mountains.

3. Though, as Leakey notes, woman-woman marriage "was not rare" among the Kikuyu before 1903, there has been little historical study of this practice. One of the best works on this subject is Oboler 1980.

4. "The wild gourd when ripe contains a soft pulp in which are its seeds. This pulp resembles the liquid fat obtained by melting the sheep's tail" (Katherine Routledge 1910: 294).

5. I am not sure what the exact phrase is in Kikuyu, but it is clear from Davison's recent text (1989), the Routledges' 1910 work, and my own notes that "talking nonsense" is related to absence of knowledge gained during the initiation ceremony and in large part has to do with lack of sexual knowledge and rules for proper conduct in the presence of those senior to you.

6. Anthropologist Greet Kershaw, who finds this tale about greed and laziness with the moral "Once wrong, always wrong," in a personal communication agrees that Wachera must be made a wife and mother through the transfer of property: "By being abducted and not paid for Wachera *is not married,* does not belong to her 'husband' and her child is thus neither her 'husband's' child, nor in the legal sense Wamwea's sister's child. Without brideprice the child is legally the child of Wamwea's and Wachera's *father.* This comes out in the fact that, when they try to rectify the situation, Wachera's 'husband' begins by offering the *'kenda,'* the ten goats which signal the beginning of the *ruracio* [bridewealth] negotiations. He does not accept the goats, nor the same kenda in cows, and so the 'husband' must continue to offer larger and larger payments."

7. By the time of the establishment of the Kenya colony, relations between the Maasai and Kikuyu had worsened, and it is likely that the story intimates a Maasai warrior party on a raid for women. But two things argue against that interpretation: Why

would Maasai take only the sister and not the cattle? And neither Maasai nor Kikuyu typically took women as war booty in the precolonial period. Writing of an expedition in 1883–84, under the Imperial British East African Company charter, Joseph Thomson remarks in amazement: "Curiously enough, though they are eternally at war to the knife with each other, there is a compact between them not to molest the womenfolk of either party. Hence, the curious spectacle is exhibited of Masai women wending their way with impunity to a Kikuyu village, while their relatives are probably engaged in a deadly fight close at hand. In the same way the Kikuyu women frequently carry grain to the Masai kraals to exchange for hides" (Thomson 1962 [1885]: 83).

8. In a personal communication, anthropologist Greet Kershaw advised me that "Kikuyu in the Southern, and I would venture in the other areas as well, *are* goat-linked to their sisters to the degree that he can call her 'my *mburi*' [goat] and that in some way or other *mburi* received for her will make part of the *ruracio* [bridewealth] given to another *mbari* [family] for his wife."

3. Kikuyu Women and Sexuality

1. Leakey refers to the last act before admission into adulthood performed by some male initiates (those in the Kikuyu guild as opposed to the Maasai guild—two initiation categories for the Kikuyu) as *kwīhaka mūūnyū* (1977: 24, 687, 691-92, 1364), which means literally to paint oneself with the white saline earth found in swampy places. In this "ceremony" groups of initiates searched for and gang raped or performed other sexual abuses on "a married woman and not an unmarried girl, [who] had to be a complete stranger to them" (1977: 691). Leakey explains: "They might not, of course, ever again rape anyone without penalty, but this sex act performed at the instigation of their elders indicated that all the prohibitions of their boyhood were now laid to one side and that they were about to enter a stage of life in which sex played one of the most important parts" (1977: 692). On the day of the "ceremonial rape," the young women initiates stayed at home. The next day, they, with young men, put on the cloak of adulthood.

Father Cagnolo, who concurs that a boy must commit "rape on a stranger" to legally become a man (1933: 257), further states, in a discussion of Kikuyu morals, that "the warriors boast of and exercise, with public consent, certain rights over the girls, even if their parents be unwilling, *even if the girls themselves are in opposition*" (1933: 257, emphasis added).

2. The term commonly used in sub-Saharan Africa for female genital mutilation is "female circumcision." This term is sometimes used to cover three different kinds of operations: (1) clitoridectomy, the removal of the prepuce or hood of the clitoris; (2) excision, removal of the clitoris and parts of the labia minora (the inner lips of the vulva); and (3) infibulation or pharaonic circumcision, removal of the clitoris and labia minora and majora (inner and outer lips of the vulva) and stitching or suturing together the two sides of the vulva, leaving a small orifice to permit urine and menstrual flow. Only clitoridectomy is analogous to male circumcision, and often more than the hood of the clitoris is removed in the actual operations. The other two operations are more comparable, in terms of physiology and anatomy, to removing or cutting part of the penis.

Kikuyu typically perform clitoridectomy. Though sometimes the tip of the clitoris is cut and parts of the labia are removed, the vulva is not stitched or sutured.

I most often use the specific term "clitoridectomy" to refer to the Kikuyu practice, even though they say "female circumcision," "initiation," and "irua." *Irua* refers to initiation, the circumcision ceremony, and is also used to refer to the operation itself. The phrase "female genital mutilation" is gaining ground with women organized against these practices.

4. Louis Leakey and the Kikuyu

1. *The Southern Kikuyu before 1903* was edited by Gladys Beecher and Jane Ensminger, whose combined knowledge on East Africa, cultural anthropology, the Kikuyu language, and botany enabled them to correct, edit, and reorganize Leakey's magnum opus. In the book's foreword, Mary Leakey, on behalf of her sons and herself, thanks the editors for their "dedication and unremitting hard work."

6. Mau Mau Discourses

1. I read the most recent work on the colonial period by Bruce Berman and John Lonsdale, *Unhappy Valley: Conflict in Kenya and Africa* (London: J. Cumley, Nairobi: Heineman Kenya, and Athens: Ohio University Press, 1992), after I had finished writing this book. Their work on Mau Mau is stunningly comprehensive and incisive, especially Lonsdale's previously unpublished chapters on the moral economy of Mau Mau.

Notable work by women scholars has begun to fill in the picture of women in Kenya and particularly women's activities during the Mau Mau period. Examples of this outstanding scholarship are Presley (1988, 1992), L. White (1990a, 1990b), and Wipper (1977, 1989).

While every topic I investigate is looked at for what it reveals about race, class, gender, and sexuality, my study of Mau Mau discourse opens the way for further examination of the production of images and discourse by and about Kenyan women.

7. Race, Class, Empire, and Sexuality

1. The following summary of the development of East African sport hunting is taken from John M. MacKenzie (1988). MacKenzie sees the European nineteenth-century hunting world as part of the development of athleticism in the British middle and upper classes, and as one of the manifestations of romanticism, bringing humans face to face with nature in the raw. In Kenya, animal meat, hide, and trophies were a part of military campaigns, and the meat was especially vital in provisioning the patrols. Trade in ivory, which had gone on for centuries in East Africa, received a boost when the Imperial British East Africa Company combined its pacification plan with elephant hunting. While some colonialists wanted to restrict all Africans to reserves, as reserves of labor, preservationists believed that the British should maintain humans and wildlife in their natural condition. The foundation of game preservationist policies led directly to the encouragement of elite sport hunting. Winston Churchill in 1907 and U.S. President Theodore Roosevelt in 1909 hunted in Kenya, adding to the allure of big game hunting. The transformation of hunting into elite sport hunting was accomplished, in part, by the systematic exclusion of Africans from subsistence and independent commercial hunting.

2. The relationship between power and knowledge is well played out here: theories of degeneracy accompany the rising number of prostitutes, and the increase in the crime rate is concomitant with the advances of industrial capitalism.

3. I am grateful to my University of California, Santa Cruz, colleague Diane Gifford-Gonzalez for laying out this formula for the noble savage as marginalized other. Professor Gifford-Gonzalez, who has spent a great deal of time in Kenya among a pastoralist group related to the Maasai, also brought me the "Out of Africa" coffee label that appears in this volume.

4. Students of human physical variation recognize the sociopolitical origins of many of the theories of racial difference and are reluctant to place great meaning on the concept of geographic race in explaining species variation. In studying clinal distribution—the geographic range of a phenotype or genetic characteristic—they caution that sharp differences between adjacent populations may be overlooked, and that sampling problems may skew the frequencies for any population (Molnar 1992: 204-8). Hiernaux, who prefers to chart genetic and phenotypic differences in "breeding populations," places the Maasai within the category "elongated Africans," people with an ancestral adaptation to hot, dry climates—tending to give them, on the whole, a slender build, light weight, and narrow heads and noses (1974: 141). The viability of this category for Kenyan Maasai, with their inclusive "mating circle," is questionable. In this case, it is especially important to note the great plasticity of human development (see Molnar 1992: 136-82).

5. See Sobania (1993) for a discussion of the late-nineteenth-century residents in the Laikipia section. Trzebinski (1986) observes that the resignations of two colonial governors were connected with issues involving the Maasai, especially the eviction of the Maasai from their second home. Maasai pastoralists put on pressure for more pasturage as their herds increased and as they refused to use the road linking the northern and southern reserves because of the outbreak of rinderpest and other cattle diseases in the area of the road. At the same time, colonialists were finding the land just outside Laikipia unsuitable for grazing and were petitioning the colonial government to allow them to settle in the Laikipia reserve itself.

6. Trzebinski credits the British writer Cyril Connolly with coming up with the phrase "alcohol, altitude, and adultery" as "the three As" that most influenced Kenya settlers (1986: 86).

Bibliography

Abrahams, Peter. 1956. *A Wreath for Udomo* (1971 edition). New York: Collier.

Abu-Lughod, Lila. 1986. *Veiled Sentiments: Honor and Poetry in a Bedouin Society.* Berkeley and London: University of California Press.

———. 1991. Writing against Culture. In *Recapturing Anthropology: Working in the Present,* edited by Richard G. Fox, 137–62. Santa Fe, N.M.: School of American Research Press.

Achebe, Chinua. 1959. *Things Fall Apart.* New York: Fawcett Crest.

Aidoo, Ama. 1970. *No Sweetness Here.* London: Longman.

Ambler, Charles H. 1989. The Renovation of Custom in Colonial Kenya: The 1932 Generation Succession Ceremonies in Embu. *Journal of African History* 30 (1): 139-56.

Appadurai, Arjun. 1991. Global Ethnoscapes: Notes and Queries for a Transnational Anthropology. In *Recapturing Anthropology: Working in the Present,* edited by Richard G. Fox, 191-210. Santa Fe, N.M.: School of American Research Press.

Aptheker, Bettina. 1982. *Woman's Legacy: Essays on Race, Sex, and Class in American History.* Amherst: University of Massachusetts Press.

Arab Women's Solidarity Association. 1988. Women and Health in Sudan. In *Women of the Arab World: The Coming Challenge,* edited by Nahid Toubia, translated by Nahed El Gamal, 98-109. London: Zed.

Armstrong, Nancy, and Leonard Tennenhouse. 1992. *The Imaginary Puritan: Literature, Intellectual Labor, and the Origins of Personal Life.* Berkeley and Oxford: University of California Press.

Armstrong, Sue. 1990. Female Circumcision: Call to Outlaw Needless Mutilation. *New Scientist,* December 15, 11.

Bailey, Paul. 1984. Review of *Out of Africa,* by Isak Dinesen. *Contemporary Literary Criticism* 29:164. (Originally printed September 11, 1981, in the *Times Literary Supplement,* 1025.)

Barnett, Donald, and Karari Njama. 1966. *Mau Mau from Within: Autobiography and Analysis of Kenya's Peasant Revolt.* London: MacGibbon and Kee.

Baudrillard, J. 1983. *Simulations.* New York: Semiotext(e).

Beecher, Leonard J. 1938. The Stories of the Kikuyu. *Africa* 11 (1): 80-87.

Benjamin, Walter. 1969. The Storyteller: Reflections on the Work of Nikolai Leskov *and* Thesis on the Philosophy of History. In *Illuminations*, edited by Hannah Ardent, translated by Harry Zohn, 83-100, 253-64. New York: Schocken.

Bennett, Lynn. 1983. *Dangerous Wives and Sacred Sisters: Social and Symbolic Roles of High-Caste Women in Nepal.* New York: Columbia University Press.

Berman, Bruce J. 1976. Bureaucracy and Incumbent Violence: Colonial Administration and the Origins of the "Mau Mau" Emergency in Kenya. *British Journal of Political Science* 6 (2): 143-75.

——. 1990. *Control and Crisis in Colonial Kenya: The Dialectic of Domination.* London: James Currey; Nairobi: Heinemann Kenya; Athens: Ohio University Press.

Berman, Bruce J., and John Lonsdale. 1991. Louis Leakey's Mau Mau: A Study in the Politics of Knowledge. *History and Anthropology* 5 (2): 143-204.

Best, Nicholas. 1979. *Happy Valley: The Story of the English in Kenya.* London: Secker and Warburg.

Black and Red Magic. *Time,* September 1, 1952, 25.

Bledsoe, Caroline. 1976. Women's Marital Strategies among the Kpelle of Liberia. *Journal of Anthropological Research* 32 (4): 372-89.

Bloodshed. *Time,* April 6, 1953, 40.

Boddy, Janice. 1982. Womb as Oasis: The Symbolic Context of Pharaonic Circumcision in Rural Northern Sudan. *American Ethnologist* 9 (4): 682-98.

——. 1989. *Wombs and Alien Spirits: Women, Men, and the Zar Cult in Northern Sudan.* Madison: University of Wisconsin Press.

Bourdieu, Pierre. 1990. *The Logic of Practice.* Translated by Richard Nice. Stanford, Calif.: Stanford University Press.

Boyles, Denis. 1988. *African Lives: White Lies, Tropical Truth, Darkest Gossip, and Rumblings of Rumor—from Chinese Gordon to Beryl Markham, and Beyond.* New York: Ballantine.

Braudel, Fernand. 1975. *Capitalism and Material Life, 1400-1800.* Translated by Miriam Kockan. New York: Harper Colophon.

——. 1981. *The Structures of Everyday Life: The Limits of the Possible.* Translation revised by Sian Reynolds. New York: Harper & Row.

Brown, Richard C., Judith E. Brown, and Okako B. Ayowa. 1992. Vaginal Inflammation in Africa. Letter to the *New England Journal of Medicine*, August 20, 572.

Buijtenhuijs, Robert. 1982. *Essays on Mau Mau.* Leiden, The Netherlands: African Studies Centre.

Bujra, Janet M. 1975. Women "Entrepreneurs" of Early Nairobi. *Canadian Journal of African Studies* 9 (2): 213-34.

Burning Spears. *Time,* April 20, 1953, 42.

Bwana Tom Goes to Court. *Time,* June 23, 1958, 23.

Cagnolo, Father C. 1933. *The Akikuyu: Their Customs, Traditions and Folklore.* Nyeri, Kenya: Mission Printing School.

Campbell, David J. 1993. Land as Ours, Land as Mine: Economic, Political and Ecological Marginalization in Kajiado District. In *Being Maasai: Ethnicity and Identity in East Africa*, edited by Thomas Spear and Richard Waller, 258-72. London: James Currey; Dar Es Salaam: Mkuki na Nyota; Nairobi: EAEP; Athens: Ohio University Press.

Bibliography

Campbell, Donald T. 1967. Stereotypes and the Perception of Group Differences. *American Psychologist* 22 (10): 817-29.

Carothers, John. 1954. *The Psychology of Mau Mau.* Nairobi: Printed by the government printer.

Cary, Joyce. 1951. *Mister Johnson.* New York: Harper.

Caveat Emptor. Review of *Something of Value,* by Robert Ruark. *Time,* May 2, 1955, 108.

Challenge, Then Shoot. *Time,* April 13, 1953, 38-39.

Chamberlin, J. Edward, and Sander L. Gilman. 1985. *Degeneration: The Dark Side of Progress.* New York: Columbia University Press.

Chatterjee, Partha. 1986. Nationalism as a Problem in the History of Political Ideas. In *Nationalist Thought and the Colonial World: A Derivative Discourse?* 1-35. London: Zed.

Clark, Carolyn M. 1975. *Kinship Morality in the Interaction Pattern of Some Kikuyu Families.* Ann Arbor: University Microfilms.

———. 1978. Female Productivity and Male Position Analysis of a Kikuyu Folktale. Paper presented to the Southwestern Anthropological Association, San Francisco.

———. 1980. Land and Food, Women and Power, in Nineteenth Century Kikuyu. *Africa* 50 (4): 357-70.

———. 1989. Louis Leakey as Ethnographer: On *The Southern Kikuyu before 1903. Canadian Journal of African Studies* 23 (3): 380-98.

———. 1990. Race, Class, Gender, and Sexuality: On Angela Y. Davis' *Women, Culture, and Politics. Social Justice* 17 (3): 195-202.

Clifford, James. 1982. *Person and Myth: Maurice Leenhardt in the Melanesian World* (1992 edition). Durham, N.C., and London: Duke University Press.

———. 1986. Introduction: Partial Truths *and* On Ethnographic Allegory. In *Writing Culture: The Poetics and Politics of Ethnography,* edited by James Clifford and George E. Marcus, 1-26, 98-121. Berkeley: University of California Press.

Clough, Marshall S., and Kennell A. Jackson, comps. 1975. *Mau-Mau Syllabus: Part I* and *A Bibliography on Mau-Mau, Syllabus: Part II.* Sacramento, Calif.: Clough.

Cohen, David William, and E. S. Atieno Odhiambo. 1989. *Siaya: The Historical Anthropology of an African Landscape.* London: James Currey; Nairobi: Heinemann Kenya; Athens: Ohio University Press.

Cole, Johnetta B. 1980. Women in Cuba: The Revolution within the Revolution. In *Comparative Perspectives of Third World Women,* edited by Beverly Lindsay, 162-78. New York: Praeger.

Cole, Sonia. 1975. *Leakey's Luck: The Life of Louis Seymour Bazett Leakey, 1903-1972.* New York and London: Harcourt Brace Jovanovich.

Collier, Jane F. 1974. Women in Politics. In *Woman, Culture, and Society,* edited by Michelle Zimbalist Rosaldo and Louise Lamphere, 89-96. Stanford, Calif.: Stanford University Press.

Colonialism's Challenge: In Asia—and now Africa—the West Is in Trouble. *Newsweek,* October 31, 1955, 40-46.

Cooke, Philip. 1990. Locality, Structure, and Agency: A Theoretical Analysis. *Cultural Anthropology* 5 (1): 3-15.

Bibliography

Corfield, F. D. 1960. *Historical Survey of the Origin and Growth of Mau Mau*. London: H.M. Stationery Office.

Coward, Rosalind. 1983. *Patriarchal Precedents: Sexuality and Social Relations*. London and Boston: Routledge and Kegan Paul.

Davidson, Basil. 1987. The Ancient World and Africa: Whose Roots? *Race and Culture* 29 (2): 1-15.

Davis, Angela Y. 1981. *Women, Race, and Class* (1983 edition). New York: Vintage.

—————. 1989. *Women, Culture, and Politics*. New York: Random House.

Davis, Natalie Zemon. 1975. *Society and Culture in Early Modern France: Eight Essays*. Stanford, Calif.: Stanford University Press.

Davison, Jean. 1989. *Voices from Mutira: Lives of Rural Gikuyu Women*. London and Boulder, Colo.: Lynne Rienner.

Deal with Mau Maus. *Newsweek*, March 15, 1954, 38-40.

D'Emilio, John, and Estelle B. Freedman. 1988. *Intimate Matters: A History of Sexuality in America*. New York: Harper & Row.

Dening, Greg. 1993. The Theatricality of History Making and the Paradoxes of Acting. *Cultural Anthropology* 8 (1): 73-95.

Desmond, Jane. 1993. Where Is "The Nation?": Public Discourse, the Body, and Visual Display. *East/West Film Journal* 7 (2): 81-109.

Dickson, Kwesi Abotsia. 1982. Mission in African Countries. In *Christian Mission–Jewish Mission*, edited by Martin A. Cohen and Helga Croner, 187-206. New York: Paulist Press.

di Leonardo, Micaela, ed. 1991. Introduction. In *Gender at the Crossroads of Knowledge: Feminist Anthropology in the Postmodern Era*, 1-48. Berkeley and Los Angeles: University of California Press.

Dinesen, Isak [Karen Blixen]. 1937. *Out of Africa* (1989 edition). New York: Random House.

—————. 1960. *Shadows on the Grass* (1989 edition). New York: Random House.

Dobson, Barbara. 1954. Woman's Place in East Africa. *Corona*, December, 454-57.

Douglas, Mary. 1966. *Purity and Danger: An Analysis of Concepts of Pollution and Taboo*. New York and Washington, D.C.: Praeger; London: Routledge and Kegan Paul.

Drake, St. Clair. 1978. Reflections on Anthropology and the Black Experience. *Anthropology and Education Quarterly* 9 (2): 85-109.

Duberman, Martin B. 1988. *Paul Robeson*. New York: Knopf.

Dudley, Edward, and Maximillian Novak, eds. 1972. *The Wild Man Within: An Image in Western Thought from the Renaissance to Romanticism*. Pittsburgh: University of Pittsburgh Press.

Edemikpong, Hannah. 1989. Education and Female Circumcision. Newsletter from the Women's Centre, Akwa Ibom State, Nigeria.

Edgerton, Robert B. 1989. *Mau Mau: An African Crucible*. New York: Free Press; London: Collier Macmillan.

Ehrenreich, Barbara. 1983. *The Hearts of Men: American Dreams and the Flight from Commitment*. Garden City, N.Y.: Doubleday.

El Dareer, Asma. 1982. *Woman, Why Do You Weep? Circumcision and its Consequences*. London: Zed.

El Saadawi, Nawal. 1980. *The Hidden Face of Eve: Women in the Arab World*. Translated by Sherif Hetata. London: Zed.

Enloe, Cynthia. 1990. *Bananas, Beaches, and Bases: Making Feminist Sense of International Politics*. Berkeley and Los Angeles: University of California Press.

Epstein, A. L. 1958. *Politics in an Urban African Community*. Manchester: Rhodes-Livingstone Institute, Manchester University Press.

————. 1981. *Urbanization and Kinship: The Domestic Domain on the Copperbelt of Zambia, 1950–1956*. London and New York: Academic Press.

————. 1992. *Scenes from African Urban Life: Collected Copperbelt Essays*. Edinburgh: Edinburgh University Press.

Esedebe, P. Olisanwuche. 1982. *Pan-Africanism: The Idea and Movement, 1776-1963*. Washington, D.C.: Howard University Press.

Etienne, Mona, and Eleanor Leacock, eds. 1980. *Women and Colonization: Anthropological Perspectives*. New York: Praeger.

Feierman, Steven. 1990. *Peasant Intellectuals: Anthropology and History in Tanzania*. Madison: University of Wisconsin Press.

Ferrell, J. E. 1987. Bone Wars. *Image* magazine, *San Francisco Chronicle*, August 23, 14-20, 34-35.

Ford, Clellan S., and Frank A. Beach. 1951. *Patterns of Sexual Behavior*. New York: Harper & Row.

Foucault, Michel. 1979. *Discipline and Punish: The Birth of the Prison*. Translated by Alan Sheridan. New York: Random House.

————. 1980. *The History of Sexuality*. Vol. 1, *An Introduction*. Translated by Robert Hurley. New York: Random House.

————. 1986. *The History of Sexuality*. Vol. 2, *The Use of Pleasure*. New York: Random House.

Fox, James. 1988. *White Mischief: The Murder of Lord Erroll*. New York: Random House.

Fox, Richard G., ed. 1991. Introduction: Working in the Present *and* For a Nearly New Culture History. In *Recapturing Anthropology: Working in the Present*, 1-16, 93-113. Santa Fe, N.M.: School of American Research Press.

Frayser, Suzanne G. 1985. *Varieties of Sexual Experience: An Anthropological Perspective on Human Sexuality*. New Haven, Conn.: HRAF Press.

From Kenya to Cape Town, Race Unrest Inflames Africa. *Newsweek*, November 3, 1952, 44-45.

Fruzzetti, Lina M. 1990. *The Gift of a Virgin: Women, Marriage, and Ritual in a Bengali Society*. Delhi: Oxford University Press.

Furedi, Frank. 1989. *The Mau Mau War in Perspective*. London: James Currey; Nairobi: Heinemann Kenya; Athens: Ohio University Press.

Galaty, John G. 1993. Maasai Expansion and the New East African Pastoralism. In *Being Maasai: Ethnicity and Identity in East Africa*, edited by Thomas Spear and Richard Waller, 61-86. London: James Currey; Dar Es Salaam: Mkuki na Nyota; Nairobi: EAEP; Athens: Ohio University Press.

Gecau, Rose. 1970. *Kikuyu Folktales*. Nairobi: East African Literature Bureau.

Geertz, Clifford. 1973. The Growth of Culture and the Evolution of Mind. In *The Interpretation of Cultures*, 55-83. New York: Basic Books.

Bibliography

General China and Friends. *Time*, March 15, 1954, 28-29.

Gessain, Monique. 1963. Coniagui Women. In *Women of Tropical Africa*, edited by Denise Paulme, translated by H. M. Wright, 17-46. London: Routledge and Kegan Paul.

Gilroy, Paul. 1991. *"There Ain't No Black in the Union Jack": The Cultural Politics of Race and Nation*. Chicago: University of Chicago Press.

Ginsburg, Faye, and Anna Lowenhaupt Tsing, eds. 1990. Introduction. In *Uncertain Terms: Negotiating Gender in American Culture*, 1-16. Boston: Beacon.

Gluckman, Max. 1940. *Analysis of a Social Situation in Modern Zululand* (1958 edition). Manchester: Rhodes-Livingstone Institute, Manchester University Press.

———. 1955. *The Judicial Process Among the Barotse of Northern Rhodesia*. Manchester: Rhodes-Livingstone Institute, Manchester University Press.

Goody, Jack. 1971. Class and Marriage in Africa and Eurasia. *American Journal of Sociology* 76 (4): 485-603.

———. 1973. Bridewealth and Dowry in Africa and Eurasia. In *Bridewealth and Dowry*, edited by Jack Goody and S. J. Tambiah, 1-58. Cambridge: Cambridge University Press.

———. 1993. *The Culture of Flowers*. Cambridge: Cambridge University Press.

Goody, Jack, and S. J. Tambiah, eds. 1973. *Bridewealth and Dowry*. Cambridge: Cambridge University Press.

Gordon, Daniel. 1991. Female Circumcision and Genital Operations in Egypt and the Sudan: A Dilemma for Medical Anthropology. *Medical Anthropology Quarterly* 5 (1): 3-14.

Griaule, Marcel. 1965. *Conversations with Ogotemmeli: An Introduction to Dogun Religious Ideas* (1975 edition). New York: Oxford University Press.

Gruenbaum, Ellen. 1982. The Movement against Clitoridectomy and Infibulation in Sudan: Public Health and the Women's Movement. *Medical Anthropology Newsletter* 13 (2): 4-12.

———. 1988. Reproductive Ritual and Social Reproduction: Female Circumcision and the Subordination of Women in Sudan. In *Economy and Class in Sudan*, edited by Norman O'Neill and Jay O'Brien, 308-25. Aldershot: Avebury.

Hackett, Alice, and James Burke. 1977. *80 Years of Best Sellers, 1895-1975*. New York and London: Bowker.

Hansen, Karen Tranberg. 1989. *Distant Companions: Servants and Employers in Zambia, 1900-1985*. Ithaca, N.Y., and London: Cornell University Press.

Haraway, Donna. 1988. Situated Knowledges: The Science Question in Feminism and the Privilege of Partial Perspective. *Feminist Studies* 14 (3): 575-601.

———. 1989. *Primate Visions: Gender, Race, and Nature in the World of Modern Science*. New York and London: Routledge.

Harrison, Faye V. 1991. Anthropology as an Agent of Transformation: Introductory Comments and Queries *and* Ethnography as Politics. In *Decolonizing Anthropology: Moving Further toward an Anthropology for Liberation*, edited by Faye V. Harrison, 1-14, 88-109. Washington, D.C.: American Anthropological Association.

Hartsock, Nancy C. M. 1988. Epistemology and Politics: Developing Alternatives to Western Political Thought. Paper presented to the International Political Science Association.

Bibliography

Hastrup, Kirsten. 1987. The Reality of Anthropology. *Ethnos* 52 (3-4): 287-300.

Haug, Frigga. 1984. Morals Also Have Two Genders. *New Left Review* 143:51-67.

Hicks, Esther K. 1993. *Infibulation: Female Mutilation in Islamic Northeastern Africa.* New Brunswick, N.J., and London: Transaction.

Hiernaux, Jean. 1974. *The People of Africa.* New York: Scribner.

Hobley, C. W. 1922. *Bantu Beliefs and Magic* (1967 edition). London: Frank Cass.

Hobsbawm, Eric, and Terence Ranger, eds. 1988. *The Invention of Tradition.* Cambridge: Cambridge University Press.

Hoffer, Carol. 1974. Madam Yoko: Ruler of the Kpa Mende Confederacy. In *Woman, Culture, and Society,* edited by Michelle Zimbalist Rosaldo and Louise Lamphere, 173-87. Stanford, Calif.: Stanford University Press.

Huxley, Elspeth. 1935. *White Man's Country: Lord Delamere and the Making of Kenya.* London: Macmillan.

————. 1939. *Red Strangers, A Novel.* New York and London: Harper Bros.

————. 1959. *Flame Trees of Thika: Memories of an African Childhood* (1986 edition). New York: Viking-Penguin.

————. 1980. Introduction. In *Out of Africa,* by Isak Dinesen, 7-12. London: Folio Society.

————. 1987. *Out in the Midday Sun.* New York: Penguin.

Isichei, Patrick. 1973. Sex in Traditional Asaba. *Cahiers d'Etudes Africaines* 13 (52): 682-99.

Jackson, Kennell A. 1976. Review of *A History of the Kikuyu, 1500-1900,* by Godfrey Muriuki. *International Journal of African Historical Studies* 9 (4): 658-65.

Jacobson, David. 1991. *Reading Ethnography.* Albany: State University of New York Press.

Jordan, Glen H. 1991. On Ethnography in an Intertextual Situation: Reading Narratives or Deconstructing Discourse? In *Decolonizing Anthropology: Moving Further toward an Anthropology for Liberation,* edited by Faye V. Harrison, 42-67. Washington, D.C.: American Anthropological Association.

Kaggia, Bildad. 1975. *Roots of Freedom, 1921-1963: The Autobiography of Bildad Kaggia.* Nairobi: East African Publishing House.

Kanogo, Tabitha. 1987. *Squatters and the Roots of Mau Mau 1905-1963.* London: James Currey; Nairobi: Heinemann Kenya; Athens: Ohio University Press.

Kapferer, Bruce, ed. 1976. *Transaction and Meaning: Directions in the Anthropology of Exchange and Symbolic Behavior.* Philadelphia: Institute for the Study of Human Issues.

Kennedy, Dane. 1987. *Islands of White: Settler Society and Culture in Kenya and Southern Rhodesia, 1890-1939.* Durham, N.C.: Duke University Press.

————. 1992. Constructing the Colonial Myth of Mau Mau. *International Journal of African Historical Studies* 25 (2): 241-60.

Kennedy, John G. 1970. Circumcision and Excision in Egyptian Nubia. *Man* 5 (2): 175-91.

————. 1978. Circumcision and Excision Ceremonies *and* Mushahara: A Nubian Concept of Supernatural Danger and the Theory of Taboo. In *Nubian Ceremonial Life: Studies in Islamic Syncretism and Cultural Change,* edited by John G. Kennedy,

Bibliography

125-70. Berkeley and Cairo: University of California Press and The American University in Cairo Press.

Kenya. *Newsweek,* August 22, 1960, 44.

Kenyatta Goes "Free." *Time,* April 27, 1959, 26.

Kenyatta, Jomo. 1938. *Facing Mt. Kenya* (1968 edition). London: Secker and Warburg.

———. 1966. *My People of the Kikuyu* and *The Life of Chief Wangombe.* Nairobi and London: Oxford University Press.

———. 1968. *Suffering without Bitterness: The Founding of the Kenya Nation.* Nairobi: East African Publishing House.

———. 1977. The Gentlemen of the Jungle. In *Winds of Change: Modern Short Stories from Black Africa,* simplified by N. P. F. Machin, 22-26. Hong Kong: Longman Group.

Kielty, Bernardine. 1952. Introduction. In *Out of Africa,* by Isak Dinesen, xi-xv. New York: Modern Library.

Kirby, Vicki. 1987. On the Cutting Edge: Feminism and Clitoridectomy. *AFS* 5 (Summer): 35-55.

Kitching, Gavin. 1980. *Class and Economic Change in Kenya: The Making of an African Petite-Bourgeoisie.* New Haven, Conn., and London: Yale University Press.

Klumpp, Donna, and Corinne Kratz. 1993. Aesthetics, Expertise, and Ethnicity: Okiek and Maasai Perspectives on Personal Ornament. In *Being Maasai: Ethnicity and Identity in East Africa,* edited by Thomas Spear and Richard Waller, 195-221. London: James Currey; Dar Es Salaam: Mkuki na Nyota; Nairobi: EAEP; Athens: Ohio University Press.

Kopytoff, Igor, ed. 1987. The Internal African Frontier: The Making of African Political Culture. In *The African Frontier: The Reproduction of Traditional African Societies,* 3-84. Indianapolis and Bloomington: Indiana University Press.

Koso-Thomas, Olayinka. 1987. *The Circumcision of Women: A Strategy for Eradication.* London and Atlantic Highlands, N.J.: Zed.

Kratz, Corinne A. 1980. Are the Okiek Really Masai? or Kipsigis? or Kikuyu? *Cahiers d'Etudes Africaines* 20 (79): 355-68.

Krymkowski, Daniel H., and Russell Middleton. 1987. Social Stratification in East Africa: Bases of Respect among Kipsigis and Kikuyu Men in Rural Kenya. *Rural Sociology* 52 (3): 379-88.

Kuklick, Henrika. 1991. *The Savage Within: The Social History of British Anthropology 1885-1945.* Cambridge: Cambridge University Press.

Kuper, Adam. 1988. *The Invention of Primitive Society: Transformations of an Illusion.* London and New York: Routledge.

Laclau, Ernesto, and Chantal Mouffe. 1985. *Hegemony and Socialist Strategy: Towards a Radical Democratic Politics.* London: Verso.

———. 1987. Post-Marxism without Apologies. *New Left Review* 166:79-106.

Lambert, H. E. 1956. *Kikuyu Social and Political Institutions.* London: Oxford University Press.

Lancaster, Chet S. 1976. Women, Horticulture, and Society in Sub-Saharan Africa. *American Anthropologist* 78 (3): 539-64.

Land of Murder and Muddle. *Time,* March 30, 1953, 30-31.

Langbaum, Robert. 1984. Review of *Out of Africa,* by Isak Dinesen. *Contemporary Lit-*

erary Criticism 29:156. (Originally printed in *Isak Dinesen's Art: The Gayety of Vision,* R. Langbaum, 1964.)

Laquer, Thomas W. 1989. Bodies, Details, and the Humanitarian Narrative. In *The New Cultural History,* edited by Lynn Hunt, 176-204. Berkeley and Los Angeles: University of California Press.

Larcom, Joan. 1983. Following Deacon: The Problem of Ethnographic Reanalysis, 1926-1981. In *Observers Observed: Essays on Ethnographic Fieldwork,* edited by George W. Stocking, 175-95. Madison: University of Wisconsin Press.

Lasson, Frans, ed. 1981. *Isak Dinesen, Letters from Africa 1914-1931.* Translated by Anne Born. Chicago: University of Chicago Press.

Lawren, William L. 1968a. An Historical Analysis of the Dissemination of Masai Culture to Five Bantu Tribes, with Special Emphasis on the Kikuyu. Ph.D. dissertation, University of California, Los Angeles.

————. 1968b. Masai and Kikuyu: An Historical Analysis of Culture Transmission. *Journal of African History* 9 (4): 571-83.

Leacock, Eleanor. 1978. Women's Status in Egalitarian Society: Implications for Social Evolution. *Current Anthropology* 19 (2): 247-75.

————. 1981. *Myths of Male Dominance: Collected Articles on Women Cross-Culturally.* New York and London: Monthly Review Press.

Leakey, Louis S. B. 1937. *White African.* London: Hodder and Stoughton.

————. 1952. *Mau Mau and the Kikuyu.* London: Methuen.

————. 1953. Mau Mau Terror: Fear, Freedom—and Magic. *Nation,* April 25, 345-46.

————. 1954. *Defeating Mau Mau.* London: Methuen.

————. 1961. *The Progress and Evolution of Man in Africa.* London and New York: Oxford University Press.

————. 1974. *By the Evidence: Memoirs 1932-1951.* New York and London: Harcourt Brace Jovanovich.

————. 1977. *The Southern Kikuyu before 1903.* Vols. 1-3. London and New York: Academic Press.

Leakey, Mary. 1984. *Disclosing the Past, An Autobiography.* New York: McGraw-Hill.

Leddy, Thomas. 1988. Gardens in an Expanded Field. *British Journal of Aesthetics* 28 (4): 327-40.

Leigh, Ione. 1954. *In the Shadow of the Mau Mau.* London: Allen.

LeVine, Robert. 1959. Gusii Sex Offenses: A Study in Social Control. *American Anthropologist* 61 (6): 965-90.

Lincoln, Bruce. 1989. *Discourse and the Construction of Society: Comparative Studies of Myth, Ritual, and Classification.* New York and Oxford: Oxford University Press.

Lingis, Alphonso. 1983. Savages. In *Excesses: Eros and Culture,* 17-46. Albany: State University of New York Press.

Llewellyn, Richard. 1961. *A Man in a Mirror.* New York: Doubleday.

Llewelyn-Davies, Melissa. 1978. Two Contexts of Solidarity among Pastoral Maasai Women. In *Women United, Women Divided: Cross-Cultural Perspectives on Female Solidarity,* edited by Patricia Caplan and Janet Bujra, 206-37. London: Tavistock.

Lofgren, Orvar. 1989a. Anthropologizing America. *American Ethnologist* 16 (2): 366-75.

————. 1989b. The Nationalization of Culture. *Ethnologia Europaea* 19 (1): 5-24.

Bibliography

Lonsdale, John. 1979. Review of *The Southern Kikuyu before 1903*, by Louis Leakey. *African Affairs* 78 (313): 570.

———. 1982. A State of Agrarian Unrest: Colonial Kenya. In *Agrarian Unrest in British and French Africa, British India and French Indo-China in the Nineteenth and Twentieth Centuries*, 1-8. Conference in London. Oxford: Past and Present Society.

———. 1989. African Pasts in Africa's Future. *Canadian Journal of African Studies* 23 (1): 126-46.

———. 1990. Mau Maus of the Mind: Making Mau Mau and Remaking Kenya. *Journal of African History* 31 (3): 393-421.

Loosening the Strings. *Newsweek*, March 7, 1960, 43-44.

Lyons, Harriet. 1981. Anthropologists, Moralities, and Relativities: The Problem of Genital Mutilations. *Canadian Review of Sociology and Anthropology* 18 (4): 499-518.

Mabro, Judy. 1991. *Veiled Half-Truths: Western Travellers' Perceptions of Middle Eastern Women.* Selected and introduced by Judy Mabro. London and New York: Tauris.

MacKenzie, Fiona. 1986. Local Initiatives and National Policy: Gender and Agricultural Change in Murang'a District, Kenya. *Canadian Journal of African Studies* 20 (3): 377-401.

MacKenzie, John M. 1988. *The Empire of Nature: Hunting, Conservation and British Imperialism.* New York and Manchester: Manchester University Press.

Mann, Judy. 1994. Refusing to Blink in the Face of Horror. Review of *Warrior Marks*, by Alice Walker and Pratibha Parmar. *San Jose Mercury News*, February 13, 23.

Marcus, George E., and Michael M. J. Fischer. 1986. *Anthropology as Cultural Critique: An Experimental Moment in the Human Sciences.* Chicago: University of Chicago Press.

Martin, Emily. 1987. *The Woman in the Body: A Cultural Analysis of Reproduction.* Boston: Beacon.

Masters, William, and Virginia Johnson. 1966. *Human Sexual Response.* Boston: Little, Brown.

Mathu, Mohamed. 1974. *The Urban Guerrilla: The Story of Mohamed Mathu.* Recorded and edited by Don Barnett. Richmond, B.C., Canada: LSM Information Center.

Maughan-Brown, David. 1985. *Land, Freedom and Fiction: History and Ideology in Kenya.* London: Zed.

Mau Mau in the Cathedral. *Time*, March 21, 1955, 32-33.

Mau Mau Terror. *Time*, October 20, 1952, 49.

Mayer, Philip. 1961. *Townsmen or Tribesmen; Conservatism and the Process of Urbanization in a South African City.* Capetown: Institute of Social and Economic Research, Rhodes University, Oxford University Press.

McCarthy, Thomas. 1992. Doing the Right Thing in Cross-Cultural Representation. *Ethics* 102 (3): 635-49.

McGregor, Gaile. 1988. *The Noble Savage in the New World Garden: Notes Toward a Syntactics of Place.* Bowling Green, Ohio: Bowling Green State University Popular Press.

Meinertzhagen, Richard. 1957. *Kenya Diary 1902-1906.* London: Eland; New York: Hippocrene.

Meow-Meows, The. *Time*, November 3, 1952, 36.

Bibliography

Middleton, John, and Greet Kershaw. 1965. *The Central Tribes of the North Eastern Bantu.* London: International African Institute.

Molnar, Stephen. 1992. *Human Variation: Races, Types, and Ethnic Groups.* Englewood Cliffs, N.J.: Prentice-Hall.

Morgan, Edmund. 1975. *American Slavery, American Freedom: The Ordeal of Colonial Virginia.* New York and London: Norton.

Morgen, Sandra, ed. 1989. Gender and Anthropology: Introductory Essay. In *Gender and Anthropology: Critical Reviews for Research and Teaching,* 1-20. Washington, D.C.: American Anthropological Association.

Morrison, Toni. 1989. Unspeakable Things Unspoken: The Afro-American Presence in American Literature. *Michigan Quarterly Review* 28 (1): 1-34.

Mosse, George L. 1985. *Nationalism and Sexuality: Middle-Class Morality and Sexual Norms in Modern Europe.* Madison: University of Wisconsin Press.

Mow Them Down. *Time,* May 25, 1953, 36.

Mullen, Harryette R. 1990. Gender and the Subjugated Body: Readings of Race, Subjectivity, and Difference in the Construction of Slave Narratives. Ph.D. dissertation, University of California, Santa Cruz.

————. 1991. "Indelicate Subjects": African-American Women's Subjugated Subjectivity. Feminist Studies Focused Research Activity, University of California, Santa Cruz.

Mullings, Leith. 1976. Women and Economic Change in Africa. In *Women in Africa: Studies in Social and Economic Change,* edited by Nancy J. Hafkin and Edna G. Bay, 239-64. Stanford, Calif.: Stanford University Press.

Mungeam, G. H. 1970. Masai and Kikuyu Responses to the Establishment of British Administration in the East Africa Protectorate. *Journal of African History* 11 (1): 127-43.

Munitions Makers, The. *Time,* May 27, 1957, 39.

Muriuki, Godfrey. 1974. *A History of the Kikuyu, 1500-1900.* Nairobi, London, New York: Oxford University Press.

Murray-Brown, Jeremy. 1972. *Kenyatta.* London: Allen & Unwin.

Nash, Gary B. 1974. *Red, White, and Black: The Peoples of Early America.* Englewood Cliffs, N.J.: Prentice-Hall

Nash, June. 1975. Nationalism and Fieldwork. *Annual Review of Anthropology* 4:225-45.

Nelson, Cynthia. 1974. Public and Private Politics: Women in the Middle Eastern World. *American Ethnologist* 1 (3): 551-63.

News in Pictures. *Time,* November 10, 1952, 30-31.

No. 2. *Time,* January 25, 1954, 26.

Oath Takers, The. *Time,* June 13, 1960, 30-31.

Obbo, Christine. 1976. Dominant Male Ideology and Female Options: Three East African Case Studies. *Africa* 46 (4): 371-89.

Obeyesekere, Gananath. 1992. *The Apotheosis of Captain Cook: European Mythmaking in the Pacific.* Princeton, N.J.: Princeton University Press.

Oboler, Regina. 1980. Is the Female Husband a Man? *Ethnology* 19 (1): 69-88.

O'Brien, Denise. 1977. Female Husbands in Southern Bantu Societies. In *Sexual Stratification: A Cross-Cultural View,* edited by Alice Schlegel, 109-26. New York: Columbia University Press.

Bibliography

O'Brien, Jay, and William Roseberry, eds. 1991. *Golden Ages, Dark Ages: Imagining the Past in Anthropology and History.* Berkeley and Oxford: University of California Press.

Okonjo, Kamene. 1976. The Dual-Sex Political System in Operation: Igbo Women and Community Politics in Midwestern Nigeria. In *Women in Africa: Studies in Social and Economic Change,* edited by Nancy J. Hafkin and Edna G. Bay, 45-58. Stanford, Calif.: Stanford University Press.

Ole Saitoti, Tepilit. 1988. *The Worlds of a Maasai Warrior: An Autobiography.* Berkeley and Los Angeles: University of California Press.

Oppong, Christine. 1974. *Marriage among a Matrilineal Elite: A Family Study of Ghanaian Senior Civil Servants.* Cambridge: Cambridge University Press.

Ortner, Sherry. 1974. Is Female to Male as Nature Is to Culture? In *Woman, Culture, and Society,* edited by Michelle Zimbalist Rosaldo and Louise Lamphere, 67-87. Stanford, Calif.: Stanford University Press.

———. 1978. The Virgin and the State. *Feminist Studies* 4 (3): 19-35.

———. 1981. Gender and Sexuality in Hierarchical Societies: The Case of Polynesia and Some Comparative Implications. In *Sexual Meanings: The Cultural Construction of Gender and Sexuality,* edited by Sherry Ortner and Harriet Whitehead, 359-409. Cambridge: Cambridge University Press.

Ottenberg, Simon. 1959. Ibo Receptivity to Change. In *Continuity and Change in African Cultures,* edited by William Bascom and Melville Herskovits, 130-43. Chicago and London: University of Chicago Press.

Out of Africa. Universal City, Calif.: Universal Pictures Limited, 1985; MCA Home Video, 1986. Videorecording.

Owusu, Maxwell. 1978. Ethnography of Africa: The Usefulness of the Useless. *American Anthropologist* 80 (2): 310-34.

Parker, Richard G. 1991. *Bodies, Pleasures, and Passions: Sexual Culture in Contemporary Brazil.* Boston: Beacon.

Pieterse, Jan Nederveen. 1992. *White on Black: Images of Africa and Blacks in Western Popular Culture.* New Haven, Conn., and London: Yale University Press.

Potash, Betty. 1989. Gender Relations in Sub-Saharan Africa. In *Gender and Anthropology: Critical Reviews for Research and Teaching,* edited by Sandra Morgen, 189-227. Washington, D.C.: American Anthropological Association.

Presley, Cora. 1986. Labor Protest among Kikuyu Women, 1912-1947. In *Women and Class in Africa,* edited by Claire Robertson and Iris Berger. New York: Holmes & Meier.

———. 1988. The Mau Mau Rebellion, Kikuyu Women, and Social Change. *Canadian Journal of African Studies* 3 (3): 502-27.

———. 1992. *Kikuyu Women, the Mau Mau Rebellion, and Social Change in Kenya.* Boulder, Colo.: Westview.

Question Man. *San Francisco Chronicle,* March 15, 1990, A33.

Rafael, Vicente L. 1993. *Contracting Colonialism: Translation and Christian Conversion in Tagalog Society under Early Spanish Rule.* Durham, N.C., and London: Duke University Press.

Ranger, Terence. 1979. White Presence and Power in Africa. *Journal of African History* 20 (4): 463-69.

———. 1985. Introduction: Laying the Comparative Foundations *and* The Great Depression and the Zimbabwean Peasantry. In *Peasant Consciousness and Guerrilla War in Zimbabwe*, edited by Terence Ranger, 1-17, 54-98. London: James Currey; Berkeley: University of California Press.

———. 1988. The Invention of Tradition in Colonial Africa. In *The Invention of Tradition*, edited by Eric Hobsbawm and Terence Ranger, 211-62. Cambridge: Cambridge University Press.

Rapp, Rayna, ed. [Rayna Reiter]. 1975. *Toward an Anthropology of Women*. New York: Monthly Review Press.

Ready or Not: Kenya's Tom Mboya (cover story). *Time*, March 7, 1960, 22-34.

Rigby, Peter. 1985. *Persistent Pastoralists: Nomadic Societies in Transition*. London: Zed.

———. 1989. Ideology, Religion, and Ilparakuyo-Maasai Resistance to Capitalist Penetration. *Canadian Journal of African Studies* 23 (3): 416-40.

Rogers, Peter. 1979. The British and the Kikuyu 1890-1905: A Reassessment. *Journal of African History* 20:255-69.

Rogers, Phyllis. 1989. Captivity, Transculturation and Puritan Society. In *Occasional Papers No. 2, Group for the Critical Study of Colonial Discourse*. Santa Cruz: University of California.

Roots of the Fig Tree, The. *Time*, March 16, 1959, 30.

Rosaldo, Renato. 1986. From the Door of His Tent: The Fieldworker and the Inquisitor. In *Writing Culture: The Poetics and Politics of Ethnography*, edited by James Clifford and George E. Marcus, 77-97. Berkeley: University of California Press.

Rosberg, Carl G., and John Nottingham. 1966. *The Myth of "Mau Mau": Nationalism in Kenya*. New York and London: Praeger.

Rosenau, Pauline Marie. 1992. *Post-Modernism and the Social Sciences: Insights, Inroads, and Intrusions*. Princeton, N.J.: Princeton University Press.

Ross, Ellen, and Rayna Rapp. 1981. Sex and Society: A Research Note from Social History and Anthropology. *Comparative Studies in Society and History* 23 (1): 51-72.

Routledge, W. Scoresby, and Katherine Routledge. 1910. *With a Prehistoric People: The Akikuyu of British East Africa* (1968 edition). London: Frank Cass.

Ruark, Robert. 1955. *Something of Value*. Garden City, N.Y.: Doubleday.

Rubin, Gayle. 1975. The Traffic in Women: Notes on the Political Economy of Sex. In *Toward an Anthropology of Women*, edited by Rayna Rapp [Reiter], 157-210. New York and London: Monthly Review Press.

Sacks, Karen. 1979. *Sisters and Wives: The Past and Future of Sexual Equality*. Westport, Conn., and London: Greenwood.

Said, Edward. 1978. *Orientalism*. New York: Vintage.

———. 1993. *Culture and Imperialism*. New York: Knopf.

Samkange, Stanlake J. T. 1971. Introduction. In *A Wreath for Udomo*, by Peter Abrahams, 9-14. New York: Collier.

Sandoval, Chela. 1991. U.S. Third World Feminism: The Theory and Method of Oppositional Consciousness in the Postmodern World. *Genders* 10 (Spring): 1-24.

Santilli, Kathy. 1977. Kikuyu Women in the Mau Mau Revolt: A Closer Look. *Ufahamu* 8 (1): 143-74.

Schlegel, Alice, ed. 1977. Toward a Theory of Sexual Stratification. In *Sexual Stratification: A Cross-Cultural View*, 1-40. New York: Columbia University Press.

Schneider, Jane. 1971. Of Vigilance and Virgins: Honor, Shame and Access to Resources in Mediterranean Societies. *Ethnology* 10 (1): 1-24.

Schuster, Ilsa. 1979. *New Women of Lusaka.* Palo Alto, Calif.: Mayfield.

Scott, Joan. 1988. *Gender and the Politics of History.* New York: Columbia University Press.

Shakespeare, William. 1975. The Merchant of Venice. In *The Complete Works of William Shakespeare,* 203-28. New York: Avenel.

Shannon, Mary. 1957. Rebuilding the Social Life of the Kikuyu. *African Affairs* 56 (225): 276-84.

Slater, Montagu. 1955. *The Trial of Jomo Kenyatta.* London: Secker and Warburg.

Slight Change for the Worse. *Time,* December 8, 1952, 32-35.

Sobania, Neal. 1993. Defeat and Dispersal: The Laikipiak and Their Neighbours at the End of the Nineteenth Century. In *Being Maasai: Ethnicity and Identity in East Africa,* edited by Thomas Spear and Richard Waller, 105-19. London: James Currey; Dar Es Salaam: Mkuki na Nyota; Nairobi: EAEP; Athens: Ohio University Press.

Something of Value. New York: Loew's, MGM/UA Home Video, 1986 (originally made in 1957). Videorecording.

S.O.S. *Time,* October 27, 1952, 40.

Southall, Aidan. 1960. On Chastity in Africa. *Uganda Journal* 24 (2): 207-16.

Spear, Thomas. 1993. Introduction. In *Being Maasai: Ethnicity and Identity in East Africa,* edited by Thomas Spear and Richard Waller, 1-24. London: James Currey; Dar Es Salaam: Mkuki na Nyota; Nairobi: EAEP; Athens: Ohio University Press.

Spear, Thomas, and Richard Waller, eds. 1993. *Being Maasai: Ethnicity and Identity in East Africa.* London: James Currey; Dar Es Salaam: Mkuki na Nyota; Nairobi: EAEP; Athens: Ohio University Press.

Spivak, Gayatri. 1980. The Revolutions That as yet Have No Model. *Diacritics* 10 (4): 47-48.

————. 1988. Can the Subaltern Speak? In *Marxism and the Interpretation of Culture,* edited by Cary Nelson and Lawrence Grossberg, 271-313. Chicago: University of Illinois Press.

Stallybrass, Peter, and Allon White. 1986. *The Politics and Poetics of Transgression.* Ithaca, N.Y.: Cornell University Press.

Stamp, Patricia. 1986. Kikuyu Women's Self-Help Groups: Toward an Understanding of the Relation Between Sex-Gender System and Mode of Production in Africa. In *Women and Class in Africa,* edited by Claire Robertson and Iris Berger, 27-46. New York and London: Africana, Holmes & Meier.

Stocking, George W. 1992. *The Ethnographer's Magic and Other Essays in the History of Anthropology.* Madison: University of Wisconsin Press.

Stoler, Ann L. 1989. Making Empire Respectable: The Politics of Race and Sexual Morality in 20th-Century Colonial Cultures. *American Ethnologist* 16 (1): 634-60.

————. 1991. Carnal Knowledge and Imperial Power: Gender, Race, and Morality in Colonial Asia. In *Gender at the Crossroads of Knowledge: Feminist Anthropology in the Postmodern Era,* edited by Micaela di Leonardo, 51-101. Berkeley and Los Angeles: University of California Press.

Strathern, Marilyn. 1987. Out of Context: The Persuasive Fictions of Anthropology. *Current Anthropology* 28 (3): 251-81.

Bibliography

Sudarkasa, Niara. 1973. *Where Women Work: A Study of Yoruba Women in the Marketplace and in the Home.* Ann Arbor: University of Michigan Anthropological Papers.

Swartz, Marc J. 1960. "Situational Determinants of Kinship Terminology," *Southwestern Journal of Anthropology* 16 (4): 393–97.

———. 1966. Introduction. In *Political Anthropology*, edited by Marc J. Swartz, Victor W. Turner, and Arthur Tuden, 1-41. Chicago: Aldine.

Tanner, Nancy. 1974. Matrifocality in Indonesia and Africa and among Black Americans. In *Woman, Culture, and Society*, edited by Michelle Zimbalist Rosaldo and Louise Lamphere, 129–56. Stanford, Calif.: Stanford University Press.

Taussig, Michael. 1987. *Shamanism, Colonialism, and the Wild Man: A Study in Terror and Healing.* Chicago and London: University of Chicago Press.

Thompson, E. P. 1966. *The Making of the English Working Class.* New York: Vintage.

Thomson, Joseph. 1962. *Through Masailand with Joseph Thomson.* Edited and abridged by Roland Young. From the original narrative. Evanston, Ill.: Northwestern University Press.

Throup, David. 1988. *Economic and Social Origins of Mau Mau 1945-53.* London: James Currey; Athens: Ohio University Press.

Tignor, Robert. 1972. The Maasai Warriors: Pattern Maintenance and Violence in Colonial Kenya. *Journal of African History* 13 (2): 271-90.

———. 1976. *The Colonial Transformation of Kenya: The Kamba, Kikuyu, and Maasai from 1900 to 1939.* Princeton, N.J.: Princeton University Press.

Todorov, Tzvetan. 1993. *On Human Diversity: Nationalism, Racism, and Exoticism in French Thought.* Translated by Catherine Porter. Cambridge, Mass., and London: Harvard University Press.

Torgovnick, Marianna. 1990. *Gone Primitive: Savage Intellects, Modern Lives.* Chicago: University of Chicago Press.

Trouillot, Michel-Rolph. 1991. Anthropology and the Savage Slot: The Poetics and Politics of Otherness. In *Recapturing Anthropology: Working in the Present*, edited by Richard G. Fox, 17–44. Santa Fe, N.M.: School of American Research.

Trzebinski, Errol. 1986. *The Kenya Pioneers.* New York: Norton.

Turner, Victor. 1957. *Schism and Continuity in an African Society: A Study of Ndembu Village Life.* Manchester: Rhodes-Livingstone Institute, Manchester University Press.

———. 1969. *The Ritual Process: Structure and Anti-Structure.* Chicago: Aldine.

Tyler, Stephen. 1986. Post-Modern Ethnography: From Document of the Occult to Occult Document. In *Writing Culture: The Poetics and Politics of Ethnography*, edited by James Clifford and George W. Marcus, 122-40. Berkeley: University of California Press.

Vincent, Joan. 1971. *African Elite: The Big Men of a Small Town.* New York and London: Columbia University Press.

———. 1978. Political Anthropology: Manipulative Strategies. *Annual Review of Anthropology* 7:175-94.

———. 1991. Engaging Historicism. In *Recapturing Anthropology: Working in the Present*, edited by Richard G. Fox, 45-58. Santa Fe, N.M.: School of American Research.

Bibliography

Walker, Alice, and Pratibha Parmar. 1993. *Warrior Marks: Female Genital Mutilation and the Sexual Blinding of Women.* New York: Harcourt Brace.

Waller, Richard. 1976. "The Maasai and the British, 1895-1905: The Origins of an Alliance," *Journal of African History* 17: 529-53.

———. 1993. Acceptees and Aliens: Kikuyu Settlement in Maasailand. In *Being Maasai: Ethnicity and Identity in East Africa,* edited by Thomas Spear and Richard Waller, 226-57. London: James Currey; Dar Es Salaam: Mkuki na Nyota; Nairobi: EAEP; Athens: Ohio University Press.

Ware, Vron. 1992. *Beyond the Pale: White Women, Racism and History.* London and New York: Verso.

wa Thiong'o, Ngugi [James Ngugi]. 1964. *Weep Not Child* (1969 edition). New York: Collier.

———. 1965. *The River Between.* London and Nairobi: Heinemann.

———. 1978. *Petals of Blood.* New York: Dutton.

wa Thiong'o, Ngugi, and Micere Githae Mugo. 1976. *The Trial of Dedan Kimathi.* Harare: Zimbabwe Publishing House.

Watson, Graham. 1991. Rewriting Culture. In *Recapturing Anthropology: Working in the Present,* edited by Richard G. Fox, 73-92. Santa Fe, N.M.: School of American Research.

Weiner, Annette. 1976. *Women of Value, Men of Renown: New Perspectives in Trobriand Exchange.* Austin: University of Texas Press.

White, Hayden. 1979. Michel Foucault. In *Structuralism and Since: From Lévi-Strauss to Derrida,* edited by John Sturrock, 81-115. Oxford and New York: Oxford University Press.

White, Luise. 1983. A History of Prostitution in Nairobi, Kenya c. 1900-1952. Ph.D. thesis, Cambridge University.

———. 1984. Women in the Changing African Family. In *African Women South of the Sahara,* edited by Margaret Hay and Sharon Stichter, 53-68. London and New York: Longman.

———. 1990a. Bodily Fluids and Usufruct: Controlling Property in Nairobi, 1917-1939. *Canadian Journal of African Studies* 24 (3): 418-38.

———. 1990b. *The Comforts of Home: Prostitution in Colonial Nairobi.* Chicago and London: University of Chicago Press.

Whyte, Martin. 1978. *The Status of Women in Preindustrial Societies.* Princeton, N.J.: Princeton University Press.

Willard, Sherri. 1993. Facial Discrimination: How Do We Recognize One Another, and Why Do the Members of Other Races All Seem to Look Alike? *Science Notes from the University of California, Santa Cruz* 19 (1): 10-12.

Wilson, Edward Thomas. 1974. *Russia and Black Africa before World War II.* New York and London: Holmes & Meier.

Wipper, Audrey. 1977. *Rural Rebels: A Study of Two Protest Movements in Kenya.* New York: Oxford University Press.

———. 1989. Kikuyu Women and the Harry Thuku Disturbances: Some Uniformities of Female Militancy. *Africa* 59 (3): 300-36.

Witch Doctors and the Courts Fail to Halt African Tension. *Newsweek,* November 24, 1952, 33.

Wolf, Eric R. 1982. *Europe and the People without History*. London and Berkeley: University of California Press.

Wolfe, Tom. 1970. *Radical Chic and Mau-Mauing the Flak Catchers*. New York: Farrar, Straus & Giroux.

Yeazell, Ruth Bernard. 1982. Podsnappery, Sexuality, and the English Novel. *Critical Inquiry* 9 (December): 339-57.

Index

Compiled by Eileen Quam and Theresa Wolner

Abrahams, Peter, 127; *A Wreath for Udomo*, 128-29, 147
Abu-Lughod, Lila, 18
Achebe, Chinua: *Things Fall Apart*, 219n
Action Group, 152
African Americans: cultures of, 15; as spiteful servants, 189-91; stereotypes in European culture, 185
Ahoi (tenants), 53, 122, 137; food distribution to, 42; gifts by, 40; and *githaka*, 40, 42; and land, 38-39; and marriage, 48. *See also Mbari*
Akikuyu, The (Cagnolo), 31-32
Allegory: and ethnography, 113-14, 115, 135; women as, 3, 60-63
Angola: Leakey in, 95-100
Anti-Semitism, 186-88
Aristotle, 136
Arthur, John, 135-36
Assimilation, 184, 190, 191, 198, 207
Athoni (in-laws), 39, 122

Barkham, John, 162
Barnett, Donald, 157
Batuni (warrior/killing oath), 151, 167, 169
Baudrillard, Jean, 16
Beach, Frank, 88
Beecher, Gladys, 222n
Beer: importance to Kikuyu, 45
Benjamin, Walter, 115
Berman, Bruce: *Unhappy Valley*, 222n
Best, Nicholas, 194, 211, 214, 215

Blacks. *See* African Americans
Bliven, Bruce, Jr., 162
Blixen, Karen, 1, 12, 213, 214; on immortality, 182; on nature, 183; *Out of Africa*, 9-10, 27, 180-81, 182, 188, 192-96; romanticism of, 192; *Shadows on the Grass*, 188
Block, Abraham, 188
Boddy, Janice, 70
Boyles, Denis, 194-95
Breeding populations, 223n
British: colonization of Kikuyu, 109; influence on Kikuyu, 29-31
Buijtenhuijs, Robert, 169-70
By the Evidence (Leakey), 95, 97, 157

Cagnolo, C., 29; *Akikuyu*, 31-32
Campbell, David, 205
Carter Land Commission (1932), 110
Cary, Joyce: *Mister Johnson*, 219n
Churchill, Winston, 162, 179
Circumcision. *See* Clitoridectomy; Male circumcision
Class: and black-white relations, 180; landscape as metaphor for, 180-84
Class and Economic Change in Kenya (Kitching), 119
Clifford, James, 60, 113, 115, 135
Clitoridectomy, 221-22n; as being about sex, 76; importance in Kikuyu culture, 61; as initiation ceremony, 68, 69, 87, 132-33; political support of, 63-64, 138; and sexuality, 76-82; and sex-

ual pleasure, 80; support of, 63-71 passim; as symbol for pure/true, 65; and virginity, 85-88; as warrior marks, 70. *See also* Infibulation

Clough, Marshall S.: *Mau-Mau Syllabus,* 160

Cold war: and Mau Mau news coverage, 171

Cole, Sonia, 63, 102

Colonialism: discourse/culture, 4-13; and social theory, 13-25. *See also* Interculturality

Comintern, 127

Communalism: vs. individualism, 141

Communism: and Mau Mau movement, 170, 172-73, 174

Connolly, Cyril, 223n

Corfield Report, 173, 178

Cultigens, 183

Culture, 13-16; colonial, 4-13; definitions and usage of term, 15, 115; and ethnography, 28, 115

Culture and Imperialism (Said), 5

Davidson, Basil, 162

Desegregation, 171

Dinesen, Isak. *See* Blixen, Karen

Discipline and Punish (Foucault), 20

Discourse, 18-22; analysis, 20; and anthropology, 18; and power, 19

Douglas, Mary, 91

Drake, St. Clair, 129

Du Bois, W. E. B., 127

East African Association, 124, 125

Edgerton, Robert B., 128, 136

Egalitarianism: among Kikuyu men, 2, 118

El Dareer, Asma, 87

Elders, Kikuyu, 35-36, 39-40, 42, 85, 106-12, 115

El Saadawi, Nawal, 88

Emilio, John: *Intimate Matters,* 166

Ensminger, Jane, 222n

Ethnography: and allegory, 113-14, 115, 135; colonial, 28; communist, 165; and

culture, 115; vs. history, 118-19, 144; vs. news/journalism, 170-71; as poetry, 108; and postmodernism, 107-8; redemptive, 143

Eugenics, 181

Eunoto ceremony, 205

Excesses (Lingis), 69-70

Excision, 221n

Extramarital relations, 62

Facing Mt. Kenya (Kenyatta), 3, 26, 63, 65, 123, 128, 129-38, 146-47, 177; audience for, 136; as blueprint for terror, 160; cover of, 125, *126,* 128; as cultural nationalist tract, 2, 3, 136; European bias in, 134-35; and functionalism, 3; introduction to, 132; major theme in, 136; memory/nostalgia in, 133, 138; as political, 26, 135; preface to, 133, 137-38; as reference source, 131; second and subsequent printings, 136; suppressed anger of, 146; topics highlighted in, 138

Female circumcision. *See* Clitoridectomy; Infibulation

Female power: vs. male dominance of Kikuyu, 28, 35, 40, 43, 46, 58-59

Flame Trees of Thika (Huxley), 8-9, 27, 181-82, 198, 209, 210-11

Flowers: and civilized life, 183; and cultures of luxury, 181-82. *See also* Gardens; Landscape

Food distribution/presentation: of Kikuyu women for work parties, 28, 34, 42-46

Ford, Clellan, 88

Fort Hall Screening Center, 158-59

Forty Group, 152

Foucault, Michel, 18-22; *Discipline and Punish,* 20

Fox, James, 213; *White Mischief,* 189, 214

Freedman, Estelle B.: *Intimate Matters,* 166

Garden of Eden, Kikuyu, 120, 121, 140, 220n

Gardens: and civilized life, 183; and class hierarchy, 181-82; as metaphor for transplanting of whites into Africa, 182; vs. wilderness, 181, 183. *See also* Flowers; Landscape
Gecau, J., 174
Gecau, Rose, 54
Geertz, Clifford, 115
Gender roles: of Kikuyu women, 34-36, 44, 60, 61; and politics of Kikuyu, 28-59
Genital mutilation. *See* Clitoridectomy; Infibulation; Male circumcision
Gifford-Gonzalez, Diane, 223n
Golden past: longing for, 31
Goody, Jack, 90, 91, 92, 181
Gordon, Daniel, 76
Gruenbaum, Ellen, 66, 77

Haddon, A. C., 96
Happy Valley, 27, 209-10, 212, 213, 214, 217
History of the Kikuyu, A (Muriuki), 29, 36, 119, *120*
Hobley, C. W., 34
Homophobia, 166
Homosexuality, 166-67
How Green Was My Valley (Llewellyn), 201
Hunting. *See* Sport hunting
Huxley, Elspeth, 1, 8, 160, 195, 209; *Flame Trees of Thika*, 8-9, 27, 181-82, 198, 209, 210-11; ideal woman, 60; on Mau Mau, 174; *Out in the Midday Sun*, 27, 198, 213; *Red Strangers*, 27, 196-201; *White Man's Country*, 198
Hypergamy, 90-91, 93

IBEA. *See* Imperial British East Africa Company (IBEA)
Ice people, 189
Igbo: clitoridectomy practice of, 86; on virginity, 85, 88, 89
Imperial British East Africa Company (IBEA), 219n, 222n
Indians. *See* Native Americans

Infibulation, 66, 70, 78, 221n. *See also* Clitoridectomy
Initiation. *See* Clitoridectomy; Male circumcision
Interculturality: in colonial Kenya, 1, 12-13, 22-24, 27, 149, 180, 184; Mau Mau movement as, 149
In the Shadow of the Mau Mau (Leigh), 167, 168
Intimate Matters (D'Emilio and Freedman), 166
Irua, 54, 69, 133, 222n
Isichei, Patrick, 89
Islands of White (Kennedy), 6-8
Itũĩka ritual, 33, 110, 111, 113, 116, 141
Ivory trade, 222n

Jackson, Kennell, 131; *Mau-Mau Syllabus,* 160
Jacobson, David, 17
Jews: as other, 186; stereotypes of, 186-87

Kabetũ, 111-12, 141-43
Kafka, Franz: *Penal Colony,* 69
Kamau, Johnstone. *See* Kenyatta, Jomo
Kamba people/traders, 121-22
KAU. *See* Kenya African Union (KAU)
KCA. *See* Kikuyu Central Association (KCA)
Kencaffe instant coffee: label, *197*
Kennedy, Dane: *Islands of White,* 6-8
Kenya: landscape, 180-84, 218; map of central Kenya, *ii*; as official colony (1920), 124
Kenya African Union (KAU), 151, 154, 155-56, 165
Kenya Land Commission, 107
Kenya Pioneers (Trzebinski), 183-84, 203-4, 215, 223n
Kenyatta, Jomo, 1, 2-3, 26, 117, 118, 120, 123-38, *126*, 143-48; as authentic native, 123-31, 133, 177; as author, 123-31, 133; on clitoridectomy, 63-69; and communism, 177; and democracy, 130; *Facing Mt. Kenya,* 3, 26, 63, 65, 123, 125, *126,* 128, 129-38, 146, 147, 160,

177; as first president of Kenya, 1, 147-48, 154; on Kikuyu, 29, 34, 36, 200; location of, 33, 38-39; in London, 125, 128; and Mau Mau, 146, 149, 151, 154, 155-56; media portrayals of, 26, 160, 161-62, 170, 171, 173-74, 176-78; in Nairobi, 124-25; name change, 128, 177; research on, 29-33; in Scandinavia, 126-27; on sexual self-control, 73; and socialism, 123, 125, 138; in Soviet Union, 125-27; *Suffering without Bitterness*, 125-26, 130; on women, 3, 44, 63-67, 138, 140

Kershaw, Greet, 33, 34, 37, 220n

Kiama (hierarchical councils), 28-29, 38, 58, 136, 154

Kikuyu: as aggressive merchants, 179; bad reputation of, 121; as bureaucrats, 119, 122, 123, 179; as community, 2, 6, 144; and democracy, 136-37; description of, 33; economy of, 34; as egalitarian society, 2, 36, 118; vs. European colonialists, 137, 141; gender and politics, 28-59; gender roles, 34-35; generational rulership within, 136-37; compared to Hebrews, 139-40; history, 206-7; as horticultural vs. pastoral, 27; vs. Luo, 179; vs. Maasai, 27, 55-56, 59, 121-22, 164, 199, 203, 207-9; vs. Mau Mau, 140; myth, 206-7; nomads among, 38; political economy/politics of, 28-29, 36-42, 46-47, 122-23; precolonial, 118; society, 6, 33-36; trade with Maasai, 40-41; view of, 2. *See also Facing Mt. Kenya* (Kenyatta); *Southern Kikuyu before* 1903 (Leakey); Women, Kikuyu

Kikuyu Central Association (KCA), 64-65, 125, 150, 156

Kimathi, Dedan, 174

Kitching, Gavin: *Class and Economic Change in Kenya*, 119; continuous dialectical process of, 123; on precolonial Kikuyu, 118, 119, 122-23; as social historian, 123

Klumpp, Donna, 209

Koso-Thomas, Olayinka, 79-80, 87

Kratz, Corinne, 209

Kūingata Mūrimū, 43

Laclau, Ernesto, 206

Laikipia reserve, 203-4, 223n

Land: Kikuyu reserve, 110; meaning of to Kikuyu, 37-38

Landscape: of colonial Kenya, 180-84, 218. *See also* Flowers; Gardens

Lanwood, Thomas, 128

Larcom, Joan, 29

Leacock, Eleanor, 46, 91

Leaders, Kikuyu. *See* Elders, Kikuyu

Leakey, Louis, 1, 2, 25-26, 95-117, 138-43; in Angola, 95-100; biographical background, 100-102; *By the Evidence*, 95, 97, 157; collaboration with elders, 106-12; as colonialist, 102-5; constructing the past, 29; on extramarital relations, 61; fund-raising for museum, 97; at Kenyatta trial, 132, 157; and Kikuyu, 95-117, 200; on Kikuyu trading women, 40-41; as liberal paternalist/revivalist, 145; on magic, 107; on Mau Mau, 26, 105, 116, 145-46, 147, 155, 156-57, 160-61, 169, 174; *Mau Mau and the Kikuyu*, 139; on polygamy, 62, 140; on rape, 61; research funding, search for, 105-6; *Southern Kikuyu before 1903*, 2-3, 71, 98-99, *99*, 106-16, 139-43, 222n; subjectivity of, 98-100; *White African*, 139; on women, 3, 44, 60-63, 140

Leakey, Mary, 25, 95, 96

Leigh, Ione: *In the Shadow of the Mau Mau*, 167, 168

Lévi-Strauss, Claude: on myths, 121

Lingis, Alphonso: *Excesses*, 69-70

Livestock: as wealth for Kikuyu, 40

Llewellyn, Richard: *How Green Was My Valley*, 201

Llewelyn-Davies, Melissa, 87

Lofgren, Orvar, 220n

Lonsdale, John: on Leakey, 145-56; on Mau Mau, 145-46; on precolonial

Kikuyu, 118, 146; *Unhappy Valley*, 222n

"Lost Sister, The" (folktale), 36, 59, 47-58, 59

Lower classes, 186

Lumpenproletariat, 160

Luo: vs. Kikuyu, 179

Lyons, Harriet, 76

Lyttelton, Oliver, 172

Maasai: accommodation of, 205; arrogant black racist image of, 217; as elongated Africans, 223n; and Europeans, 203-6; vs. Kikuyu, 27, 55-56, 59, 121-22, 164, 199, 203, 207-9; as lost tribe of Israel, 201; marginality of, 201; as noble savages, 184, 191; and pastoralism, 27, 184, 201, 208; physical traits of, 201; resistance to capitalism, 205; social organization, 204; trade with Kikuyu, 40-41; on virginity, 85, 86; as wild, 184

MacKenzie, John M.: on East African sport hunting, 222n

Magic, 107

Male circumcision: as being about sex, 76; as initiation ceremony, 69, 124

Male dominance: vs. female power of Kikuyu, 28, 35, 40, 43, 46, 58-59

Malinowski, Bronislaw Kasper, 2, 130, 134-35, 137-38, 196

Malinowskian functionalism: on clitoridectomy, 67-71

Marriage: of *ahoi*, 48; consummating, 74; of unwed mothers, 74; woman-woman of Kikuyu, 41-42

Marshall, Thurgood, 165

Master-servant relationship, 124, 188

Mau Mau, 26, 148, 149-78; as bad religion, 159; as bloody savages, 179; casualty reports, 153; as civil war, 157, 174; criminal element in, 156; definitions and usage of term, 154, 159-60; forest fighters, 152; historiography in Russia and Eastern European countries, 165-66; as interculturality, 149; vs. Kikuyu, 140; media coverage of, 149, 160, 161-62, 170-78; moral economy of, 222n; as nationalism, 165, 170, 172-73, 178; vs. Nazi Germany holocaust, 171, 175; oaths/oath taking, 140, 146, 150, 155, 157, 159, 168-70, 173, 175-76, 207; and racial hatred, 172; as religious movement, 26, 157; as revolutionary struggle, 26; torture camps, 157-58; as transgression, 173

Mau Mau and the Kikuyu (Leakey), 139

Mau-Mau Syllabus (Clough and Jackson), 160

Mbari (subclan/family group), 33, 122, 153; of initiating women, 4; on land, 38-39; and wealth, 43; and women's work, 45. *See also Ahoi*

Mboya, Tom, 174, 177-78

McDaniel, Hattie, vii

McGregor, Gaile: *Noble Savage in the New World Garden*, 181, 182-83, 189

McQueen, Butterfly, vii

Men. *See* Male dominance

Merchant of Venice, The (Shakespeare), 187

Middleton, John, 33, 34, 37

Missionaries: vs. clitoridectomy, 64; mores on sexual activity, 73

Mister Johnson (Cary), 219n

Moran (warriors), 56, 203, 204, 205

Mouffe, Chantal, 232

Muhoi. See Ahoi

Mullen, Harryette, 201

Mundu mugo (medicine man), 35, 143, 197

Mungeam, G. H., 203

Murang'a District, 38

Muriuki, Godfrey: *History of the Kikuyu*, 29, 119, *120;* on immigration of Kikuyu, 39; on Kikuyu land, 39; on precolonial Kikuyu, 36, 118, 119-22

Murray-Brown, Jeremy, 65, 123, 125, 128, 134

Muthaiga Club, 212-13

Myths: vs. history, 120, 121

Nairobi: museum, 97

Nash, Gary, 190

Nation, 161, 162
Nationalism: and Mau Mau movement, 165, 170, 172-73, 178
Native Americans: as marginalized other, 191; as noble savages, 183, 189-91
New York Times: Mau Mau coverage, 170, 174
News: defined, 170; vs. ethnography/history, 170-71
Newsweek: Mau Mau coverage, 170, 172, 173, 174
Ngugi, James, 219n
Ngweko: rules of, 72, 73, 74, 82
Njama, Karari, 157
Nkrumah, Kwame, 127, 128, 129
Noble savage: classical-aristocratic overtones of, 191; dichotomies in development of, 183; and European progress, 204; Maasai as, 184, 191, 204; as marginalized other, 191; and nationalism, 189; Native Americans as, 183, 189-91; and nature, 183, 189; and romanticism, 189
Noble Savage in the New World Garden, The (McGregor), 181, 182-83, 189
North-south discourse, 188-89
Nyandura Mountains, 39

Okiek, 209
Ole Saitoti, Tepilit: *Worlds of a Maasai Warrior*, 202
Oppression, 186
Orientalism, 180, 212
Ortner, Sherry, 90-93
Out in the Midday Sun (Huxley), 27, 198, 213
Out of Africa (Blixen), 9-10, 27, 180-81, 182, 188, 192-96; film version, 10, 194
"Out of Africa" Kencaffe instant coffee: label, 196, *197*
Owusu, Maxwell, 131

Padmore, George, 127
Pan-Africanism, 127-28, 130-31
Past/present/future: sub-Saharan view of, 115-16. *See also* Golden past

Pax Britannica, 124, 203
Peace treaties: and trading, 41
Penal Colony, The (Kafka), 69
Pharaonic circumcision, 221n
Pieterse, Jan Nederveen, 185-86
Poetry: ethnography as, 108; and social analysis, 24
Politics of Aristotle, The, 136
Politics of representation, 185-91
Polygamy, 62, 140
Population: location of Kikuyu, 38-39
Populist Land and Freedom Army, 154
Postmodernism: defined, 17; and ethnography, 107-8; and social theory, 16-18
Post-modernism and the Social Sciences (Rosenau), 16
Pravda, 173
Preservationists: vs. colonialists, 222n
Primitivism: and Mau Mau movement, 170, 171, 172; and romanticism, 183
Pritt, D. N., 156

Race: in colonial Kenya, 196-203
Racism: and stereotypes, 185-91
Radical Chic and Mau-Mauing the Flak Catchers (Wolfe), 159
Ranger, Terence, 118, 124, 216
Rape, 61
Recontextualization, 132
Red fez (worn by servants), 199
Red Strangers (Huxley), 27, 196-201
Research funding: Leakey's search for, 105-6
Rigby, Peter, 205
Rituals: and elders, 109; *irua*, 54, 133, 222n; *ituīka*, 33, 110, 111, 113, 116, 141; *Kūingata Mūrimū*, 43. *See also* Clitoridectomy; Male circumcision
Robeson, Paul, 128-29
Rogers, Peter, 219n
Romanticism: of noble savage, 189; and primitivism, 183; of sport hunting, 222n
Rosenau, Pauline Marie: *Post-modernism and the Social Sciences*, 16
Routledge, Katherine: 31, 196; on

Kikuyu, 29-31; on "The Lost Sister," 48; research methods, 30; *With a Prehistoric People,* 29-31

Routledge, W. Scoresby: 31, 196; on Kikuyu, 29-31; research methods, 30; *With a Prehistoric People,* 29-31

Ruark, Robert, 1; *Something of Value,* 26, 160-67, 168, 170, 216

Said, Edward: *Culture and Imperialism,* 5

Sanders of the River (film), 128-29

Savages. *See* Noble savage

Schneider, Jane, 90, 92

Self-determination: for colonial Africa, 173; and Mau Mau movement, 150, 173

Servants. *See* Master-servant relationship; Spiteful servants

Sexual freedom: of Kikuyu women, 61, 63

Sexual Meanings, 90

Sexual morality, Kikuyu, 71-72; premarital, 72-75, 82, 86, 89

Sexuality: in colonial Kenya, 209-18; in "The Lost Sister," 54-55

Shadows on the Grass (Blixen), 188

Shakespeare, William, 188; *The Merchant of Venice,* 187

Shamanism, Colonialism, and the Wild Man (Taussig), 103-4

Shona: on virginity, 88

Singh, Makhan, 165

Slaves: as spiteful servants, 189-91

Social Science Citation Index, 131

Social theory: and colonialism, 13-25; guidelines for social analysis, 24-25

Sodomy, 163, 166

Something of Value (Ruark), 26, 160-67, 168, 170, 216; film version, 162

Southern Kikuyu before 1903, The (Leakey), 2-3, 71, 98-99, 106-16, 139-43; as collaborative, 107; cover of, *99;* editing of, 222n; major themes of, 140-41; political conditions surrounding, 139

Spiteful servants: African Americans/black slaves as, 189-91

Sport hunting, 181, 195-96, 222n; as athleticism, 222n; and romanticism, 222n

Stereotypes, 185-91

Stoler, Ann, 188, 215

Subjugation, 185

Subordination, 207

Suffering without Bitterness (Kenyatta), 125-26, 130

Sun people, 189

Taussig, Michael, 115-16; *Shamanism, Colonialism, and the Wild Man,* 103-4

Things Fall Apart (Achebe), 219n

Thuku, Harry, 124

Tignor, Robert, 205

Time: Mau Mau coverage, 170, 171, 173-78 passim

Trading: by Kikuyu, 40-41

Trafford, Raymond, 214

Tribalism: in colonial Kenya, 4-6, 121

Trzebinski, Errol: *Kenya Pioneers,* 183-84, 203-4, 215, 223n

Tyler, Stephen, 108

Tylor, Edward B., 29

Uhuru (freedom/independence), 11-12, 154

Unhappy Valley (Berman and Lonsdale), 222n

Villagization, 153, 178

Vincent, Joan, 44-45

Virginity, 82-85, 88-89; Africa vs. Europe/Asia on, 89-94; anthropological interpretations of, 84; and clitoridectomy, 85-88; and objectification, 83; and prestige, 85; and property, 90; proof of, 88; and sexual play, 72-75, 89; as sign, 83

Walker, Alice, 70, 77

Warrior oath. *See* Batuni

Waugh, Evelyn, 214

Wealth: for Kikuyu, 37, 40

White, Hayden, 18-19

White African (Leakey), 139

White Man's Country (Huxley), 198
White Mischief (Fox), 189, 214
With a Prehistoric People (Routledge and
  Routledge), 29-31
Wolf, Eric, 4-5
Wolfe, Tom: *Radical Chic and Mau-
  Mauing the Flak Catchers,* 159
Women: anthropology of, 14-15; ideal
  Victorian, 60; and nature, 198
Women, Kikuyu: as allegory, 3, 60-63;
  and political economy, 40-42, 46-47;
  power of, 28, 35, 40, 43, 46, 58-59;
  productivity of and male dependence,

56-58; and rituals, 43; trading by, 40-
41, 89; and traditions, upholding, 140;
Western views of, 84; woman-to-
woman marriage, 41-42. *See also* Gen-
der roles
Wood, Percy, 165
Worlds of a Maasai Warrior, The (Ole
  Saitoti), 202
Wreath for Udomo, A (Abrahams), 128-
  29, 147

Yeazell, Ruth Bernard, 202

Carolyn Martin Shaw, formerly known as Carolyn M. Clark, is an associate professor of anthropology at the University of California, Santa Cruz, where she is also chair of the Board of Studies in Anthropology and provost of Kresge College, one of the eight residential colleges of the campus. She completed ethnographic fieldwork among the Kikuyu in central Kenya and was awarded a Fulbright Fellowship at the University of Zimbabwe. Recognized as a distinguished teacher, at Kresge College she introduced the central academic theme of the college, "Cultural Intersections: Race, Class, Gender, and Sexuality," which explores the space of surprise created when competing ideas and discourses bump up against each other. Her writings and presentations include works on women in Kenya and Zimbabwe, cross-cultural studies of sexuality, and works on race and sexuality in the United States.